LETTERS

FROM

PORT ROYAL

1862-1868

Selected from
THE AMERICAN NEGRO: HIS HISTORY AND LITERATURE
William Loren Katz
GENERAL EDITOR

LETTERS
FROM
PORT ROYAL
1862-1868

Edited by Elizabeth Ware Pearson

With a new preface by James M. McPherson

ARNO PRESS and THE NEW YORK TIMES
NEW YORK 1969

THE LETTERS IN THIS VOLUME PROVIDE VALUABLE insights into one of the most important sidelights of the Civil War—"the Port Royal experiment." This was nothing less than an experiment in freedom for the ten thousand slaves who had worked the long-staple cotton plantations on the South Carolina Sea Islands lying just off the coast south of Charleston. Port Royal Island, containing the town of Beaufort, is the largest of the islands. The basis of South Carolina's antebellum cotton aristocracy, these plantations were abandoned by the white population when the Union Army and Navy captured them in November, 1861. Cotton agents from the United States Treasury descended on the islands to collect the crop, but the status of the Negroes, no longer slaves but not yet freedmen, was still uncertain. Into this breach stepped northern abolitionists and philanthropists, aided by antislavery forces in the Union government. "Here, within the protection of the arms of the United States, might a new experiment of tropical culture by free labor be tried," declared one abolitionist. "Succeeding there, as succeed it must and would, how simple the process by which it might be extended wherever the arms of the nation may be predominant!"

Societies were formed in Boston, New York, and Philadelphia to send teachers and labor superintendents to the Sea Islands. In the spring of 1862 these abolitionist missionaries of freedom and Yankee culture, soon called "Gideonites," began arriving, setting up schools, and establishing themselves as superintendents of plantations on which black people who had once worked as slaves now worked for wages. As Laura Towne, one of the Gideonites, put it when she arrived at Port Royal: "We have come to do anti-slavery work, and we think it noble work and mean to do it earnestly."

Here were the beginnings of an experiment in freedom that gradually spread to other parts of the occupied Confederacy during the war, and to the entire South when emancipation was consummated in 1865. In other respects also the Port Royal experience established precedents for the transformation of chattels into free men, soldiers, and citizens. The first regiment of freed slaves was recruited on the islands. The sale of land once owned by slaveholders to the former slaves was first carried out there. The education of the freedmen was undertaken more intensively on the islands than anywhere else during the war. The first experience of former slaves in the democratic process of voting took place at Beaufort when the Sea Islands elected delegates, including four black men, to the Republican National Convention in 1864 (the delegates were not seated, however, since South Carolina was not considered a state while the war was still in progress).

All of these developments are discussed in this volume; perhaps the most interesting and controversial issue being the question of land for the freedmen. In 1863 and 1864 the Union government sold at auction several thousand acres of land confiscated from their Confederate owners. Many of the Gideonites wanted the government to grant twenty or forty acres to each Negro family, "who so long have tilled them without wages," or to give the freedmen first option to buy prime land at special low prices. But others, led by Edward S. Philbrick and William C. Gannett, two of the central figures in this book, opposed special consideration for the freedmen on the grounds that charity would weaken their moral fiber and undermine their independent initiative. Philbrick, an aggressive entrepreneur from Boston who came south with the first boatload of Gideonites, is the most arresting personality in this volume. At the land auctions in 1863 he bought several thousand acres of plantation property for himself and in behalf of Boston investors for whom he was agent, and hired the freedmen as laborers to raise cotton on the land. Philbrick cleared a large profit on his cotton, and was accused by some of the other Gideonites and by northern abolitionists of selfishly exploiting the freedmen.

It is difficult to determine Philbrick's real motives in opposing special grants or sales of land to the freedmen. He may simply have wished to buy as much land as possible for himself. But in his letters, reprinted here, he naturally portrayed his purposes in the best possible light: He wanted to prove that black people would work more efficiently for wages and raise more cotton as free laborers than they had as slaves, and he saw himself as the benevolent employer under whom this experiment could be carried out. Many of the freedmen themselves, on the other hand, thought the experiment could best succeed if they were independent owners of the land rather than wage laborers; one of them said that "Every colored man will be a slave, and feel himself a slave until he can raise him own *bale of cotton* and put him own mark upon it and say *dis is mine!*"

Philbrick was perfectly willing for the freedmen to own land; indeed, the Negroes bought over four thousand acres in competitive bidding during the war, and Philbrick himself sold them several thousand more acres of his land after the war. But he disapproved of special favors for the freedmen: "The fact is that no race of men on God's earth ever acquired the right to the soil on which they stand without more vigorous exertions than these people have made," he wrote in 1864. "This is apparently the wise order of Providence as a means of discipline, or the misfortune of man, as a consequence of his failings, perhaps both; but I cannot see why these people should be excepted from the general rule. . . . No man or race of men ever truly appreciate freedom who do not fight for it, and no man appreciates property who does not work for it, on the same terms with those around him. I think they would be better off for paying ten dollars an acre for land, if the land is worth it, rather than one dollar, because they would use the land for which they had paid the full price economically, would be

likely to get more out of it, and would be taught
a feeling of independence more readily than by being made the recipients of charity." Here was a perfect expression of the New England Puritan ethic:
hard work, thrift, and self-denial were "the wise
order of Providence" and a "means of discipline"
by which man is "taught a feeling of independence."

All but a few of the letters in this volume were
written by four of the Gideonites: Philbrick, William C. Gannett, Harriet Ware, and Charles Preston
Ware. The editor, Elizabeth Ware Pearson, was the
daughter of Charles and niece of Harriet Ware. In
designating the names of people who were still alive
when this book was first published in 1906, Mrs.
Pearson used initials: thus W.C.G. was Gannett;
H.W. was Harriet Ware; C.P.W. was Charles P.
Ware. Another person of some importance whose
name is indicated only by initials is T. Edwin Rug-
gles (T.E.R.), a Gideonite plantation superintendent.

Philbrick, Gannett, and the Wares were Boston-
ians; most of the other white people in these letters
were also New England Yankees. They all shared,
to some degree, the Puritan paternalism toward the
freedmen explicitly expressed by Philbrick, but to
assume that such an attitude was typical of all the
Gideonites does them an injustice. Some of the most
prominent northern missionaries on the Sea Islands,
such as Laura Towne, Ellen Murray, and Mansfield
French, were more warm, friendly, and equalitarian
in their attitudes toward the people of the islands.
Nevertheless, this volume fills an important niche

in a shelf of books on American Negro history, for it illustrates the selfishness and pettiness, as well as devotion and self-sacrifice that have characterized efforts by white liberals to help black people. The men and women of both races who come alive in this volume of letters were human beings, with all the frailties and foibles of the species. There are no ivory saints here, nor ebony saints either. This is history in the flesh.

James M. Mc Pherson
DEPARTMENT OF HISTORY
PRINCETON UNIVERSITY

CONTENTS

INTRODUCTION

WITH Commodore Dupont's capture, on November 7, 1861, of two earth forts which the rebels had recently thrown up at Hilton Head and Bay Point, South Carolina, the Sea Island region became Union territory. The planters and their families having fled precipitately, the United States Government found itself in possession of almost everything that had been theirs, the two chief items being the largest cotton crop ever yet raised there, nearly ready for exporting, and several hundred demoralized, destitute slaves, the number of whom was daily being increased by refugees and returned fugitives. The negroes were plainly a burdensome problem, the cotton a valuable piece of property. The first thing to do was obvious, and fortunately the same " cotton-agents " who were despatched by the authorities at Washington to collect and ship the property were able, by employing negroes for the purpose, to make a beginning towards solving the problem.

In another month the next step was taken; the Secretary of the Treasury sent down Edward L. Pierce, of Milton, Massachusetts, as a special agent charged with the duty of getting under way some method of managing the negroes and starting a cotton crop for 1862. Mr. Pierce, who the summer before had had charge of the contrabands at Fortress Monroe, did his work quickly and well, and his suggestions for organization were promptly adopted and put into practice by the Government. Meanwhile he had written to " bene-

volent persons in Boston," setting forth the instant
need of the negroes for clothing and for teachers,
meaning by the term "teachers" quite as much superintendents of labor as instructors in the rudiments of
learning. The response to this appeal was immediate.
An "Educational Commission for Freedmen" [1] was
organized in Boston, New York and Philadelphia were
quick to follow, and on March 3, 1862, there set sail
from New York for Port Royal [2] a party of men and
women who were almost without exception inspired
purely by the desire to help those who had been slaves.
Government made them an allowance of transportation, subsistence, and quarters; and, since few could
afford to give their services, the Commissions paid
them salaries of from $25 to $50 a month.

There was a good deal of courage in what these
people did. The climate of the Sea Islands is unwhole-
some; the rebels were more than likely, from across the
narrow Coosaw River, to invade the territory held by
Northern troops; it was not improbable that the negroes
might refuse utterly to work; it was not impossible
that they might wreak vengeance for their wrongs on
every white man who should try to control them. Fur-
thermore, as a rule these men and women knew little
of any kind of agriculture, and still less of the local
conditions under which they were to do their work,

---

[1] Later "The New England Freedmen's Aid Society."

[2] The name Port Royal, in ante-bellum days used only of the island
on which Beaufort is situated and of the entrance to the Beaufort
River, was given by the United States Government to the military
post and the harbor at Hilton Head, and to the post-office there.
Hence the Sea Island district came to be referred to in the North as
"Port Royal."

or of the people with whom they were to deal. They had, in fact, no other guides to action than enthusiasm and good sense, and of the latter, in particular, they carried widely differing amounts. Some, who went supplied with too little of either, were back in their Northern homes before summer was under way; the majority, making what they could of the means, or lack of means, at their disposal, had within the same period of time got about thirty-eight hundred laborers at steady work on fifteen thousand acres of corn, potatoes, and cotton. For the first time in our history educated Northern men had taken charge of the Southern negro, had learned to know his nature, his status, his history, first-hand, in the cabin and the field. And though subsequently other Southern territory was put into the hands of Northern men and women to manage in much the same fashion, it was not in the nature of things that these conditions should ever be exactly reproduced. The question whether or not the freedman would work without the incentive of the lash was settled once for all by the "Port Royal Experiment."

Of the many thousand letters that must have been written by these people to their Northern homes, those of one small group only are represented by the extracts here printed. The writers were New Englanders and ardent anti-slavery people; W. C. G. and C. P. W. were Harvard men just out of college, H. W. was a sister of the latter. A few of the later letters were written by two other Massachusetts men, T. E. R., a Yale graduate of 1859, and F. H., who remained on the islands longer than the three just mentioned. All five are still living. Richard Soule, Jr., now dead for many years

was an older man, a teacher, a person of great loveliness
of character and justice of mind. The principal figure
in the letters, Edward S. Philbrick of Brookline, who
died in 1889, was in one sense the principal figure in
the Sea Island situation. He began by contributing a
thousand dollars to the work and volunteering his services on the ground, where he was given charge by Mr.
Pierce of three plantations, including the largest on the
islands; being a person of some means, with an established reputation as an engineer and a very considerable
business experience, he was from the first prominent
among the volunteers. When, in the following year, he
became personally and financially responsible for a
dozen plantations, this prominence was increased a
hundredfold. Thus he found himself the victim of the
vituperation hurled by many Northern friends of the
blacks at the "professed philanthropists" who went to
Port Royal to "make their fortunes" out of the labor
of the "poor negro." The integrity of Mr. Philbrick's
motives stands out in his letters beyond the possibility
of misinterpretation. This record is a witness of what
sort of thing he and his kind were ready to do to redress
the wrongs of slavery.

The extracts have been arranged in chronological
order, except in a few cases where chronology has
seemed less important than subject-matter. They tell
a complete story, the greater part of which falls within
the period of the Civil War. They give a vivid notion of
the life from the midst of which they were written;
of the flat, marsh-riddled country, in which few Northerners saw any lasting charm; of the untidy, down-at-
the-heels plantations; of the "people," wards of the

nation, childish, irritating, endlessly amusing; of the
daily toil of Northern men in managing farms and of
Northern women in managing households under
Southern and war-time conditions; of the universal
preoccupation with negro needs; of the friendly interchange of primitive hospitality; of the underlying sense
in the writers' minds of romantic contrast between their
own to-day and the yesterday of the planters, — or a
possible to-morrow of the planters. It is not with matters military or political that these letters deal. They
record the day to day experiences of the housekeeper,
the teacher, the superintendent of labor, and the land-
owner. For this reason they form a new contribution to
the history of the Port Royal Experiment.

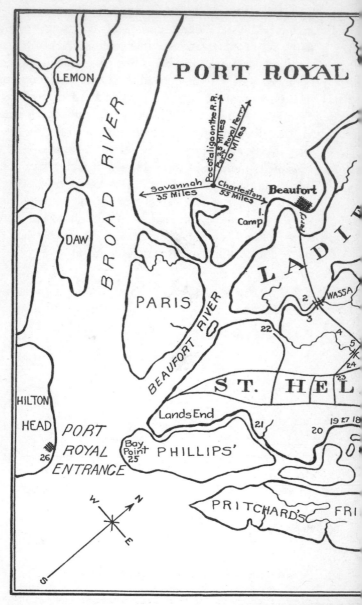

THE SEA ISL.

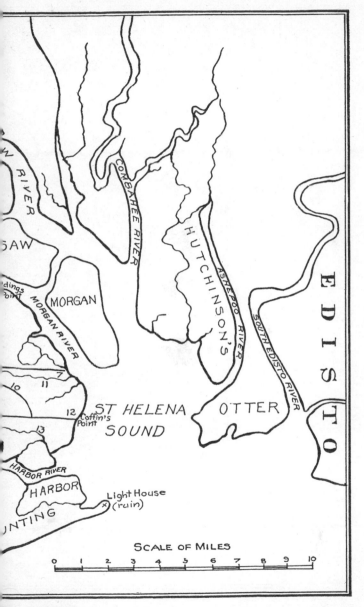

COMBAHEE RIVER

HUTCHINSON'S

ASHEPOO RIVER

SOUTH EDISTO RIVER

E D I S T O

RIVER

SAW

dings
Point

MORGAN

MORGAN RIVER

7

10   11

12   Coffin's
      Point

13

ST HELENA
SOUND

OTTER

HARBOR RIVER

HARBOR

NTING

Light House
× (ruin)

SCALE OF MILES

0 1 2 3 4 5 6 7 8 9 10

KEY TO MAP OF THE SEA ISLANDS OF
SOUTH CAROLINA

PLANTATIONS.

LETTERS FROM PORT ROYAL

1862

FROM E. S. PHILBRICK

Boston, February 19, 1862. Dear ——: I think you will not be greatly astonished when I tell you that I am off for Port Royal next week. I go under the auspices of the Educational Commission to make myself generally useful in whatever way I can, in reducing some amount of order and industry from the mass of eight or ten thousand contrabands now within our lines there. Boston is wide awake on the subject, and I am determined to see if something can't be done to prove that the blacks will work for other motives than the lash.

The Treasury Department offer subsistence, protection, transportation, and the War Department offer their hearty coöperation to the work undertaken here by private citizens, but can't take any more active part at present for reasons obvious. They ridicule the idea that these blacks can ever again be claimed by their runaway masters, which is a satisfactory foundation for our exertions in overseeing their labor and general deportment.

You don't know what a satisfaction it is to feel at last that there is a chance for me to *do something* in this great work that is going on.

The next letter describes the sailing of the first party of superintendents and teachers.

E. S. P. TO MRS. PHILBRICK

New York City, Sunday, March 2. We have a rather motley-looking set. A good many look like broken-down schoolmasters or ministers who have excellent dispositions but not much talent. As the kind of talent required where we are going is rather peculiar, the men may be useful, but I don't believe there will be a great deal of cotton raised under their superintend-ence.

Str. Atlantic, March 5. We all repaired to the Col-lector's [1] house Sunday evening, and were sworn in squads of half a dozen with our hands on the Bible, after which our passports were made out and signed by Mr. Barney in his library with the whole thirty-three of us standing about.

[The next morning] I found Collector Barney on the pier with his Bible and papers, swearing in the rest of the New York delegation. The last of the cargo was slung aboard about eleven, and we started off at quarter past, in a drizzling rain, freezing fast to everything it touched. Our Boston party consisted of twenty-nine

[1] Collector Barney of the Port of New York.

men and four women; the New York one of twenty-three men and eight women, including those from Washington, making sixty-four in all. At dinner (2 P. M.) we found some one hundred and twenty cabin passengers, besides a lot of recruits, perhaps one hundred in all, who live forward. The larger part of the *Atlantic's* staterooms have been taken out to make room for stowing troops or cargo, leaving enough for only about half our number. These rooms were assigned by the Steward and Mr. Pierce[1] to the ladies and the oldest of us gentlemen; so I got one with Uncle Richard,[2] for most of our party are quite youthful. Half a dozen ladies sat on the bare deck (no other seats provided), during most of the evening, singing Methodist hymns and glory hallelujah till after nine o'clock. I have talked with several of our party, and got slightly acquainted, chiefly with Messrs. Hooper,[3] G—,[4] and Mack; also with Mr. Forbes.[5] There is a general medley of cabin passengers, recruits, sutlers' and quartermasters' agents, and crew, the latter not being dressed in uniform, but in nondescript old garments such as can be found at any old Isaac's shop. Those passengers who are outside our party are coarse-looking and disagreeable, — Mr. Forbes and Mr. Augustus Hurd of Boston being almost the only exceptions. I had some talk with Mr. Pierce yesterday about your coming on, and he said as soon as

[1] Edward L. Pierce (see Introduction).

[2] Richard Soule, Jr.

[3] Edward W. Hooper, afterwards for many years Treasurer of Harvard College.

[4] G. is W. C. G. of these letters.

[5] John M. Forbes, who had hired a house at Beaufort for a few months.

I found it advisable he would send you a pass, but I am very glad you are not here now, for I don't believe these ladies will find anything but bare boards to sleep on.

Thursday evening, March 6. We had a sort of lecture from Mr. Pierce before dinner, consisting of some very appropriate and sensible advice and suggestions, expressed simply and with a good deal of feeling. Mr. French [1] followed in his vein of honest, earnest Methodism. He is the head of the New York delegation, and a worthy man, though not so practical as Mr. Pierce.

Our Boston party improves upon acquaintance, and the longer I think of the matter the more wonderful does it seem that such a number of disinterested, earnest men should be got together at so short a notice to exile themselves from all social ties and devote themselves, as they certainly do, with a will, to this holy work. It must and with God's help it *shall* succeed! The more I see of our fellow-passengers and co-workers, the more do the party from Boston stand eminent in talent and earnestness, as compared with those from New York, and I can't help thinking that the former were more carefully selected. The Boston Commission acted with more deliberation than that of New York, and I think the result will be shown in the end. But it's early to form any such opinions, and out of place to draw any comparisons in disparagement of any of our colleagues. We are all yoked together and must pull together. The work is no trifle. It is Herculean in all its aspects — in its reactive effects upon our country and its future destiny, as well as in its difficulties.

[1] Rev. Mansfield French had already spent some weeks at Port Royal.

Yet never did men stand in a position to do more lasting good than we, if we act with a single eye to the
object in view and pray God to guide us aright.

Friday, March 7. We waked this morning still adrift
off Port Royal Bar, where we had been tossing all night,
near the lightship. The wind was blowing cold and clear
from the northwest just as it does at home in March,
almost cold enough for a frost. We continued to drift
till the tide was near the flood, about noon, when a
pilot came out and took us in to Hilton Head. Here
in this magnificent harbour, larger than any other on our
coast, lay some fifty transports and steamers at anchor,
and here we dropped our anchor, almost directly between the two forts[1] taken by Dupont last November.
These forts, by the way, are so inconspicuous as to be
hardly perceptible to a passer-by, and would certainly fail
to attract the attention of a person not on the lookout
for them. The shore is as flat as flat can be, sand-banks
and beaches being the only variety, backed by long dark
green masses of foliage of the pitch-pine, reminding
me forcibly of the coast of Egypt, with its sand and
palm forests. Yet even Egypt was sufficiently enter-
prising to line its coast with windmills, while this state
has not yet arrived at a stage of civilization sufficiently
advanced to provide them. So, there being no water-
power and no steam, every negro grinds his peck of
corn in a handmill as in the year one. We came to
anchor about one P. M. and have been waiting for the
necessary passes from the quartermaster to enable us to
proceed up to Beaufort, the only town in possession of
our forces. Here we lie in the still harbour under the

[1] Thrown up by the island planters after the outbreak of the war.

splendid moon, surrounded by the regiments encamped
on the neighboring islands, with the prospect of another
day afloat, before we can begin to be distributed over
our field of labor.

8 P. M. The acting Provost Marshal has just come
aboard with our passports viséed, enabling us to land
here, but I don't care to do that to-night, there being
nothing but sand-banks to sleep on, while we have
tolerable berths aboard. To-morrow I may go, if there
is time before going upstream to Beaufort, though I
imagine there is little to see but sand and tents, which
look quite as well at a distance.

March 8. We spent the greater part of the day
transferring freight and baggage to the *Cosmopolitan*,
a white river-steamer. We got started at last about
three P. M. The distance to Beaufort can't be more
than fifteen miles, and we had already made half of it
at a tolerable rate of speed when we ran aground in the
mud, about two hours before ebb tide. We were in the
middle of a creek called Beaufort River, between Cat
Island and Port Royal Island, whose flat shores did not
look very inviting. I fell to reading about cotton-culture
in my book, but some of our companions got a boat and
went ashore on St. Helena Island, bringing back their
hands full of beautiful flowers from some private garden,
peach-blossoms, orange-blossoms, hyacinths, fleur-de-
lis, etc. We succeeded in getting afloat about 9.30 P. M.
and arrived at Beaufort about midnight, after poking
slowly along the crooked channel under the glorious
moonlight. On getting up in the morning, which we
did betimes, we found the deck slippery with hoar-
frost, and are told that it is the coldest night of this

winter. Somebody has told me that Beaufort was on a bluff, and that its environments were not so flat as the rest of the islands.

Beaufort, Sunday, March 9. But I can't find any place over ten feet above tide-water, and no hill over six feet high. So things are judged of by comparison. We all went ashore soon after sunrise and walked about the town, which is laid out in rectangular streets, lined with pleasant but weedy orange-gardens and often shaded by live-oak and sycamore trees, *i. e.*, when the latter leave out, as they will soon. The soil is a fine sand, very like ashes, and the streets are ankle-deep with it already, wherever the grass does n't grow. Dilapidated fences, tumble-down outbuildings, untrimmed trees with lots of dead branches, weedy walks and gardens and a general appearance of *unthrift* attendant upon the best of slaveholding towns, was aggravated here by the desolated houses, surrounded by heaps of broken furniture and broken wine and beer bottles which the army had left about after their pillage. Quantities of negro children lay basking in the morning sun, grinning at us as we passed. We saw a chain-pump in a yard and walked in to wash our faces, there having been no chance on the steamer, and were waited upon by an old negro, who brought us bowls, soap, and towels. Mr. Pierce succeeded in getting us some bread and coffee from one of the regiments; having no time to go to headquarters. They were carried to an old negro cabin in the remotest corner of the town, where the coffee was made and served up in the poultry-yard in our tin mugs.

Our quarters are in a very fine house in the east end

of the town, bordering on the river, against which is a garden wall, built of oyster-shells and mortar, there being no stone to be had here.

We are to wait here till our positions are assigned to us by Mr. Pierce, which will be done in a few days. He told me he wanted me to take the most important one, which I suppose means Coffin's.[1]   I am to have W—— G—— for my clerk and assistant. He is a very agreeable, quiet fellow, and works like a beaver, but like several others, is too young to take charge of the organization of the labor to good advantage.

There is something very sad about these fine deserted houses. Ours has Egyptian marble mantels, gilt cornice and centre-piece in parlor, and bath-room, with several wash-bowls set in different rooms. The force-pump is broken and all the bowls and their marble slabs smashed to get out the plated cocks, which the negroes thought pure silver. Bureaus, commodes, and wardrobes are smashed in, as well as door-panels, to get out the contents of the drawers and lockers, which I suppose contained some wine and ale, judging by the broken bottles lying about. The officers saved a good many pianos and other furniture and stored it in the jail, for safe-keeping. But we kindle our fires with chips of polished mahogany, and I am writing on my knees with a piece of a flower-stand across them for a table, sitting on my camp bedstead.

I am anxious to get to work, as I hope to in a few days. Mr. Eustis [2] has gone to his plantation, a few

[1] Thomas A. Coffin's large plantation at the eastern end of St. Helena Island.

[2] F. A. Eustis of Milton, who was part owner of the plantation in question.

miles distant on Ladies Island, and Mr. Hooper is spending a few days with him. The latter is to be Mr. Pierce's private secretary at present.

Beaufort, March 10. I can't tell until I get settled at my post what to say about your coming on here. If my post should be exposed to any of the rebels' scouting-parties you had better stay at home. I must say it seems rather *near* to live within rifle-shot of their outposts, as some of the plantations are.

March 11. We had a visit from the Provost Marshal last evening. He has had a good deal to do with the contrabands and came to give us some advice about them. He thinks that rebel spies may come among us, but don't apprehend any trouble, says we can govern the negroes easily enough by firm and judicious treatment, and says the officers in charge are very glad to have them taken off their hands.

Hilton Head,[1] *March* 13. This is a most desolate-looking place, flat and sandy, and covered with camps and storehouses for a mile along the river. A line of intrenchments encloses the whole, some seven miles long, resting on the river at each end. There is a long wharf just built out to deep water, at the end of which the *Atlantic* is discharging. This is the general dépôt for stores for the whole army on the Atlantic coast and the blockading fleet.

March 14. A fortnight has passed since I left Brookline, without my being able to get at my work. This loafing about and waiting upon the movements of Government officials is the hardest work I ever tried to do.

---

[1] Mr. Philbrick had gone down to Hilton Head again to see about his luggage.

If you can't come early in April you had better not come at all, for it will be too hot for even me to live on the plantations later than June 1. They say the planters never lived on the plantations in summer months, though they were acclimated, for fear of fevers. Beaufort is the healthiest place on these islands and their resort when leaving their plantations. Yet, if H—— W—— will come with you, *and not without*, and you think it will pay, come as soon as you can. I shall probably be on Coffin's plantation then, about fifteen miles east of Beaufort, on St. Helena Island, coast of St. Helena Sound. This plantation is one of the most secure from any interference from the rebels, so I don't feel the slightest uneasiness on that score, for the whole circumference of the island is picketed, and our forces also occupy the opposite or northeasterly coast of the sound.

Now as to outfit. Not over $5 each in money, *silver*, for you are supplied with transportation and food by Government and there's nothing here to buy. Bed-sacks and pillow ditto. Three umbrellas with light covers, fly-paper, tin cups, bowls, and tea-pot, set of wooden boxes for rice, sugar, and other stores furnished by army rations. Spring-balance that will weigh about twenty pounds, knife, fork, and spoons for each of you, *plated*, thermometer, three pounds of tea in one of the boxes. We now have plenty of rice, sugar, molasses, vinegar, hominy, potatoes, coffee, and beans, from army stores, and on plantations can get fresh lamb, mutton, chickens, eggs, milk; so we shall fare better than I thought.

Beaufort, March 17. I don't think they would let you take a servant; it's difficult enough to get you here

alone, and there are plenty of servants here which you
are supposed to teach not only to read but — what is
more immediately important — to be *clean* and industrious. If you feel any hesitation about coming in
contact with them you should n't come, for they are
sharp enough to detect apathy or lurking repugnance,
which would render any amount of theoretical sympathy about worthless. Tell your father their nature
and disposition is nothing new to me. I was with them
in Egypt long enough to get pretty well acquainted,
and though these sons of Western Africa are not exactly
of the same stock as the Nubians, they are certainly
no more degraded or lazy. In fact, from what I have
already seen here I am agreeably disappointed. Think of
their having reorganized and gone deliberately to work
here some weeks ago, without a white man near them,
preparing hundreds of acres for the new crop! The
Irish would n't have done as much in the same position.

This comparison of the negroes with the Irish is made
by the letter-writers, as will be seen, more than once,
— almost always to the disadvantage of the Irish.
Forty years ago the Irish were still merely immigrants,
and, further, they were practically the only people in
this country who suggested comparison with negroes.

The next letter is the first from W. C. G., whom Mr.
Philbrick has already mentioned as destined to be his
assistant.

March 24. Coffin's Point. It is the largest plantation on the Islands, numbering in its full days over 250
hands, or head, as the negroes call themselves.

A large amount of cotton is still in store here, for
which the boat I hope will call this week; meanwhile

the cotton-agent [1] and a guard occupy the house with us. The former has been on the place three or four months in charge of a large district with several plantations; he is a smart young fellow, very dashing and jockey-like. We were received by the guard with shouldered arms and by this agent, who did their best to induce or rather bluff us into leaving the premises and taking possession of another house; for we have two plantations besides this, — estates belonging to William Fripp's sons.[2] We stayed, however, and are now occupying two rooms, with plenty of furniture of different kinds stored by the agent, probably for removal. The whole business of our Commission and all its agents are much disliked by the cotton-agents, partly because they don't sympathize with our purposes,—partly because we seem about to usurp their authority, to which of course we do succeed.

The cotton-agents have started the corn-planting on most of the estates, — and almost everywhere the whole condition of people and land is much better than I expected to find it. The present state of a plantation depends on the previous character and age of the people, the influence of the drivers,[3] and the circumstances to which they have been exposed since the soldiers came. If the people are on the whole old and steady, if the drivers are intelligent and strong-minded, if their masters have been humane and fatherly, and if they have seen few soldiers, — then the work has usually

[1] See page v.

[2] Pine Grove and Fripp Point.

[3] The drivers, negroes holding a position next below the white overseers, were found by the Northerners still keeping the keys and trying to exert their authority.

been kept up pretty well and the negroes are still at
home and willing to go a-field, — and their condition
varies as those items vary. On the larger number, as
I have said, things are much better than I expected to
see them. As is proper, more attention has as yet been
paid to the *corn* lands, and very little to the cotton.
Two precious months have been lost for that crop. On
most of the plantations corn enough remains to last
through the next crop, — so there is little danger of
much suffering for want of food. But everything except corn, and their own eggs and poultry, is wanting,
— no molasses, no sugar, no salt, no tobacco, — and
no clothing.

On two of our three plantations things are doing
well, but this big Coffin place is in a very miserable,
demoralized condition. It used to be very successful
in cotton — and of late, especially, the hands have
been worked very hard. There are many *young* people — so all the more likely to leave. They are within
a few miles of Bay Point opposite Hilton Head, so the
temptation to leave is very pressing, for smart fellows
can get money there, — one York with whom I was
talking yesterday got over $30 a month by cooking
for two or three messes; he is sick now and thinks he
had better come home for the good of his *soul*. And
perhaps as evil an influence as any was the early presence of the guards from the 19th N. Y .V., a regiment
rather notorious for wild ways, I believe, — certainly
one which greatly injured these people by their talk
about *freedom* and no need of work, etc., and their
rampant deeds. We are therefore in a hard place here, —
and shall take pretty energetic measures and do the

best we can. Mr. Philbrick has charge of the farming,
etc., — I of the teaching. We were not all sent out
two by two; small plantations had single men. Some
men are expected to overlook several estates lying near
each other.

March 29. The women work much better than the
men, but very few are faithful. Nor can we hope for
any regularity and real improvement till we are delivered from our cotton-agent and the influences which
emanate from him and his interests.

The people are very discontented here, and as they
have logic and need on their side, it is hard to meet
their complaints. In fact, they can't be met, — very
few do full work, many half or none. They need *clothing* very badly. They need salt and tobacco, — this
summer they need a little molasses and some bacon.
These things [1] they have been accustomed to receive
in stated quantities at stated times, — at Christmas,
and in April or May. If we could supply them simply as they have been supplied by their masters, the
majority I think would be contented and would work
well. The *promises* to pay to which they have been
treated by the agents of the Government for the last
three months have n't kept them warm. The agent
here will probably soon give them some cloth in part
payment. Money they don't know the value of — and
especially now can't spend it to advantage; besides,
as I said, I think few desire it.

The following fragment of a letter, from which the

---

[1] For clothing their masters had been in the habit of giving them
material for two suits a year; a pair of blankets every few years made
up the sum of gratuities.

date and the beginning are missing, was written from Pine Grove at about this time; its subject is, of course, the negroes.

FROM E. S. P.

They have not yet got any diseased appetite for alcoholic stimulants, and are happy in their comparative ignorance of such things.

They are a simple, childlike people, almost ignorant of malice, patient and easily influenced by an appeal to their feelings. There is far less family feeling and attachment to each other than among the ignorant Irish, apparently, though I don't know how much allowance to make for their being so much less demonstrative in their emotions, and more inured to suffering. They are most eminently a religious people, according to their light, and always refer their sufferings to Divine Providence, though without the stoical or fatalist ideas of their Mohammedan brethren, whom I got to know pretty well in Nubia and Egypt.

We find it very difficult to reach any motive that will promote cleanliness as a habit. It requires more authority than our position gives us as employers to make any police regulations very effectual in their quarters. This plantation is the neatest one I have seen anywhere in respect to their houses and yards, but there is room for great improvement here. They have the same dread of fresh air in sickness which is common to poor people at home, but there is very little sickness among them. Only one death has occurred since we came here, among a population of 420, and that was an infant. They place great trust in our doctors and keep them pretty busy jogging about.

The next letter, the first from H. W., records her arrival with Mrs. Philbrick.

Beaufort, April 15. The sail up was very beautiful, the green beyond description brilliant, and now and then the deeper shade of palmetto or live-oak. Some of the plantations were very picturesque. Roses and azaleas were plainly visible. An hour and a half, very quickly passed, brought us to the wharf, where Mr. Pierce and Mr. Hooper met us with the information that we were to go to Mr. Forbes's, whither we walked a long half-mile, a sentry at the street-corners, darkies bowing in every direction, birds and the scent of flowers filling the air, everything like a June day after a shower. Mr. Philbrick hopes to be ready for us on Saturday. A cotton-agent in his house prevents us from going just yet to the Coffin house, but we shall be established for the present on one of the smaller plantations adjoining.

The letter that follows, written at Pine Grove several days later, narrates the events of these days, beginning with April 16, in Beaufort.

FROM H. W.

Pine Grove, St. Helena, April 21. H.[1] and Miss Towne [2] carried the letters to the post-office, Caroline, Mr. Forbes's chamber-girl, following to show them the way there, take them to the schools and into some negro quarters. They were derided by the soldiers,

[1] Mrs. Philbrick.
[2] Miss Laura E. Towne of Philadelphia. She never returned to live in the North. The school she started in 1862 is still in existence, under the name of the Penn Normal, Industrial, and Agricultural School.

they said, who called after them, "See the Southern Aristocracy with their nigger behind them!" which amused Caroline very much.

Mr. Forbes took me in his open wagon, a tumble-down affair he has from a negro to avoid the annoyance of always having to make a requisition upon Government, the only owner in these regions of anything, and drove me down the river to a plantation [1] we had noticed as we came up on the boat, and where there was a cotton-gin Mr. Forbes wanted me to see. The greater part of the way our road was shaded by woods on the water-side, live-oaks with their ornamental moss, gum-trees and pines with quantities of cat-brier and trumpet honeysuckle in full bloom. The cotton-fields were un-shaded, of course, and very large, containing from one to three hundred acres. We passed some freshly planted, but most of them were covered with the old bushes, dry and dead, at which I was much surprised until I found that it was the habit to leave the fields as they are after the cotton is picked, for a year, planting on the same land only every other year. It makes dreary, desolate-looking fields, for though a few weeds spring up, no grass grows in this region, and they are brown instead of green all summer. The Smith Plantation is about five miles from town, the house in the centre of a live-oak grove, beautiful and beyond description, open underneath, and so hanging with moss that you can scarcely see any leaves as you look up. A little chapel on the place I got out to look at, made very roughly of boards whitewashed, inside an earth floor covered with straw, rough wooden benches, the pulpit

[1] Known as the Smith Plantation.

and altar made in the same way, but covered entirely with the grey moss, as we trim for Christmas. The house looked rough and ordinary to us, as they all do, except a few in the town; we did not go in. I believe there are cotton-agents there attending to the ginning, which process we saw in a little house by itself, where a steam gin worked four stands tended by one hand each. The funny thing was to see them pack the bales. There was a round hole in the second-story floor and a bag was fastened to the edges, into which a man gets and stamps the cotton down. I saw it swinging downstairs, but did not know what it was till, on going up, I found a black head just above the floor, which grinned from ear to ear with pleasure at the sight of a white lady, and ducked and bobbed in most convulsive fashion.

We drove through the negro quarters, or "nigger-house," as they themselves call the whole settlement, and they flocked to the doors to look at us, bowing and smiling as we went by. There were eight or ten separate houses just raised from the ground so that the air could pass underneath, and, as we looked in at the doors, apparently with very little furniture, though in some we saw chairs which were evidently Massa's. Dirty and ragged they all were, but certainly no more so than poor Irish, and it seemed to me not so dirty.

I saw palmetto-trees for the first time on this drive near enough to know what they really looked like. They stand alone in the cotton-fields like our elms in a meadow, though there are fewer of them, and they are stiff and straight. The Spanish dagger, looking

like a miniature palmetto, was planted for hedges
round the garden and fish-pond. Mistletoe I saw for
the first time.

Mr. Hooper came over in the morning [of the next
day] and told us he should come for us at 12.30, but it
was five before we got into the boat.[1] The negroes
sang to us in their wild way as they rowed us across
— I cannot give you the least idea of it. Indeed, I can't
give you the least idea of anything, and you must not
expect it. The town looked very pretty from the boat,
some of the houses are large and quite imposing in
appearance. We found Mr. Pierce and his carriage
waiting for us, having been there without any dinner
since one o'clock. (This is the land of waiting, we have
discovered — patience is a virtue our Northern people will have to learn here.) We drove at once to Pope's
plantation, passing Mr. Eustis on the way at his overseer's house, bedaubed from head to foot with molasses, which he had been selling all day to the negroes,
a pint to a hand. Here Mr. Philbrick was waiting with
his sulky (a two-wheeled jockey-cart), an ox-team for
the baggage, and a dump-cart in which he and H.
were to drive, while I drove the sulky alone in my glory.
But it was too late for us to think of driving ten miles
farther, so we laid our beds down and prepared for
another halt. The next morning Mr. Pierce sent us
home in his carriage.

We reached here not long before two, and went to
work to try and muster up some dinner. I had a cup
and saucer, tumbler and three knives and forks, and

---

[1] The ferry to Ladies Island, across which ran the road to St. Helena
Island and Mr. Philbrick's plantations.

the rennet, which soon supplied one dish; the negroes
brought china in limited quantities; we opened a box
of sardines, and coffee, and, with the army bread we
brought from Beaufort, fried eggs, and hominy, made a
most excellent meal; a tablecloth, napkins, and silver
spoons forming some of the appointments. Joe, the carpenter, young and handy, made a very good waiter, but
when he went out and cut a bough of sycamore and
began to brush the flies as we ate, it was almost more
than I could stand. Then we went to work to put
what things we had to rights, H. got her servant, and
moreover we had to receive and shake hands with any
number of negroes, who came flocking round us at
once, following the carriage as we drove up in true
Southern style, and coming into the house to satisfy
their curiosity.

W. G—— was here and aided us with a will, and
about five o'clock I went with him to the praise-house,[1]
where he has his school. The children were all assem-
bled by Cuffy, and he was teaching them when we
went in. Mr. G—— read in the Bible, substituting
words that they could understand, made a very simple prayer, all kneeling, and then heard them their
letters and words for an hour, with a great deal of tact
and ability — strange words, you may think, to use
in such a connection, but you have little idea how

---

[1] The plantation "praise-house," as the negroes' church was called,
was often merely "a rather larger and nicer negro hut than the others.
Here the master was an exemplary old Baptist Christian, who has
left his house full of religious magazines and papers, and built
his people quite a nice little house, — the best on this part of the
Island."

(Letter of W. C. G., April 22, 1862.)

much it needs of both. We are not used to these people
— it is even very difficult to understand what they
say. They have been born and brought up just
here, in the most isolated way, for generations, with
no chance of improvement, and there is not a single
mulatto [1] on the place — they are black as the blackest,
and perfect children — docile, and with "faith enough
to live by," W—— G—— says. I find I have no
shrinking from them, and hope I shall be able to do
my part. I take this school off his hands — he has two
other plantations to teach on and has been working
like a beaver. I made my first attempt this afternoon
and got along comfortably. Flora, the house-servant
(that is, ours, — she is a field hand), took me on my
way to see the old mammas, and I went into several
of the cabins and came home with a present of nine
eggs!

These houses are all built of hard pine, which is handsome on the floors, but the rest of the woodwork is
painted, in this house an ugly green, which is not pretty
or cheerful. The walls are always left white. Clap-
boards are unknown, but hard-pine boards, a foot or
more broad, are put on in the same way, and everything outside is whitewashed. The place is very at-
tractive-looking, grapevines and honeysuckles and pine
woods near.

April 25. The house is raised high from the ground,
as all are here, and boarded in loosely underneath.
There is a circle of orange-trees round the house, and
roses in abundance, but no grass, which is dreary.

[1] Pine Grove was in this respect an exception among the Sea Island
plantations.

The quarters are a quarter of a mile off, and the praise-house is near them, where I have school twice a day. It is very interesting, and I enjoy it much, though of course there is nothing to teach but the alphabet and little words. They sing their letters very nicely now. They are much better-mannered than the Irish, and I have had no trouble as yet.

Perhaps when I get to understanding things better I shall be able to tell you some things they say. They were uneasy till they discovered our first names, and were pleased that mine was that of the "old Missus." They have brought me presents of eggs two or three times.

FROM W. C. G.

Pine Grove Plantation, April 22. You see that we have changed our home. The ladies have arrived. The house is in better condition than that at Coffin's, the people better disposed, and the locality is more retired and does not boast of a cotton-agent. In a month or two we shall probably move to our old quarters, if it does n't take longer to clean it. Miss W—— will be a grand helper. It will be a pretty rough life for them, and New England comforts and neatness and intelligence will be sadly missed, but we certainly have been well, — our table is the most refined thing on the Island, I fancy.

FROM H. W.

Pine Grove, April 29. Our days pass pretty much after this fashion. Mr. Philbrick gets up about six, calls me, and I obey, having stipulated for a full hour in

which to dress. After we get downstairs it takes the
united efforts of most of the family to get the breakfast
on the table, and we are fortunate if we get up from
that meal by half-past eight. It generally consists of
hominy, very delicious eaten with either milk, butter, or
molasses, corn-cake, or waffles of corn-flour — the best
of their kind — concentrated coffee, chocolate, or tea,
army bread — when we can get it — crackers, when
we can't, and boiled eggs or fried fish, as the case may
be. The important operations of dish-washing and
arranging the rooms upstairs take longer than you can
imagine, and things are not always done when I go
to school at ten, which with our simple style of living
is rather a nuisance. H. begins to pity the Southern
housekeepers. This morning, after making the starch
in our little kitchen in the house, she waited about for
two hours, before she could get hold of one of the three
servants. They were all off at the kitchen, smoking and
talking and taking things easy. Joe was nominally
cleaning knives, Flora had gone to empty a pail of water,
and Sukey had no thought about her starched clothes!

Well, I walk off to school, under the white umbrella
if the sun shines, dressed as warmly as I can if it does
not. My way lies between a row of large "Hesha-
berry" trees, as the negroes call them; a corruption,
I suppose, of Asia Berry, as it is the "Pride of Asia,"
in full blossom now, with scent something like our
lilac, but more delicate. On each side of these trees
are the corn-houses, stables, cotton-houses, and near
the house a few cabins for house-servants, and the
well. They stretch an eighth of a mile, when a gate
(left open) shuts off the nigger-house and field. An-

other eighth brings me to the cabins, which have trees
scattered among them, figs and others. The children
begin to gather round me before I get there, with
their bow and curtsey and "goo' mornin, Marm," and
as I go through the quarters I send them in to wash
their hands and faces. The praise-house reached, one
of the children rings the bell out of the door to summon
all, and they gather quickly, some to be sent off to
wash their faces — alas, they cannot change their
clothes, which are of the raggedest. But now enough
clothes have come to begin to sell, I hope to have a
better dressed set before long. I keep them in for about
two hours — there are about thirty of the little ones
who come in the morning, ten and under; all older
are in the field, and come in the afternoon, as they finish
work by noon always.

I go back to lunch at half-past twelve, a cold one
generally, sometimes a few waffles or some hominy
for variety, but crackers, sardines, and blackberries
which we have in abundance now, make a refreshing
meal, with tea or coffee when we please. Shop [1] has
to be tended in the afternoon principally, and I sometimes take a turn at it till I go off at half-past three to
school again. We use for shop the little room between
Mr. G.'s and the entry, selling out of the window over
a box for a counter, to the groups on the porch. It is
a funny sight and funny work for us, albeit interesting,
for they have had no clothes for a year, and buy eagerly.
Mr. Philbrick has not been able to let them have any
clothing before, as there has only been enough to give
a garment to one in ten, and they have been so used to

[1] See p. 33.

being treated alike that their jealousy is very easily roused, and it is a difficult matter to deal with them. For the same reason the clothes have to be sold, the money going back to the Commission, to be used again for their benefit. It would be very much better if only the goods were sent, for they prefer to make their own clothes and all know how to sew.

These people show their subserviency in the way they put Marm or Sir into their sentences every other word and emphasize it as the one important word, and in always agreeing to everything you say. In school it is rather annoying to have them say, "Yes Marm, 'zackly Marm," before it is possible for an idea to have reached their brains.

Flora, our housemaid, who is a character, has a great deal of dignity and influence among the other negroes, and takes the greatest care of us. She is most jealous for what she considers our interests, and moreover is quite an interpreter, though it is hard enough to understand her sometimes. "Learning" with these people I find means a knowledge of medicine, and a person is valued accordingly. Flora wanted to know how much "learning" Miss Helen [1] had had, and it was a long time before I could make out what she meant.

H. says she never saw me look so well, so you see I thrive in spite of fleas, which have almost flayed me alive. I understand what it means by eels' getting *used* to being skinned.

May 1. Took a ride through the quarters. We stopped to see Doll and her week-old baby. H. had quite a talk with Mily, the nurse, who told her it did them

---

[1] Mrs. Philbrick.

good to see white ladies about, and hoped we were going to stay. She seemed very much disappointed when H. told her we should be here [at Pine Grove] only a short time longer. I think it does them good just to have me walk through the quarters four times a day — they always curtsey and say a word.

In the afternoon, as I came out of school, Cuffy said, "You promise to jine praise with we some night dis week, Missus," so I told him I would go up in the evening if Mr. G. would go with me. When we went up after eight they were just lighting the two candles. I sat down on the women's side next a window, and one of the men soon struck up a hymn in which the others joined and which seemed to answer the purpose of a bell, for the congregation immediately began to assemble, and after one or two hymns, Old Peter offered a prayer, using very good language, ending every sentence with "For Jesus' sake." He prayed for us, Massa and Missus, that we might be "boun' up in de belly-band of faith." Then Mr. G. read to them and made a few remarks to which they listened very attentively; then some hymn-singing, Cuffy deaconing out the lines two at a time. Then some one suddenly started up and pronounced a sort of benediction, in which he used the expression "when we done chawing all de hard bones and swallow all de bitter pills." They then shook hands all round, when one of the young girls struck up one of their wild songs, and we waited listening to them for twenty minutes more. It was not a regular "shout,"[1]

[1] "The true 'shout' takes place on Sundays or on 'praise'-nights through the week, and either in the praise-house or some cabin in which a regular religious meeting has been held. Very likely more

but some of them clapped their hands, and they stamped
in time. It was very difficult to understand the words,
though there was so much repetition that I generally
managed to make out a good deal, but could not remember it much, still less the music, which is inde-
scribable, and no one person could imitate it at all. As
we walked home we asked Cuffy if they considered
the "shout" as part of their religious worship; he
said yes, that "it exercise the frame." Mr. G. told
him that some of the old people had told him they did
not like the shouts, or think them religious, but he said
old Binah did not object to them in the praise-house,
but she did not like the shout "out in de world," *i. e.* before they joined the Church or came to "strive behind

than half the population of the plantation is gathered together. Let
it be the evening, and a light-wood fire burns red before the door to
the house and on the hearth. . . . The benches are pushed back to
the wall when the formal meeting is over, and old and young, men
and women, sprucely-dressed young men, grotesquely half-clad field-
hands — the women generally with gay handkerchiefs twisted about
their heads and with short skirts — boys with tattered shirts and
men's trousers, young girls barefooted, all stand up in the middle
of the floor, and when the 'sperichil' is struck up, begin first walking
and by-and-by shuffling round, one after the other, in a ring. The
foot is hardly taken from the floor, and the progression is mainly due
to a jerking, hitching motion, which agitates the entire shouter, and
soon brings out streams of perspiration. Sometimes they dance silently,
sometimes as they shuffle they sing the chorus of the spiritual, and
sometimes the song itself is also sung by the dancers. But more frequently a band, composed of some of the best singers and of tired
shouters, stand at the side of the room to 'base' the others, singing
the body of the song and clapping their hands together or on the knees.
Song and dance are alike extremely energetic, and often, when the
shout lasts into the middle of the night, the monotonous thud, thud
of the feet prevents sleep within half a mile of the praise-house."
(New York *Nation*, May 30, 1867.)

the Elders." He makes his own hymns, "praying to
de Lord Jesus to teach him as he in de woods — jine one
word 'ginst toder." They were almost unintelligible
as he deaconed them out, but I daresay they were his
own, unconsciously caught, perhaps, in part from what
he had heard in the white people's church. The only
song I could remember ran somewhat after this fashion:

> Oh, Jacob's ladder.
> Climb high, climb higher!
> Oh sodier of de jubilee,
> When you git dere 'member me,
> Oh! sodier of de cross!

In the introduction to "Slave Songs of the United
States," a collection made chiefly at Port Royal and
published in 1867, this particular song is set down as
spurious, that is, as being sung to a well-known "white
folks'" tune. But most of the negro music is described
as "civilized in its character, partly composed under
the influence of association with the whites, partly
actually imitated from their music. In the main it
appears to be original in the best sense of the word."
The same writer goes on:
"On the other hand there are very few which are of
an intrinsically barbaric character, and where this
character does appear, it is chiefly in short passages,
intermingled with others of a different character. . . .
It is very likely that if we had found it possible to get
at more of their secular music, we should have come
to another conclusion as to the proportion of the barbaric element. . . . Mr. E. S. Philbrick was struck
with the resemblance of some of the rowing tunes at
Port Royal to the boatmen's songs he had heard upon
the Nile. . . .
"The words are, of course, in a large measure taken
from Scripture, and from the hymns heard at church;
and for this reason these religious songs do not by any

means illustrate the full extent of the debasement of
the dialect." Of words funnily distorted through failure
to understand their meaning there are, however, many
examples. "Paul and Silas, bound in jail," was often
sung "Bounden Cyrus born in jail;" "Ring Jerusa-
lem" appeared as "Ring Rosy Land," etc. etc. "I never
fairly heard a secular song among the Port Royal freedmen, and never saw a musical instrument among them.
The last violin, owned by a 'worldly man,' disappeared
from Coffin's Point 'de year gun shoot at Bay Pint.'"

The negroes' manner of singing is pretty well suggested by the following:

"The voices of the colored people have a peculiar
quality that nothing can imitate; and the intonations
and delicate variations of even one singer cannot be
reproduced on paper. And I despair of conveying any
notion of the effect of a number singing together,
especially in a complicated shout. . . . There is no
singing in *parts*, as we understand it, and yet no two
appear to be singing the same thing — the leading
singer starts the words of each verse, often improvising,
and the others, who 'base' him, as it is called, strike
in with the refrain, or even join in the solo, when the
words are familiar. When the 'base' begins, the leader
often stops, leaving the rest of his words to be guessed
at, or it may be they are taken up by one of the other
singers. And the 'basers' themselves seem to follow
their own whims, beginning when they please and
leaving off when they please, striking an octave above
or below (in case they have pitched the tune too low or
too high), or hitting some other note that chords, so as
to produce the effect of a marvellous complication and
variety, and yet with the most perfect time, and rarely
with any discord. And what makes it all the harder to
unravel a thread of melody out of this strange network
is that, like birds, they seem not infrequently to strike
sounds that cannot be precisely represented by the
gamut, and abound in 'slides from one note to another,
and turns and cadences not in articulated notes.'"

How the same songs could be sung equally well at all sorts of work is explained by another writer,[1] as follows: "Of course the *tempo* is not always alike. On the water, the oars dip 'Poor Rosy' to an even andante, a stout boy and girl at the hominy-mill will make the same 'Poor Rosy' fly, to keep up with the whirling stone; and in the evening, after the day's work is done, 'Heab'n shall-a be my home' [a line from 'Poor Rosy'] peals up slowly and mournfully from the distant quarters. One woman — a respectable house-servant, who had lost all but one of her twenty-two children — said to me: 'Pshaw! don't har to dese yer chil'en, misse. Dey just rattles it off, — dey don't know how for sing it. I likes "Poor Rosy" better dan all de songs, but it can't be sung widout a full heart and a troubled sperrit!'"

FROM H. W.

Saturday, May 3. Directly after breakfast I mounted the pony, followed by Tom to open the gates. In this way we proceeded to Fripp Point, the plantation which belongs to this one. Just before we reached the Point, Tom started my horse, and before I knew it I was on the ground from the saddle's having turned under me. The horse behaved perfectly well, and I mounted and rode on towards the quarters (there is no white people's house here), where I could see St. Helena Village across the creek — a Deserted Village of a dozen or more mansions with their house-servants' cabins behind them, and two churches in a large pine wood, free from underbrush, where there are only one mulatto woman and her two children, belonging to this place,

[1] Miss Lucy McKim, in a letter to the Boston *Journal of Music*, November 8, 1862.

the sole occupants.[1] The village is directly on the creek on a bluff like that on which Beaufort is situated, about eight feet high, and is the place where the white people used to spend the summers for health and society — those who did not go North to travel, or to Beaufort. This Fripp family had a house in each place, besides this one at Pine Grove. As he [Tom] walked alongside the horse, I questioned him about the old family, and found that it consisted of William Fripp and his wife Harriet, their four sons and a daughter. The old man they all speak of with respect as a "good marn." Mass' Washington they represent as not liking the war,[2] and papers have been found which prove this true. Mass' Clan's was a doctor and very kind, and lived at the village — "bes' young massa we hab." Mass' Eden lived alone on this place, and was from all accounts a very bad man. With only one meal a day, he lived on whiskey, and, beyond his own control most of the time, he used to "lick wus 'an fire." The tree in the yard to which they were tied, their feet a foot or more from the ground, while he used the raw cowhide himself, has the nails in it now which prevented the rope from slipping — Flora showed it to me from my window. They do not talk much unless we question them, when they tell freely. As I opened shop this afternoon, old Alick, head-carpenter and a most respectable man, opened the cupboard door in the entry,

---

[1] This old woman Mr. Philbrick had found "keeping guard over her late master's household goods — i. e., selling them."

[2] A few weeks earlier than this, one of the drivers told Mr. Philbrick that Washington Fripp had just been shot near Charleston for refusing to enlist.

but when he saw our dishes shut it with an apology, saying that it was an old acquaintance and he wanted to see what it was used for now. "I get sixty lash for makin' dat two year Christmas, and hab to work all Christmas day beside." Well, Alick, those days are over for you now. "Tank de Lord, missus, tank de Lord."

By afternoon my hip was swollen and painful. I did not go downstairs again that night; but hearing them laugh at the dinner-table over some experience of Mr. G.'s, found it was this. He had been telling them [his pupils] that it was necessary that they should be punctual, study hard, and behave well in order to have a good school, and talking to them Saturday night about the fresh week that was coming, in which they must try hard, asked what three things were necessary for a good school. A question which was received in profound silence, for it is almost impossible to make them put that and that together, till one boy about nineteen rose and said very solemnly, "Father, Son and Holy Ghost!"

FROM W. C. G.

Pine Grove, May 3. Sunday, besides its other virtues, in this place brings us bread, and an opportunity to send and receive letters. Mr. Eustis takes a large bag of loaves in his carriage, which are shared out to hungry superintendents after service. Eustis's house and his plantation serve as general caravanserai to our whole establishment. His overseer house — a mile from his own — is the dépôt for supplies for these outside islands.

Our cotton-agent has at last paid off our plantations and will probably say farewell this coming week. We also have made a small payment to the hands of $1.00 per acre for all the cotton they had planted up to a certain date. The slight sum has had a very good effect. Other things have aided it. The cotton-agent paid them partly in goods. As soon as they had received the money from him and ourselves, we opened store, putting our goods at cheap prices. The stock consisted of the clothes I brought with me, those which K. sent me, and some pieces Mrs. Philbrick brought with her, with some furnished by the Commission; also a barrel of molasses, some tobacco, and shoes. The " sweetening " and the clothing were at cheaper prices than anything they have been accustomed to, so they were greatly pleased and we have sold out rapidly. The good effect is already quite noticeable, —but they are by no means all clothed. The men and boys, especially, stick to their rags. [The money] obtained from our private boxes will be expended in buying other articles for the negroes, to be sold again, or distributed to them, as may seem best. A vast deal of dissatisfaction among the people has been saved by this method of distributing the clothing. The faithful workers have all had money. All understand and like the arrangement.

I have made a rather elaborate explanation of all this, because to some perhaps it will seem to be a strange and suspicious operation.

The natural impulse to treat the negroes as objects of charity was thus early found to be a mistaken one; by the end of November the Government, too, had ceased to give them anything, the system of rations having done, as is remarked in one of the letters, "too much harm already." The time never came, however, when there was not heard from the North abundant criticism of the kind which H. W., in her letter of April 29, and W. C. G. here are trying to disarm, and the superintendents had to outgrow their fear of being blamed for "strange and suspicious operations."

FROM H. W.

Sunday, May 4. They had had a "Shout," which I had heard distinctly at three o'clock in the morning when I happened to wake up. They come from all the plantations about, when these meetings take place for the examination of new members, "prodigals and raw souls," as 'Siah said, he being an elder and one of the deacons. They do not begin till about ten o'clock Saturday night, when the examinations commence and the other services, after which they keep up the shout till near daylight, when they can see to go home. They admitted two this time, and, as Uncle Sam remarked, "they say there is joy in Heaven over one sinner that repenteth, so we rejoice over these souls that have come in."

A good many of the girls came up. They lay round the floor or squatted about as I read and sung hymns to them; they were very much surprised that I was not afraid to sleep alone in such a big room — said Miss Juliana and Miss Lynch, Mass' Sam and Mass' Willie and their Mamma used to sleep there. These people do not use any feminine adjective, and their "hims" are very confusing sometimes. Harriet walked down to the house behind me from school the other day for some sugar

for a sick baby, and I asked her the name of a bird
that flew across our path. "Him de Red bird." I
thought the Red bird was all red, I said. "Him de
'oman bird, marm, de marn bird all red, him de 'oman
bird, marm." The girls hung round till the faithful
Flora appeared to "wash me down" with the tide.
Everything here depends on the tide; Susan will not
make butter when the tide is going out — it would take
it all day to come; and Flora would bathe the swelling
when the tide was going out, that it might carry it
with it.

No letters when they came from church — four
weeks from home, and never a word.

In the afternoon I walked out in the yard a few steps,
and it was pleasant and touching to see how eagerly
they watched me and passed the word, "Miss Hayiot's
comin'," with bow and curtsey, asking, "How you find
yourself to-day, Missus?" "Glad to see you on you
feet, marm."

May 5. I had the school come up to me on the piazza,
a plan I shall adopt for the future; it is cool and pleasant, saves me a walk which will be warm by and by,
and also from the fleas of the praise-house. Louisa
came up to give me two eggs, carefully wrapped in
her apron. This makes over a dozen I have had brought
to me by my grateful pupils.

May 6. In the afternoon Flora brought me a letter
to read to her, which proved to be from her husband,
who is cook to some officers at Bay Point. I am quite
curious to see him — she is so fine and the children
are among the brightest here. Some soldier had written
it for him, and she was too pleased for anything at her

first letter. It was signed "York polite," which she
told me was his title. I can't make out whether they
give each other surnames, and this is his, or whether
it is really a title, as she says, like "Philip the Fair." [1]
She told me what to say, and I wrote an answer for
her.

May 8. A Baptist minister, who came out with us
and has been appointed the pastor of the island, came
to lunch, went to the other plantations with Mr. Philbrick, and has come back to spend the night. He had
been up to the praise-meeting by Uncle Peter's invitation. He is very much puzzled what to do about the
religious feeling of these people and their habits and
customs. I hope he will let them alone.

May 9. Went up to the praise-house for school in
the morning; it is so hard to get the little things together
and then, like as not, they have *half* of them to be sent
back to wash their faces and hands. Asked the little
children questions, such as "What are your eyes
for?" "For see 'long." "Teeth?" "For chaw 'long,"etc.

Sunday, May 11. In the morning a number of the
women had come up to the house to see us. It seems
they have always been in the habit of coming into the
yard on Sundays. Tira, Sim's wife, brought me three
little fish fried. The women said that all the people
here were born on the place, and no new hands had
ever been bought, only one sold, and his master allowed
him that privilege because his wife belonged in Charleston and he wanted to belong to the same man.

Flora said at lunch, as she brushed off the flies, that
her husband York was at work on the "main" (land),

[1] A "title" was a negro surname of whatever derivation.

she did not know where, on a house, with five of their
carpenters, when the war broke out, or rather, before
the Fort here was "taken away," as they say, and that
then the white people had not food enough to feed the
blacks, and she is quite sure all her brothers and sisters
who were carried off were dead before this — starved.
York was five weeks getting back here, and arrived
about Christmas.

Limus came for a reading-lesson, a man about fifty,
driver on one of Mr. Soule's plantations next this, who
comes over almost every day for me to teach him. He
has a wife here and grown children, and another on
the other plantation, the rascal. He is very smart and
learns well.[1]

Mr. Philbrick had business with Mr. Pierce, and
did not come home to dinner. But he got into more
business than he expected before he came back, and

[1] The following description of Limus and his subsequent doings
is copied from a letter of W. C. G.'s (June 12, 1863), which was printed
by the Educational Commission in one of a series of leaflets containing extracts from Port Royal letters:

"He is a black Yankee. Without a drop of white blood in him, he
has the energy and '*cuteness* and big eye for his own advantage of a
born New Englander. He is not very moral or scrupulous, and the
church-members will tell you 'not yet,' with a smile, if you ask whether
he belongs to them. But he leads them all in enterprise, and his ambition and consequent prosperity make his example a very useful
one on the plantation. Half the men on the island fenced in gardens
last autumn, behind their houses, in which they now raise vegetables
for themselves and the Hilton Head markets. Limus in his half-acre
has quite a little farmyard besides. With poultry-houses, pig-pens,
and corn-houses, the array is very imposing. He has even a stable,
for he made out some title to a horse, which was allowed; and then
he begged a pair of wheels and makes a cart for his work; and not
to leave the luxuries behind, he next rigs up a kind of sulky and bows

I never saw a poor man show suffering more than he did when he came in after ten o'clock and told us what he had received orders to do the next day. While he was at Mr. Pierce's, writing, young Hazard Stevens came over with despatches from General Hunter [1] ordering all the agents to send him in the morning all the able-bodied black men between the ages of 18 and 45, capable of bearing arms, on the plantations. There was no explanation whatsoever of the reasons for the demand, no hint of what was to be done with them, and to the white men from his carriage. As he keeps his table in corresponding style, — for he buys more sugar . . . than any other two families, — of course the establishment is rather expensive. So, to provide the means, he has three permanent irons in the fire — his cotton, his Hilton Head express, and his seine. Before the fishing season commenced, a pack of dogs for deer-hunting took the place of the net. While other families 'carry' from three to six or seven acres of cotton, Limus says he must have *fourteen*. To help his wife and daughters keep this in good order, he went over to the rendezvous for refugees, and imported a family to the plantation, the men of which he hired at $8 a month. . . . With a large boat which he owns, he usually makes weekly trips to Hilton Head, twenty miles distant, carrying passengers, produce and fish. These last he takes in an immense seine, — an abandoned chattel, — for the use of which he pays Government by furnishing General Hunter and staff with the finer specimens, and then has ten to twenty bushels for sale. Apparently he is either dissatisfied with this arrangement or means to extend his operations, for he asks me to bring him another seine for which I am to pay $70. I presume his savings since 'the guns fired at Bay Point' — which is the native record of the capture of the island — amount to four or five hundred dollars. He is all ready to buy land, and I expect to see him in ten years a tolerably rich man. Limus has, it is true, but few equals on the islands, and yet there are many who follow not far behind him."

[1] Major-General David Hunter, who on March 31 had taken command of the newly created Department of the South, consisting of the states of South Carolina, Georgia, and Florida.

nothing but our confidence in General Hunter's friend-
liness to the race gave us a shadow of comfort. But
that would avail little to the negroes, who would lose
the confidence they are beginning to feel in white
men. Yet there was but one thing for us to do, and it
was with heavy, aching hearts that at midnight we
separated. Companies of soldiers were to be sent from
Beaufort in the night and distributed to the different
plantations to prevent the negroes from taking to the
woods, so that we were not surprised at being roused
about two hours after by thundering knocks at the
front door, echoing through all these empty rooms with
a ghostly sound. This proved to be Captain Stevens again,
alone, who had stopped to enquire the way to some
of the other plantations he had to notify, and say that
the soldiers would be here in about an hour. We had
scarcely got to sleep again before we all were roused
by their arrival, and eight men, a Captain and Sergeant
of the New York 79th Highlanders, tramped through the
house. Mr. Philbrick gave them a pail of water and
some hardtack, for they had had a long walk, and then
they stretched themselves on the floor of one of our
empty parlors as quietly as could be, considering themselves in luxury. We slept as best we could the rest of
the night, and were up early to get the soldiers their
breakfast and get ready for the heart-sickening work.
You never saw a more wretched set of people than sat
down to our breakfast-table. I *could not* eat, for about
the first time in my life. Nothing had been said to any
one. Joe saw the soldiers on the floor when he opened
the house door in the morning, and wore a sober face
when we came down, but no one asked any questions,

and we moved about, seeing to the breakfast, trying to
look as usual (and failing), getting out tobacco and
crackers to give the men on all these plantations when
they went off. It had been arranged that Mr. G. should
see to these two plantations after Mr. Philbrick had
taken part of the soldiers to Coffin's Point. When he had
gone, Mr. G. began on Joe before he went to the field
for the other hands — telling him that General Hunter
had work at Hilton Head for a great many black men,
that he did not know what for, but had received orders
in the night, and they must be obeyed and he must
march; he had to go at once to his house for his cap,
say good-bye to his wife and come to us to leave his will,
for he said he never expected to come back. We made
as light of the whole thing as we could, but did not dare
to say anything (as we knew nothing) which might make
them feel afterwards as if we had deceived them, for the
thing they dread is being made to fight, and we knew
that there had been men about trying to recruit for Hunter's pet idea, a regiment of blacks. *One* man had been
obtained on this island! We told Joe that Mr. Philbrick
knew nothing about it and was going with them himself,
and gave him a letter Mr. Philbrick had written asking
for him to be returned as a personal favor, as he was a
house-servant. He did the same thing with each of the
drivers, for the good of the plantation crops. The men
were easily collected, ten here, and went off after all with
much less emotion than we expected; the soldiers behaved admirably, delighted with the treatment they had
received, and cheering the negroes with tales of money
and clothes, treating them most kindly. Mr. Philbrick
called all the hands together at Coffin's and told them

the simple fact, all that he himself knew, and named
the men who were to go, and the whole thing was accomplished with much less *apparent* suffering than we
had supposed possible. Many of the men were not averse
to trying their hands at life in the world, for many of
their number have been and still are at work for officers,
etc., at Hilton Head and Bay Point, etc., with most
desirable pecuniary results, but they are afraid of being
made to fight. Flora, our heroine, said the women and
boys could take care of all the cotton and corn if the
men did have to go — that they did not trust many
white people, but they did trust Mr. Philbrick.

The day passed in perfect quiet: the women finished
their work in the field, I kept school, Mr. G. came back
from the Point and after lunch took the driver's place,
sharing out the week's allowance of corn to the people,
while H. and I sat under the shade of the trees, watching
or talking to the women. Wil'by, Joe's wife, was the only
one who seemed really sad and heart-sick — all the rest
were as usual. Dr. Wakefield [1] came and recounted
his miseries while I set the tea-table, when, just as everything was cleared away, Mr. G. came in, with his face
all aglow, to tell us that the drivers, Joe, and one or two
others had been sent back, and in a moment Joe appeared, radiant with happiness. Mr. G. found he had
not seen his wife, so went to her cabin and told her the
ladies wanted her, and it was pretty enough to see her
simple delight as she caught sight of Joe in the door-
way. They both laughed nervously, then shook hands
shyly, and she curtseyed, then hid her face against the
wall, saying, "I so thankful I can't say a word," and

[1] Dr. Wakefield was physician for that end of St. Helena Island.

pretty soon, "Oh Joe, I could n't eat the hominy for dinner;" and Joe, "I could n't eat the biscuits, either, that Mr. Philbrick gave me, had to gi' um away — and then I was so glad, I did n't feel hungry till I got home." We sent them off to eat hominy and be happy, and sat down to write with lighter hearts ourselves.

Mr. Philbrick soon appeared. He found Mr. Pierce had been down to Hilton Head and found what he had in part suspected to be the fact. General Hunter found that the negroes misapprehended his wishes and ideas, and he could not raise as many as he wanted, so had resorted to these measures, meaning to give the men an idea of the life and drill, and after a few weeks not retain any who wished to return to their homes. All the superintendents were indignant at the way the thing was done, but it will not turn out so badly as we feared, I trust. The people are used to being made to do things, and are not in the least rebellious, as any white man would have been. If we can have blacks to garrison the forts and save our soldiers through the hot weather, every one will be thankful. But I don't believe you could make soldiers of these men at all — they are afraid, and they know it.

The cotton-agent left Coffin's Point to-day, so that we can go there now whenever we can get the house ready. Then we shall have horses and vehicles more at our disposal; you may hear of our carriage and span yet, but I shall hate to leave here. This moon is lovely. and to-night the flats are covered with water by the full moon tide, and the sea looks as if it came to our doors,

The opinion just expressed concerning the impossibility of making soldiers from Sea Island negroes was, very naturally, the view that prevailed at this time among the superintendents and teachers; in the extract that follows it is stated with even more decision. As the letters progress, the reader will see the development of a complete change of mind on this point.

FROM W. C. G.

May 27. Negroes — plantation negroes, at least — will never make soldiers in one generation. Five white men could put a regiment to flight; but they may be very useful in preventing sickness and death among our troops by relieving them of part of their work, and they may acquire a certain self-respect and independence which more than anything else they need to feel, if they are soon to stand by their own strength.

FROM H. W.

May 13. Old Peggy, the "leader" from Fripp Point, came over, and Flora brought her to see the school. She sat on the doorstep, very much interested and uttering frequent ejaculations of "Oh Lord!" H. had her sewing-school, and then I my regular session, with diminished numbers. Hope the men took their books. Saw Wil'by to-day and asked if she did not feel pretty well, when Susan answered, "She feel pretty well, Missus, but I don't; can't feel right with five boys all gone, not so much as that (pointing off the end of her finger) left of one of them; two carried off by Secesh, one with a Captain of ours at Fort Pulaski,[1] not heard from since Christmas, and now two gone yesterday." But she seemed to feel, spite of her regrets, that if they could help she was glad they should. Flora said old Peggy

[1] On Cockspur Island, Georgia.

and Binah were the two whom all that came into the
Church had to come through, and the Church supports
them, and she contributed thirty-five cents to get her
some flannel for garments, which she had always been
used to till now. Of course we gave them to her.

May 14. Our new equipage with its two horses drew
up, and I got in, while H., shocked at the rags, cut out
the lining of the top of the buggy, showering me with
sand thereby. The buggy and horses were legacies from
Mr. S., the cotton-agent, who departed yesterday.

There have been seven babies born on the three plantations since we came, and thirteen since Mr. Philbrick
came, for which we have been able to supply but little
and that only on this place. The Master always provided for the new babies two of each garment and half
a dozen diapers.

I found that they had a most heart-rending time [at
Mr. Eustis' plantation] on Monday. The two companies of soldiers coming over Sunday night had frightened
them, and they kept watch all along the creek through
the night of their own accord, for fear of Secesh. The
thing was not judiciously done the next morning, and
seems to have made a great deal of suffering which was
avoided here.

May 15. After lunch I walked down to the quarters
and stopped at all the cabins. Found two of the men
had already come back from Hilton Head and had eased
the minds of all the mothers and wives by the reports
which they brought back of comfortable quarters, good
food and clothing, confirming all our statements. I think
here a greater degree of confidence than ever will be
established by this painful episode. Mr. Philbrick says

they have not behaved so well at Coffin's Point as to-day
since he came. We walked down to the field to see them
hoeing corn in their own "nigger field" — what is
raised for the plantation, not their own private patches,
but that out of which their weekly peck comes, and
which therefore they will work on out of hours. Their
task [1] is done, often, by eleven o'clock.

Went to see Binah. She is always very glad to see us,
and to-day reached to a little shelf at the foot of the bed,
off which she took a small tin pail and gave us three eggs
— her last. I remonstrated, but she said, "You gib me
ting, I say tank 'ee," so I picked them up and thanked her.

Mr. Philbrick sent for the people to make the final
payment for cotton-planting, which is now finished, and
we stood at the window to watch them as they came up,
and help give out the money. One woman, who had
not done so much work, was disturbed at not getting as
much money as the others, and Mr. Philbrick could
not make her understand. Flora came to H. afterwards
and said, "You must excuse we niggers, we no sense,
and Mr. Philbrick *so* patient; all Secesh on these islands
could n't make so much as he has with we."

May 16. Dr. Wakefield arrived with the news of the
rebel Flag-steamer's having escaped from Charleston
through the inside passages, passed Beaufort and gone

---

[1] As the quarter-acre "task," which was all that the planters had required of their slaves each day, had occupied about four or five hours
only, it will be seen that the slaves on the Sea Islands had not been
overworked, though they had been underfed. Like the "task," the
"private patches" were also an institution retained, at E. L. Pierce's
suggestion, from slavery times, with the difference that their size was
very much increased — often from a fraction of an acre to ten times
that amount.

to Hilton Head. It was manned by blacks, who came off at two o'clock night before last with their wives and children, the officers having all gone ashore. It mounted two guns, and had four others on board which were to be taken [1] somewhere, passed Sumter with the right signals, and Beaufort with a Federal flag, and was sent back there again from Hilton Head. I should like to have been in Beaufort. It is magnificent.

The sales have been quite large, as Mr. Philbrick's denims [2] have arrived, and the negroes had yesterday their second payment. The cloth is sold at the wholesale price, as it was bought. I am afraid they will never get it as cheap again. Now we can give away the made clothes with more freedom.

Got old Peter to make me a piggin for fresh water in my chamber; as they always carry everything on their heads, a pail is no advantage. It is of a red color, and very nicely made. When I gave it to Flora to fill, she said, "him name Harriet" — whether intended as a compliment to me or to the piggin I could not understand. When we told Joe about the steamer, he exclaimed, "Gracious! 'zackly, that done beautiful," and kept exploding through the rest of dinner, "my glory," "gracious," "smartest ting done yet."

May 17. H. called me out of school this morning to see one of the crew of the *Planter*, the steamer that ran off from Charleston. He proved to be a man from McKee's plantation who had a wife and children at Coffin's Point and had come round in a boat with a crew

---

[1] By the rebels.

[2] He had already had sent down from the North a quantity of articles to sell to the negroes.

and pass from General Stevens [1] to take them to Beaufort. Almost all the men came from about here; David
had two brothers with wives at Coffin's Point who were
afraid to run the risk, and, though they belonged to the
crew, went ashore. The pilot first proposed the plan,
and they arranged a day or two beforehand with the
wives they had there, took them on board in boats I
think at two o'clock, passed Fort Sumter with the signal,
two long whistles and a short, and came round inside
the islands so that they did not encounter any of our
blockading fleet till they came off Otter Island, where
there is a vessel lying within sight of Coffin's Point.
Then they raised the Federal flag which was on board,
were boarded by our men and *cheered* as they passed
on their way. Beaufort was amazed at a steamer with
the Federal flag coming from that direction. The guns
were to be mounted between Sumter and Charleston
at the new Fort Ripley. David said they had made up
their minds to blow up the vessel rather than be taken
— they knew they should have no mercy. I hope the
men who stayed were not hung for not informing. He
said Charleston was "very interrupted," not a white
woman left in the town, as they were expecting an
attack from the Federals. He reports coffee at $1.50 a
pound, sugar 50 cents there, but I don't know how much
he is to be relied on; he was very quiet and modest — the
fireman; said he used to work in the field here, but would
"go furder" before he ever would do it again.

To-day a quantity of bacon, which was sent from Philadelphia, was given out to the hands on both the Fripp

---

[1] Brigadier-General Isaac I. Stevens, then at Beaufort, commanding the Second Division.

plantations. There has been a good deal of trouble about
their working Saturday, and the bacon was only given
to those who went into the field to-day, I hope with good
effect. They have not done a third the usual work this
year, and it is hard to bring anything to bear upon them.
I hope Captain Saxton, who we hear is coming out as
head of the whole concern, will have sufficient authority
to settle some points which have been left to the individual superintendents and with regard to which they
have not pursued the same course, making it very hard
for some.

Rufus Saxton, Captain in the United States Army,
had been a quartermaster at Hilton Head ever since
its capture. On April 29, 1862, he was assigned, as
Brigadier-General of Volunteers, "to take possession of
all the plantations heretofore occupied by the rebels"
in the Department of the South, "and take charge of
the inhabitants remaining thereon within the department, or which the fortunes of the war may hereafter
bring into it, with authority to take such measures, make
such rules and regulations for the cultivation of the land
and for protection, employment, and government of the
inhabitants as circumstances may seem to require."
He was to act under the orders of the Secretary of War,
and, so far as the persons and purposes specified were
concerned, his action was to be "independent of that
of other military authorities of the department," and
in all other cases "subordinate only to the Major-General commanding." Many of Saxton's orders are signed
"Brigadier-General and Military Governor," but of
course he was never a military governor in the sense in
which that term was used of Lincoln's military governors
of states. Doubtless Saxton was recommended for his
position by General Hunter, both being ardent anti-
slavery men.

FROM H. W.

Sunday, May 18. Started [for church] directly after
breakfast in the buggy. It is the first time I have been
up, and I am glad to have seen the sight. The church [1]
is of brick, in a grove of very beautiful live-oak trees
wreathed with grapevines and hanging moss, under
which were tied every conceivable description of horse
and vehicle, from Mr. Pierce's six-seated carriage and
pair of fine Northern horses to the one-seated sulkies,
and mules saddled with cotton-bags. Just as we arrived
the people were all pouring out of church after Sunday
School, for a short intermission before the service. I
was very sorry to lose that part of the performances.
Mr. Hooper is superintendent, and they say has an
admirable faculty at interesting the children, who are
taught besides by the white people present in classes.
We had a pleasant chat with Miss W. and Miss Towne
and the gentlemen, most of whom do not meet at all
except once a week at church, and then the people were
collected again, and when they were seated, Mr. Pierce
summoned us, the four ladies, to an empty pew with
himself. The church is painted white inside, very plain,
with galleries, and filled full of black people, — doors,
windows and aisles. Dr. French had come over from
"Biffert," as they call it, and conducted the services.
He read a hymn through, "Am I a soldier of the Cross?"
etc., and then deaconed out two lines at a time, while

---

[1] The "Brick Church" was a Baptist Church which had always
been used by both blacks and whites. Less than a mile away stood
the " White Church," Episcopalian, — closed since the flight of the
planters.

the negroes sang it in their peculiar, nasal manner, one always leading. He preached them an admirable sermon, familiar in its style. He told them of his visit to the men who had been carried to Hilton Head, which interested them very much and comforted them too, I guess. Compared them to the Israelites coming out of Egypt, as in a transition state in which everything depended upon themselves — they must not behave so ill that God would make them wander forty years in the wilderness instead of reaching Canaan in eighteen months. It was pleasant to see their interest — the "elders" all sat under the pulpit and in the front seats, and many would nod their heads from time to time in approbation, equivalent to the "'zackly" and "jus' so" of their every-day speech. They were all well dressed — a few in gaudy toggery, hoopskirts, and shabby bonnets, but mostly in their simple "head hankerchers" [which] I hope they will never give up. Many of the men on the road had their shoes in their hands to put on when they got to church. Most of them wear none. The women, many of them, came up to shake hands with us after church and·said they must come and see us. There are no white ladies on the islands beside us and those at Pope's (Mr. Pierce's).

Mr. Hooper told us of General Hunter's proclamation declaring all slaves free in South Carolina, Georgia, and Florida.[1] We got no letters or news from the North of any sort, and are waiting anxiously to know how this news is received there and what has happened since we heard last. He promises free papers to all who enlist, and gives each a chance to come home to his family if

[1] Issued May 9, and on May 19, nullified by President Lincoln.

he concludes to do so. Expresses great regret that the
thing should have been done as it was, but I don't know
what he could expect, and it will be some time before
the impression will die out, particularly among the women. The men are well contented there, and most of
them will stay, I daresay; there are over five hundred.

May 19. This evening Dr. Wakefield arrived with the
Doctor of the Roundhead Pennsylvania Regiment. Said
the pilot of the *Planter*, as he passed Fort Sumter
at daybreak, broke into the Captain's room, put on his
regimentals, and walked up and down the deck mim-
icking the Captain's gait, so that if they should use
their glasses at Fort Sumter no suspicion should be
excited!

May 20. We are fortunate in being on a plantation
so far from town, the soldiers, and the influence of the
cotton-agents. At Coffin's Point the people have shown
the effects of having soldiers quartered there so long,
though they were a less simple and quiet sort than these
in Secesh times. The quarters here are the cleanest and
prettiest I have seen, though there is room for improvement.

The day has been a very busy one. A large box of
Philadelphia clothing I overhauled, made a list of everything in it, and with H.'s help rolled up half and packed
again to go to Coffin's Point. It is the last box of clothing we shall have, I hope. We thought we should enjoy
the giving more things, now that the goods have come
by the piece which they prefer to buy, but they are so
jealous, and it is so hard to keep the run of so many
families so as to distribute the garments equally, that
it is hard work, and proves the wisdom of those who

decided it was best to sell in the first place. The old people and babies of course we give to entirely, *i. e.*, as far as we have the means. I should like a box full of baby-clothes and flannel for the old rheumaticky women, whose garments are all worn out.

Heard Joe tell Flora, "Don't call me 'Joe' again; my name Mr. Jenkins." I find they all have surnames, of one sort and another, a wife taking her husband's.

May 22. When they go into the field to work, the women tie a bit of string or some vine round their skirts just below the hips, to shorten them, often raising them nearly to the knees; then they walk off with their heavy hoes on their shoulders, as free, strong, and graceful as possible. The prettiest sight is the corn-shelling on Mondays, when the week's allowance, a peck a hand, is given out at the corn-house by the driver. They all assemble with their baskets, which are shallow and without handles, made by themselves of the palmetto and holding from half a peck to a bushel. The corn is given out in the ear, and they sit about or kneel on the ground, shelling it with cleared corn-cobs. Here there are four enormous logs hollowed at one end, which serve as mortars, at which two can stand with their rude pestles, which they strike up and down alternately. It is very hard work, but quicker than the hand process. After it is all shelled, the driver puts a large hide on the ground and measures each one's portion into his basket, and men, women, girls, and boys go off with the weight on their heads. The corn-house is in a very pretty place, with trees about it, and it is always a picturesque sight — especially when the sand-flies are about, and the children light corn-cob fires to keep them off. The corn is

ground by hand by each negro in turn for themselves;
it is hard work and there are only three hand-mills on
the place, but it makes very sweet meal and grits. The
negroes do not like the taste of that which is ground by
steam-mill at Beaufort; I suppose the heat of the stones
hurts it. The blacks at Hilton Head, who have had our
Indian-meal given them as rations, cannot eat the "red
flour." [1] They separate the coarse and fine parts after
it is ground by shaking the grits in their baskets; the
finest they call corn-flour and make hoe-cake of, but
their usual food is the grits, the large portion, boiled as
hominy and eaten with clabber.

E. S. P. TO EDWARD ATKINSON

Pine Grove, May 25. We received the Philadelphia
bacon and salt herring about a week ago and divided
it among the cotton-workers. I have also distributed
a part of the salt you sent. This allowance of bacon
was given once a fortnight and *weekly* at this season
by the different masters, and the quart of salt monthly.
Several plantations near Beaufort which had been
stripped of their corn by the army have been referred
to me for supplies. I have loaded three flat-boats from
the corn-barns here and at Coffin's, where there was
a surplus, sending off 285 bushels shelled corn in all.
The removal of this corn from my barns gave occasion for some loud and boisterous talking on the part
of some of the women, and made the driver of this
plantation feel very sober, but I pacified them by telling them the Government showed its determination
to provide for them by this very act, for here were sev-

----

[1] South Carolina corn is white flint corn.

eral plantations on Ladies Island, destitute of corn,
which might have been fed with much less trouble
from the pile of bacon and herring recently received,
but that the Government did not consider *that* a just
division of good things, so they sent me a part of the
bacon and fish, and took my corn to feed the destitute.
Thereby, said I, you are all gainers, for you have corn
enough left to last till potatoes come, and you get the
bacon besides, for which you ought to be thankful.
The noisy ones stopped their clamor and the sensible ones thanked me and hoped I would stay and
take care of them, saying they had about given up
hopes of seeing any more meat in their lives, and were
very thankful for even this bit to grease their hominy
with.

The people are taking hold of the cotton-fields with
much more heart than I had feared, after the levy of
recruits two weeks ago. The cotton has been mostly
hoed once and is growing well under the favorable
weather. Some of the corn is five feet high and it is all
hoed and ploughed except the latest portion, which
was planted this month. A small portion of the cornfields has been neglected, being the portions assigned to
some of the men who are absent. There were ten young
men belonging at Coffin's Point who escaped notice
on the day of the levy, but who, on learning that I had
called for them, came and delivered themselves up next
morning. I sent them on towards Beaufort and they
met Mr. Pierce on the road. He told them that General
Hunter did not want their service against their will,
and as they preferred to return home they did so. I
had just organized the whole gang anew after this,

when Mr. S.,[1] who I thought was gone for good, turned
up with an order to collect cotton on the mainland,
and requested me to let him have a boat's crew to ex-
plore for two days. I told him the men were all organized and at work, each on his own acre, but if he could n't
get men elsewhere I should not refuse for such a short
time. The men came back on the third day without
Mr. S. and notified me that he had hired them (and
two more joined them, making twelve in all) to collect
cotton for a month or two on the neighboring territory
beyond our previous pickets, under protection of scouting-parties detached for the purpose. The men were
offered fifty cents per day, and as I had no authority to offer *anything* definitely, except a house to live in and their
allowance of corn, I told them they were free to go
where they pleased, but advised them to stay. Of course
they all went off, but have been back twice since to
spend a night and have gone again this morning. They
are nearly all active young men and are pleased with
this roving sort of life, but you may imagine how fatal
such a state of things is to my efforts at organization,
and how demoralizing upon the general industry of
those remaining at home these visits of the rovers are,
to say nothing of the breaking up of old gangs and
abandoning allotments of land. Some of these men
who were about to go with Mr. S. told me their wives
would carry on their tasks while they were gone, and
I told them that if they would do so I would let them
avail themselves of the proceeds of their labor, but if
these patches should be neglected, I should assign them
to other men, and their planting labor would be for-

[1] The cotton-agent who had been at Coffin's Point.

feited. Thus far I find but one neglected patch, and unless this is soon hoed by some of the friends of the sick woman to whom it belongs, I shall have to assign it to some one else. It is a common practice among them to hire each other to hoe their tasks, when sickness or other causes prevent them from doing it themselves, so that most of the tasks of the lying-in women are taken care of by sisters or other friends in the absence of their husbands.

The more I see of these people the more surprised I am that they should have done so much as they have this year without any definite promise of payment on our part, and with so little acquaintance with us. The course we have been obliged to pursue [1] would not have got an acre planted by Irish laborers. I do not think it the best course, but under the existing confusion it was *only* one. If we were authorized to say that we could pay a definite sum per one hundred pounds for cotton raised, or a definite sum per month for certain services performed, we might have accomplished much more, but under the present arrangement I doubt if we can do the usual work for next year's crop, *i. e.*, in preparing manure. The only men left upon these plantations are the old ones and they are not fit to cut the marsh-grass commonly used for cotton manure. The only way I can get the cornfields ploughed is by asking the drivers to take the ploughs in their own hands, which they do very cheerfully and with good effect, each one plough-

---

[1] The Government not only had made no definite promise of payment, but it was of course unable to bring to bear on the negroes any compulsion of any sort. They worked or not, as they liked, and when they liked.

ing three or four acres per day. I do not think the
hands can be expected to work on all summer without
further payments of money or some equivalent. I wait
rather anxiously for the development of Captain or
rather *General* Saxton's instructions. He has not arrived yet, but is daily expected.

The two thousand five hundred yards of cloth you
sent me is all sold with the exception of about three
pieces, and paid for in cash; a few have said they
had no money and ask me to set it down in the book
for them to pay when they get money from the cotton.
I always trust them in this way when they desire it,
and find them very reluctant to run up a long score.
My willingness to trust them gives them confidence
that they will be paid for their cotton labor, and though
the "white folks" at Hilton Head are telling them
that the cotton crop is a mere speculation on our part,
I don't think they listen much to them. One man told
me to-day that nobody could cross the sill of my door
to harm me or my ladies while he could prevent it.
This same man was sent by his master, the day that
Hilton Head was taken, with a fleet of flat-boats, to
bring the secession soldiers away from their forts.

W. C. G. says of the situation at this time:

May 27. Between the gradual settling of affairs, the
people's growing confidence in us and in the Government as paymasters, and the absence of the unruly
men, the plantations are getting on quite nicely. The
land, both corn and cotton, has been divided and al-

lotted to the hands, — so a new system of labor [1] is — on our places — already inaugurated.

FROM H. W.

Monday, May 26. Had quite a talk with Flora over the bed-making; she asked me to hem her a muslin head-hankercher which York had sent her from Hilton Head, and re-string some beads which had come too and been broken. I promised to do it, telling her she would have things enough to remember me by — to which she responded, "Neber forget you, long as I hab breath for draw." I find they are all beginning to feel badly at our leaving,[2] now they know we shall really go so soon.

This is 'lowance day, and school is always late Monday P. M., but to-day, as they were all together, after they got through their corn, Ranty distributed some salt and mackerel Mr. Philbrick had for them, which kept them till six, our dinner-time, and they lost school altogether, greatly to their regret. We went to the porch to watch the groups, and as they passed us with their baskets on their heads and fish wrapped in green leaves in their hands, they all looked up and curtseyed, with a "tank 'ee, Massa."

When Flora came in with the tea just after, she was muttering, "Neber see a marn so payshun as Mr. Philbri'," and then, turning to H. as if she was afraid she did not appreciate his virtue, — "Miss Helen, not two

---

[1] The old system of labor — the system in force in slavery times — had been the "gang system," the laborers working all together, so that no one had continuous responsibility for any one piece of land.

[2] For Coffin's Point.

body in de worl' so payshun as him." I don't know
what had excited her admiration just then, but she
probably never saw a white man before who did not
swear, at least. For even her favorite Mass' Clan's she
does not consider as immaculate, though he would
"nebber drive nigger."

May 28. To the [Pine Grove] quarters to say good-
bye all round, stopping at each house. They seemed
quite sorry to have us go, expressing their regret by
presents of eggs. I filled my pockets and H. her hands;
then Mily held her apron and walked home with us; she
counted over three dozen in all. My children came in
the evening, and we went to bed early; and so passed
the last day at William Fripp's Pine Grove Plantation.

Coffin's Point, May 29. Before ten the two carts
were ready, and Flora and Joe mounted one to help
us get to rights. Then H. and Mr. Philbrick went off
in the buggy with the span. I was to have gone in the
sulky, but harness fell short, and I had to wait till Tom
could come back with the mule-cart. So I collected
the children and had a last school for them, and when
Tom came, locked the door, mounted the sulky (with
the white umbrella) onto which the saddles had been
tied, and, followed to the gate by the whole tribe singing "A, B, C," took my departure, the children shouting as I bid them good-bye, "We come for see you!"

As I drove up to the house [at Coffin's] the yard
really looked attractive, as it has some grass in it, though
I had not thought the house so. But a day's work has
made a vast change, and to-night it looks quite habit-
able. It was built in good style originally, but it is very
old, and has been so abused by the negroes in the first

place, and then from having had soldiers living in it for so many months, it is very shabby. It must have been handsomely furnished, to judge from the relics, for they are nothing more — rosewood tables, sideboards and washstands with marble tops, drawers and doors broken in and half gone, sofas that must have been of the best, nothing left but the frame; no one can conceive of the destruction who has not seen it. The rooms are twelve feet high, and the lower story is more than that from the ground. The air is delicious, and we shall find the blinds which are on the second story a luxury. I have my own little bed, bureau, marble-top washstand, *three* chairs and a large wardrobe, to say nothing of a piano, in my chamber, which is I should think eighteen feet square.

FROM W. C. G.

May 30. Schools are getting on pretty well, I suppose, — slowly, of course. A few are really bright, — a few really dull; the larger part — like the same proportion of white children — could creep, walk, or trot, according to the regularity with which they are driven, and the time devoted to their books. While we have been living at Pine Grove, there have been five schools daily, teaching about one hundred and forty scholars.

FROM H. W.

May 30. We have moved just in time, I guess, for the weather will grow warmer now. Between eight and eleven is the warmest part of the day; after that the sea-breeze is sure to come up.

May 31. There is a line cut through the trees all

across the islands so that they can see the light-house
from Beaufort. I asked Tom who cut it, as I rode over
the other day, and he said, "Yankee cut it." "Since
the Fort was taken?" "Long time ago." "The old
Masters cut it, then?" "No, Secesh neber cut down
trees, make nigger do it; poor white men cut 'em."
I finally came to the conclusion that it must have been
done by the Coast Survey. I daresay they think we
are all "poor white." Mary, a mulatto here, told Mr.
G. his clothes would be fifty cents per dozen for washing; that she used to have seventy-five cents in Charles-
on, "for real gentle folks!"

Sunday, June 1. H. called in Betty, Joe, and Uncle
Sam while she read, and after Mr. Philbrick had repeated the Lord's Prayer, Uncle Sam of his own accord
offered a very simple, touching prayer. He is an Elder,
and as honest and true as "Uncle Tom" himself — a
genuine specimen of that class among the negroes,
which exists in reality as well as in story. The younger
ones do not seem to be quite so religious a class, though
perhaps they are too young to tell, for young married
men like Joe and Cuffy seem to have genuine principle, and belong to the church. H. told Joe, when he
had been sulky for the first time, that she hoped he felt
better; she did not like to see him so. "Yes, Marm,
feel better now, Marm; you know de ole marn will rise
sometimes." And he told Mr. G. once that he should
not cry if his baby died, "'cause de Lord take him to
a better place — not punish him, 'cause he have no
sin;" but he said he should cry hard if Wil'by died,
because he knew she would be punished. (His wife is
not a "professor.")

June 2. An officer from the gunboat off here came ashore to see if he could hire some men, but Mr. Philbrick told him that General Hunter had taken off more than he could spare. The officer seemed to think that Hunter would be recalled and the regiment disbanded [1] — in which case Mr. Philbrick told him he did not want the men and he might take what he needed. We hear they are made sick by the change of diet; army rations can't be very good for men who have lived on hominy all their lives. He told us, moreover, a most interesting piece of news; that the firing we heard the other day was from the blockading fleet off Charleston, which captured six and sunk three of a fleet of English steamers, ten in number, laden with arms and munitions of war, which were making an attempt to run in to Charleston — thus letting only one escape. I don't know whether it got in or off.

A semiweekly *Advertiser* and *Tribune* of May 14th, with full accounts of the taking of New Orleans and the battle of Williamsburg, which we have not heard about, and the splendid doings have roused me all up to full war pitch again. We have been so peaceful I could not realize all that was going on.

E. S. P. TO EDWARD ATKINSON

Coffin's Point, June 3. I suppose we shall lose General Hunter, for even if not recalled I don't see how he could stay after Lincoln's proclamation. I must say I think his, Hunter's action, premature and uncalled for. It seemed to me very like the tadpole resolution

[1] As a result of Lincoln's proclamation of May 19 (see p. 50 n.), the regiment, all but one company, was disbanded in August.

in "Festina lente." In this case, too, the tadpoles were
quite out of our reach except the small number in these
islands, who had virtually shed their tails in course of
nature already. I have great faith in Lincoln and am
ready to leave the question with him. I think the effect
of Hunter's proclamation upon the slaves of these
states would be inconsiderable. They don't hear of
it, to begin with, and if they did they would n't care
for it. I am surprised to find how little most of these
people appreciate their present prospects. Once in a
while you find an intelligent man who does so, but the
mass plod along in the beaten track with little thought
about the future and no sort of feeling of responsibility.
They feel a sense of relief that no one stands to force
them to labor, and they fall back with a feeling of indifference as to whether they exert themselves beyond
what is necessary to supply the demands of necessity.
No better result can be hoped for till the time comes
for each to see the reward for his labor. At present they
are working upon faith, without even a definite promise as to what that payment shall be. Hunter's course
is of far greater importance in its effect upon the political world in the North than in its immediate influence upon the status of the negroes in the districts to
which it applies. The secret of such exploits as the
crew of the *Planter* have lately performed lies in the
fact that the men were forcibly .aken from this region
last November and wanted to get back home again.
If their old home had been in Charleston, they would
not have left it at the risk they incurred. In short, I
don't regard the blacks as of any account in a military
light, for they are not a military race, and have not suf-

ficent intelligence to act in concert in any way where
firmness of purpose is required.

June 5. Mr. Philbrick brought one unwelcome letter — an appointment from Mr. Pierce to Mr. G. to
some plantation at the other end of the island. He is
too valuable to be here. He is going to a hard place,
ten or twelve plantations, though with fewer negroes in
all than on these three.

The mule-cart came up and was loaded with all Mr.
G.'s things, and by nine o'clock he took his departure
on horseback, in his red flannel shirt and palm-leaf
hat looking quite Southern and picturesque.

[Later.] Here came my morning school, for the
first time, under Bacchus' conduct. I heard them singing and went to the window to watch and see how he
was bringing them from the quarters. He is a cripple
in his hands, which turn backwards, and he has but
little control of his arms, but is much looked up to by
the other children. Of course he cannot do any work,
and Mr. G. has made him a sort of schoolmaster, and
he has always kept school when Mr. G. was away. He
manages them nicely, after his fashion — leaving them
in the midst if he happens to want to eat some hominy!
They never have regular meals, but each one eats hominy
when he happens to want it. Well, soldiers have been
stationed on the place, and Bacchus had got some notion of drill, so he marched up the thirty-five children,
six or seven in a row, holding hands to keep them
straight, and with two of the oldest boys for captains
on each side to administer raps with their sticks if they

did not keep in line, walking backwards himself to
oversee the whole company, with a soldier's cap on his
head, and shouting out his orders for them to sing
their different tunes all the way, — the funniest spectacle himself imaginable.

Monday, June 9. Found that Bacchus' brother Lester
had been taken sick Sunday morning and died at night,
so he did not bring up the school. Just after dinner we
saw the people assembling at their burying-place,[1] and
H. and I went down to witness the services. Uncle Sam
followed us, book in hand and spectacles on nose, reading as he walked. As we drew near to the grave we
heard all the children singing their A, B, C, through
and through again, as they stood waiting round the
grave for the rest to assemble and for Uncle Sam to
begin. Each child had his school-book or picture-book
Mr. G. had given him in his hand, — another proof
that they consider their lessons as in some sort religious exercise. We were joined at once by Mr. Philbrick, and stood uncovered with the rest about the
grave, at the mouth of which rested the coffin, a rough
board one, but well shaped and closed. Uncle Sam
took off his hat, tied a red handkerchief round his head
and, adjusting his glasses, read the hymn through, and
then deaconed out two lines at a time for the people
to sing. He repeated the process with a second hymn,
when Abel made a prayer; then Uncle Sam read from

[1] This burying-place was "an unfenced quarter of an acre of perfectly wild, tangled woodland in the midst of the cotton-field, halfway between here [the "white house"] and the quarters. Nothing
ever marks the graves, but the place is entirely devoted to them."
[From a letter of H. W.'s, June 5, '62.]

the Burial Service and began his exordium, apologizing for his inability to speak much on account of a sore throat, but holding forth for about half an hour upon the necessity for all to prepare for "dis bed," filling his discourse with Scripture illustrations and quotations aptly and with force, using the story of "Antoninus and Suffirus" as a proof that God would not have any "half religions" — that if anybody had "hid his Lord's money in de eart' he must grabble for it before 'twas too late." He read from the service again, one of the men throwing on earth at the usual place. When they came to cover up the grave, the men constantly changed hoes with those who had not handled them before, that each might aid, women and old men stooping to throw in a handful. Abel made another prayer, they sang again and dispersed.

It was of this scene that W. C. G. wrote the following lines:

THE NEGRO BURYING–GROUND.

'Mid the sunny flat of the cotton-field
   Lies an acre of forest-tangle still;
A cloister dim, where the grey moss waves
   And the live-oaks lock their arms at will.

Here in the shadows the slaves would hide
   As they dropped the hoe at death's release,
And leave no sign but a sinking mound
   To show where they passed on their way to peace.

This was the Gate — there was none but this —
   To a Happy Land where men were men;
And the dusky fugitives, one by one,
   Stole in from the bruise of the prison-pen.

When, lo! in the distance boomed the guns,
  The bruise was over, and "Massa" had fled!
But *Death* is the "Massa" that never flees,
  And still to the oaks they bore the dead.

'T was at set of sun; a tattered troop
  Of children circled a little grave,
Chanting an anthem rich in its peace
  As ever pealed in cathedral-nave, —

The A, B, C, that the lips below
  Had learnt with them in the school to shout.
Over and over they sung it slow,
  Crooning a mystic meaning out.

A, B, C, D, E, F, G, —
  Down solemn alphabets they swept:
The oaks leaned close, the moss swung low, —
  What strange new sound among them crept?

The holiest hymn that the children knew!
  'T was dreams come real, and heaven come near;
'T was light, and liberty, and joy,
  And "white-folks' sense," — and God right here!

Over and over; they dimly felt
  This was the charm could make black white,
This was the secret of "Massa's" pride,
  And this, unknown, made the negro's night.

What could they sing of braver cheer
  To speed on his unseen way the friend?
The children were facing the mystery Death
  With the deepest prayer that their hearts could send.

Children, too, and the mysteries last!
  We are but comrades with them *there*, —
Stammering over a meaning vast,
  Crooning our guesses of how and where.

But the children were right with their A, B, C;
In our stammering guess so much we say!
The singers were happy, and so are we:
Deep as our wants are the prayers we pray.

FROM W. C. G.

Captain Oliver Fripp's Plantation, June 9. I came
here, in consequence of a letter received from Mr.
Pierce, asking me to take charge over some plantations here. There is a Mr. Sumner here, — lately arrived, — who is teaching. The place is quite at the other
end of the island from Coffin's Point. At present I am
by no means settled; it seems like jumping from the
19th century into the Middle Ages to return from the
civilization and refinement which the ladies instituted
at Coffin's to the ruggedness of bachelor existence.

June 22. In regard to danger of sickness, I hear
much about it, — but I think it is exaggerated. The
white overseer stayed on Edgar Fripp's Plantation —
close by — all summer. The planters generally went
to Beaufort or the Village, but I think very much as
we go out of town in summer. The summer was the
fashionable and social time here, when the rich people
lived together, gave parties, etc.

July 6. The people do not work very willingly, —
things are not so steady as they have become at Coffin's.
The district is even more exposed to the influence of
visits to and from the camps.

We had quite a celebration for the people on the
Fourth. A stage was erected near the old Episcopal
church in a cool grove of live-oaks, all grey with long
trails of Southern moss. A large flag was obtained and

suspended between trees across the road — it was good
to see the old flag again. The people had been notified the previous Sunday, and I should think about a
thousand were present, in gala dress and mood, from
all parts of the island. When the ladies, the invited
superintendents from Port Royal, and the General
(Saxton)[1] had taken their seats, the people marched
up in two processions from each direction, carrying
green branches and singing. Under the flag they gave
three rousing cheers, then grouped around the stage.
The children from three or four of the schools marched
in separately. After a prayer and some native songs,
Mr. Philbrick, the General, and the *Times* reporter
addressed them, and then one of the old darkies got
on the stage and in an ecstasy of obedience and gratitude exhorted them to share his feelings, I believe.

For an hour and a half there was a general press for
the hard bread, herring, and molasses and water. When
everything was devoured, the superintendents rode up
to "the Oaks," — Pierce's headquarters,[2] — and had a
collation. So much for Fourth of July. It was strange
and moving down here on South Carolina ground,
with the old flag waving above us, to tell a thousand
slaves that they were freemen,[3] that that flag was
theirs, that our country now meant their country, and

[1] Saxton's first general order, announcing his arrival, is dated
June 28.

[2] E. L. Pierce had changed his headquarters from "Pope's."

[3] From the first the anti-slavery Northerners at Port Royal had
had no hesitation in telling their employees that they were freemen.
Indeed, they had no choice but to do so, the tadpoles on these islands,
as Mr. Philbrick said, having "virtually shed their tails in course of
nature already."

to tell them how Northerners read the Declaration —
"All men are born free and equal." The people had
a grand time, they say, and seem really grateful for it.
It was a new thing for them, a Fourth of July for the
negro. In old times they worked, if with any difference,
harder than usual, while their masters met and feasted
and drank.

The rest of this extract is an expression — which
will be followed later by many like it — of the sense
that people in the North were getting too complacent
a notion of what had been done and what could be
done for the Sea Island negroes.

Pierce's report [1] has too much sugar in it. His statements are facts, but facts with the silver lining out.
The starving, naked condition of the blacks was much
exaggerated when we started to come down here.

July 25. On the whole, affairs conduct themselves
pretty quietly and regularly. The cases of discipline
are the most vexing and amusing. It is a peculiar
experience to be detective, policeman, judge, jury, and
jailer, — all at once, — sometimes in cases of assault
and battery, and general, plantation *squows*, — then
in a divorce case, — last Sunday in a whiskey-selling
affair; a calf-murder is still on the docket.

The next letter is the first from C. P. W., who went
to Port Royal early in July, on the same steamer with
Charles F. Folsom of Harvard, '62, who is often mentioned in the letters that follow, and with several other
young Massachusetts men who had volunteered as
superintendents.

[1] Pierce's second report to Secretary Chase on the Sea Islands,
dated June 2, 1862.

FROM C. P. W.

Beaufort, July 7. We got our luggage into the May-flower and started for this place [from Hilton Head] about six o'clock. It was droll enough to find a party of Boston men taking a sail in the old Hingham boat up Beaufort River under United States passes, to super-intend South Carolina plantations.

July 15. *Coffin's Point.* The nearest of my five plan-tations is three miles distant, along the shore road, and the four on that road extend about two miles; my fifth is on the upper road, to Beaufort, about four and a half miles from the Point. The roads are mere tracks worn in the fields, sometimes through woods, like our wood roads, only more sandy. In front of my plantations there are bushes on the right-hand side, for some dis-tance, the field being bounded on the other side by woods. Fields usually very long, sometimes three quarters of a mile, divided across the road by fences, gates occur-ring at every passage from one to another; the plan-tation houses and quarters at an average of one third of a mile from the road, paths through cotton-fields leading to them. Imagine a perfectly flat country, re-lieved by belts of trees, and intersected by rows of brush, single trees standing here and there in the bare, hot fields. Very little fresh water either in brooks or pools. Salt-water creeks are to be crossed on the shore roads; the richest lands in the adjoining meadows. A cotton-field looks not unlike a potato-field, the rows higher and more distinct, the plants further apart, usually two feet; the rows five feet. Corn planted on rows like cotton. You would be surprised to see the soil in which these flourish;

beach sand, in many places, is the principal ingredient.
The fields are very much the colour of the sea-beach.

We live on the fat of the land. We are allowed $5.24
per month for rations, but I do not use even that. Rice,
sugar, and molasses are our principal draughts from
the Commissary.

The colonists referred to at the beginning of the next
letter were a thousand blacks from the island of Edisto,
which the United States Government, after taking,
had evacuated, as too troublesome to hold. The place
where they were quartered, as described in the first
sentence, was St. Helena Village.

FROM C. P. W.

July 20. The Secesh houses there are insufficient
to accommodate them all, and they stow themselves
in sheds, tents, and even in the open air, as best they
can. Many of them are to be distributed on plantations where there are quarters; they will probably be
set to planting slip-potatoes and cow-pease.

Everything needs personal supervision here; every
barrel or parcel must be kept under your eye from the
time it leaves the storehouse in Beaufort till it is put
in your mule-cart, on Ladies Island. Then you must
be at home when the team arrives and see everything
brought into the storeroom. There is a good deal of
red tape, too, at Beaufort, the untying and retying
of which is a tedious and vexatious operation.[1] They
are becoming more strict here in Beaufort in several
respects; passes are needed by every one. There is

---

[1] "We have to spend more than half our time," writes Mr. Philbrick in September, "getting our limited supplies."

a great deal of running to Hilton Head and Bay Point, which is to be stopped as far as possible.

July 30. I ride right through the morning, from nine till four, without suffering from the heat so much as in one trip to town and back one of our warm, still days at home. I have my white umbrella, there is usually some breeze, often a very cool one; the motion of the sulky puts me to sleep, but the heat of the sun has not been oppressive more than once or twice on this island. If I had attempted to follow all the directions I received before leaving, concerning my health, I should have been by this time a lunatic.

Rust is such a common thing here that we get used to it. Mrs. Philbrick's needles rust in her work-bag; our guns, even after cleaning and oiling, are soon covered with a thin coating. Food moulds here very rapidly, crackers soften and dried beef spoils. Hominy, of course, is the chief article of food. I think it tastes best hot in the negro cabins, without accompaniment of molasses, sugar, or salt.

Our life here is, necessarily, very monotonous: the hired people come and go, or we go and come to and from them, and the mosquitoes and flies do very much as we do. Mosquitoes are really a great annoyance at times. They introduce themselves under the netting at night in a very mysterious way, and wake us up early with their singing and stinging. My theory is that those that can lick the others get themselves boosted through the apertures; the animal is smaller than ours at the North. I think that they are unaccustomed to human treatment; they will not be brushed away, and slapping, if not fatal, only excites their curiosity. There is also

a small fly which appears on warm days after a rain
in great numbers. Driving on my beat the other day,
and holding my umbrella in one hand and newspaper
scrap in the other, I was driven nearly wild by their continuous attentions. It is very easy to read driving here;
the roads are so sandy that the horse has to walk a great
part of the way and one is glad to be able to employ
the weary hours with literature.

This is the greatest country for false rumors that I
ever was in. Communication is very uncertain, nothing
but special messengers to bring us news from the outside world. An occasional visit to Mr. Soule [1] or to
Beaufort enlivens the long weeks, and we welcome the
gathering at church on Sunday, with the gossip and
the mail and the queer collection of black beings in
gay toggery, as the great event of our lives. If it were
not for the newspapers, I might forget the time of year.
It is very amusing to be appealed to by a negro to know
how soon the 1st of August is; to tell them it is the 20th
of July gives them very little idea.

I should like to look in upon you and bring you some
of the delicacies of the tropical clime, watermēlions,
as the "inhabitants" call them, rich and red; huge,
mellow figs, seedy but succulent; plump quails, sweet
curlew, delicate squirrels, fat rabbits, tender chickens.
We fare well here. If the wretched country only had
more rocks and less sand, better horses, more tolerable
staff officers, [2] and just a little more frequent communi-

---

[1] Richard Soule, Jr., was General Superintendent of St. Helena
and Ladies Islands, and was living at Edgar Fripp's plantation.

[2] The first of many references to the frequent lack of sympathy
shown by army officers.

cation with New England, I should perhaps be content to make quite a long stay, if I were wanted.

I will only remark at present that I find the nigs rather more agreeable, on the whole, than I expected; that they are much to be preferred to the Irish; that their blackness is soon forgotten, and as it disappears their expression grows upon one, so that, after a week or so of intercourse with a plantation, the people are as easily distinguished and as individual as white people; I have even noticed resemblances in some of them to white people I have seen. They are about as offensively servile as I expected. The continual " sur," "maussa," with which their remarks are besprinkled is trying, but soon ceases to be noticed. " Bauss " is the most singular appellation, used by a few only.

"M's Hayyet's brudder" passed through the Pine Grove "nigger-house" one day and retired, after a distinguished ovation, incubating, like a hen, upon a sulky-box full of eggs. Promises to show Miss Harriet's picture, not yet fulfilled, were received with the greatest satisfaction.

We have been making out our pay-rolls for May and June; the blanks, delayed in the printing, have just arrived. Red Tape. The money has been ready a long time. We ought to pay for July at the same time. This, understand, is only a partial payment, on account; the full payment is to be made when the crop comes in.

Aug. 7. Last Friday Mr. Philbrick and I got our money. The people generally took the payment in excellent spirit. A few seemed surprised, not knowing what to do with so much money; a few, of course, grumbled at the amount, though a clear explanation was always understood and received with reasonable satisfaction. I thought that one or two were disposed to take advantage of the fact that I had not taken the account of acres,[1] and so tried to make a difficulty by telling strange tales. But there was a great deal of manliness and fairness shown, with a degree of patience and foresight that was very gratifying.

Aug. 16. Perhaps the best way to give you a satisfactory notion of "what my work is, how I like it," etc., is to give an account of a day's work on my plantations.

Thursday, Aug. 14. I allow Mr. Philbrick to have his horse saddled first, — this was polite, — and as soon as he is out of the gate — "Robert!" — "Surr!" "Put my *smallest* horse into the sulky." I retire within, and collect the necessary equipment for a day "out," viz.: white umbrella, whip (riding, long enough for sulky use), plantation-book, spring-balance (some rations to be delivered), much stout twine, for mending harness if need be, paper of turnip-seeds, two thirds of a pound of powder, and one novel, "An Only Son," for occupation during the first weary hour, consumed in a three miles walk over a sandy road. The young horse, caught at last, — our stud of four graze on the turfy acre fenced in about the house, — is a little restive at first in the unwonted restraint of the harness, but soon gets broken in to steady work by the heavy roads. Somewhat over an hour's slow progress brings me to the rude portal ⊓ which spans the entrance of the McTureous estate. The houses of all the plantations on the Sea Side road are to be found on the eastern, or left-hand

---

[1] That is, the account had been taken before he came South.

as one rides towards Hilton Head. The character of
the fields and quarters between the road and the water
is very much the same on all the places. The "water"
is a creek, separating the island proper from salt-water
marshes and the higher islands outside, against which
latter the ocean itself beats. The distance from the road
to the creek averages half a mile. The quarters, universally called "nigger-houses," are strung along the bank
of the creek, at about 100 feet from the water, on a ridge
between the water and the corn. The "big house" is
a two-story affair, old, dirty, rickety, poorly put together and shabbily kept. Here lived old Mrs. Martha
E. McTureous, with a large household. The James
McTureous place — the other half of this one — is
all in one and the same field. On both these places the
houses are terribly out of repair, with wooden chim-
neys and mud floors, the people dirty and suffering
from the effects of much confusion and discouragement in the spring. Limus,[1] their old driver, did much
mischief by striving to keep up the old system, and at
the same time neglected the place to go and earn
money for himself. Then they suffered severely from
the black draft, their four best men being taken; from
a population furnishing only "eight men working cotton," and thirteen full hands in all. Arriving as I did
after all the mischief was done, I have had rather a
discouraging time with them.

Entering the plantation, I am aware of old Nat. He
is hoeing pease. As I approach, he shouts, and comes
to the road, and lays before me a case of menace, ill
usage, and threatened assault. I inspected convales-

[1] See page 37.

cent boy, ascertained what work had been done, —
in a general way, that is, learning that corn-blades had
been, and were being, stripped, that all the able-bodied
men were cutting marsh-grass for manure, that Tirah
had planted a task of cow-pease for the Government,
but had allowed them to go to grass, — whereupon,
after personal inspection of said task, with an injunc-
tion to strip some corn which was getting dry, I drove
over to the James McTureous place. Having received
from Mr. Soule two packages of Swedish turnip-seed,
I enquired concerning the manner of planting, how
much seed was required for a task, etc. Dismounting
from the sulky, and leaving it in charge of a returned
volunteer (I like the sarcastic phrase), who was unwell
and therefore lounging under the trees in front of one
of the nigger-houses, I went forth to the field to count
the acres of Government corn with the driver. On the
way, I counted up the tasks of pease, slip, etc., to see
if they coincided with the account given me by the people. Found one and a half of corn worthless, except
for fodder. Conversed concerning marsh-grass, found
another hook for cutting would be acceptable, glad-
dened their hearts with promise of turnip-seed, and
drove off.

Not the least curious part of the curious state of
things described in the next paragraph is the matter-of-
course view of it taken by the youthful superintendent.

By the way, Jim, driver on the James McTureous
place, used to be slave of Mr. Pritchard, residing in
Hunting Island,[1] which runs along just outside of St.

[1] The term "Hunting Island" was applied to several of the outside islands collectively.

Helena. He was a very cruel man, — there are stories
of his burning negroes, — so when the "guns fired at
Bay Point," as he could n't run from his negroes, as
the other masters did, for lack of transportation, his
negroes ran from him, and settled among their friends
on St. Helena. When matters were established at Hilton Head, Pritchard went and took the oath and got
a pass, and has since lived at home, supporting himself by fishing and raising hogs. He often visits Jim
and others of his old slaves, getting them to go fishing
with him. Now one day last year, Jim and Mr. Pritchard found a four-oared boat — I give Jim's story
— on the beach. Pritchard promised Jim half the
value of the boat, but has since refused to fulfill his
promise. Jim referred the matter to me. I told him
to send Pritchard up to me. I think there will be no
trouble, if Jim's story is straight.

Cherry Hill, one of T. A. Coffin's [1] places, comes
next to McTureous'. Cherry Hill is one of the most
encouraging places I have. The people are of a more
sensible caste, old people, almost entirely, who see the
sense and propriety of right measures, and display a
most comforting willingness to work and be content,
though with less energy, of course, than younger men.
The place owes much of its success this year to Tony,
the driver, a person of great discretion, energy, and
influence. The ingenious method by which he induced
the people to plant more cotton than they wanted to is
entertaining, though a little troublesome to us in making out the pay-roll. Mr. Palmer, Mr. Soule's assist-
tant, counted sixteen acres of cotton on the place. But

[1] Thomas Astor Coffin, of Coffin's Point.

the several accounts of the people on the place added up only fourteen and a half acres. In this perplexity, Tony was appealed to, who explained the difficulty thus. The land was laid off in rows, twenty-one to the task, each row being one hundred and five feet long. Tony staked off the tasks anew, throwing twenty-four instead of twenty-one rows into the task, thus adding twelve rows to every acre, which the people blindly tilled, never suspecting but that they were having their own way about their cotton.

Mulberry Hill, owned by Captain John Fripp, is a little place, with not many more hands than Cherry Hill, but they are younger. The driver here is an extremely nice person, hardly energetic enough, I should think, for the old system, but a very quiet, gentlemanly man, perfectly frank and open in his manner, and a little superior in his conversation to those by whom he is surrounded. He is much respected in the dark community. It is to his bounty that I owe several huge watermelons which I have brought home for our table, besides several partial favors of the same kind, enjoyed under his own roof.

To these people I was to deliver one month's rations of hard bread. It comes in fifty-pound boxes; and as a day's ration is three quarters of a pound, and there are thirty-one days in August, it requires but a simple calculation to determine that each person entitled to a full ration should receive twenty-three and one quarter pounds, and that, one child being reckoned one sixth of a grown person (monstrous, you will say, when eating is concerned, — but such is law), one box must be delivered to every two grown-persons-and-one-child.

Having the people together, I took the opportunity to enquire of them the number of tasks of cow-pease, slip-potatoes, etc., they had planted, likewise the amount of cotton they had hoed, "since Mr. Palmer took the last account." It will be a great job making up the next pay-roll. I hope the people won't lie worse than usual. If they do, if the drivers should fail me, especially, — if, as will probably happen, their own accounts, added up, do not tally within several tasks with my count of the whole, and if at the same time I shall be required to make out the whole roll in two days, and both my horses should have sore backs at once — you can imagine what a comfortable, easy time I shall have of it.

From Mulberry Hill, after looking at some doubtful cotton in the field with the driver, Paris, and finally setting it down as not properly hoed, I proceeded to the next plantation, Alvirah Fripp's, commonly called the Hope Place. It is the largest, the most distant, and, in many respects, the toughest plantation I have. There are a great many men of twenty-five to forty, "tough-nuts" many of them, and all looking so much alike that it is impossible to remember the name that belongs to any one face, though all their names and all their faces are familiar enough. I can see that it is a great drawback to my obtaining their confidence to have to ask one and another, as I ask, "how many tasks of slip have you planted for the Government, and how many for your own use?" to have to ask also, in variously modified phrase, "What's your name?" Recognize a negro, remember anything in which he has any interest, and you have his confidence at once. I not only surprised but made my fast friend a fellow on one of my

places by calling him by his name the second time
I saw him.

The men on the Hope Place are not all of a poor
stamp, of course. The driver, Isaac, is my very ideal of
a nigger-driver on a large place, made alive. Strong of
body and up to all the dodges of the plantation life,
he shows the effect — not apparent, in such a disagreeable manner at least, in Tony and Paris — of having
a good many rough fellows to manage. I do not think
he is liked on the place; I doubt his frankness; I think
he is somewhat disposed to kick against the new authorities, disputing, *e. g.*, their right to take away "his"
horse, the little one Mr. Palmer and I foraged from
him the first day I came.

Charles, the carpenter, is a man after my own heart.
He attracted me first by his dignified and respectful
demeanor, and by his superior culture. He has a little
touch of self-consideration. He, more than any other
negro I know, seems to me like a white person. I forget his color entirely while talking with him, and am
often surprised, on approaching a black man, to recognize Charles' features. I think he is a pretty able fellow, — I should like to give him some regular employment in his trade. It seems an imposition to expect
such a man to work cotton and corn.

Beaufort is neither Bofort nor Boofort nor Biufort,
but Büft, the ü pronounced like the umlauted ü in Ger-
man. Sometimes one hears Biffut. Hooper, extremist in
ridicule, says Biffit. A letter of Mrs. Philbrick's went,
"missent," to Beaufort, N. C., which is, I believe, Bofort.
Had the pronunciation been written on the envelope, as
one hears it among the "black inhabitants," it would

have gone to the Dead Letter Office, unless, by good
luck, the S. C. had brought it as far as Hilton Head.

We get, first or last, a pretty good notion of one
another (you understand I am speaking of the white
population only), though we see very little of each other,
except when we are on adjoining plantations. The
Oaks is a rendezvous where we see each other at times;
we meet occasionally in Biffut; but church is the principal meeting-house on the island, of course, and all
the gossip of the week is fully aired on Sunday.

There is very little to tell about General Saxton, except that it is a great pity that he does not come onto
the plantations himself and learn something, personally,
of their state and their wants. He was extremely surprised the other day when Mr. Philbrick represented to
him the necessity of making the last payment promptly;
it was then twenty days behind time. A good deal
of ignorance is shown in various ways in the orders
sent from headquarters — *e. g.*, the order that has
been issued concerning marketing, nothing to be sold
on the plantations except by leave of the superintendents and no boats to go to Hilton Head or Beaufort
without a "Market Pass" from the superintendent.
Until I hear that a guard is stationed [at Hilton Head],
— which I shall the day after it is done, — I shall not
order men to report to me before going over. I have
no idea of making a rule I cannot enforce.

On the whole, our work is succeeding as well as the
disappointments and hindrances [1] of the year allow

[1] The chief "hindrance" was, of course, the late date at which
work on the cotton crop had been started; the land should have been
prepared in February, and the planting begun at the end of March.

us to expect. A great deal will depend on the manner and promptness of the next payments and the treatment of the people at harvest-time.

FROM W. C. G.

Sept. 2. There is one frightful contingency, — a much talked of evacuation. Where the people will go, I know not; but possibly to Hayti. In that case I presume the superintendents will go with them, — I certainly shall. General Saxton, I am sorry to say, goes to-morrow in a gunboat — for his health. It leaves us without a head and worse — renders evacuation all the more likely. It is thought that his presence and words prevented it several weeks ago. I doubt if he comes back, — he is not satisfied with his work here, does not enjoy it. It is properly the duty of a civilian, who should have military rank merely to give him a position. Saxton and his staff understand little or nothing of the real wants of the plantations, and though affairs have of course been improved by his presence and authority, very little in proportion to our hopes and our needs has been accomplished. We need a civilian, who is a first-rate business man, — of force, of forethought, of devoted interest in this undertaking. But there is no use in writing this, — rather some harm.

FROM C. P. W.

Sept. 6. Things are in a state of suspension generally; I confess that a decidedly azure hue has prevailed during the last week. Talk of evacuation, General Saxton's departure, threatened attacks, and even successful forays on an island behind Hilton Head by the rebels, the increased inconvenience and vexation of red-tape-ism, threatened changes in the policy to be pursued towards the people in some minor matters, involving, however, infringement of our authority with them, it is feared, besides the breaking of promises already made; the difficulty of getting them promptly and properly paid, and of getting the value of their work fairly estimated; the general inefficiency, ignorance, and indecision of the authorities, wanting a defined system and hampered by prejudice and ignorance and selfishness, — all these things make the aspect of affairs dark enough at times, and one gets discouraged and disheartened and disgusted and disappointed, and is ready to part and have nothing more to do with the concern. When, in addition to actual evils, one feels that there is a strong opposition to the enterprise, and that the difficulties are made as vexatious as possible, by jealous and hostile army officers, so that, in short, the spirit of the stronger party here is against us; and when, added to injury, one has to bear

> " the law's delays,
> The insolence of office, and the spurns,
> Which patient merit of th' unworthy takes,
> One almost swears his homeward voyage to make,
> In the next steamer."

Ignorance and want of confidence are the two evils which we suffer; want of confidence by the powers in us, by us in the negroes. It is painful to note how distrust must be the rule ; how every one must take it for granted that those under him are cheats and liars. Hence the necessity of red tape, and its delays and vex-atious inconveniences. Mr. Philbrick says, " Working for a Corporation is bad enough, but working for the Government is very much worse." However, it would n't be so bad if the Government officers knew enough of the plantation work to do the proper thing at the proper time, even though they use the red-tape method in doing it. I believe I knew more after being two weeks on my places than the Heads do at Beaufort now about the details of the work.

Sept. 9. General Saxton went North last Friday. It is more than hinted that his principal purpose is to obtain greater powers for himself. Hunter has gone North too, "in disgust," it is said, and General Brannan, who is said to befriend the enemies of the United States, and has given Saxton a deal of trouble, is left at the head of the Department.

Brigadier-General John M. Brannan was in command for a fortnight only, pending the arrival of Major-General Ormsby M. Mitchel.

Sept. 18. The President having sent word not to evacuate, you need not be anxious about us. I was a little afraid that A. L. would give in to Hunter, evacuate all but Hilton Head, and colonize the negroes from the other islands; glad he has more sense.

Here follows a detailed account of the kind of magisterial power which the superintendents found themselves called upon to "assume," though they "had it not."

FROM E. S. P.

Sept. 23. Alex sent Finnie here before breakfast to request me to come over at once, for Cato was driving his, Alex's daughter Rose, his own wife, out of the house. I rode over after breakfast. Found the whole plantation excited and on the *qui vive*. Cato had broken up Rose's bedstead and thrown it out of doors and bundled up all her things. I began to talk with him, but he was very saucy and threatened to kill the first man who interfered with him in "his own house." I thought it quite time to test him, and taking hold of his arm told him he must go home with me. He hung back sulkily at first, but in a minute yielded and said he would do so. I stepped out of the house and he after. Caroline asked me to read her a letter from John at Hilton Head, and while preparing to do so Cato dodged about the house and made for the woods across the cornfield. I cried out for him to halt, but he ran the faster. I pulled out my revolver and fired two shots over his head, but he only ran the harder, and never stopped till he reached the woods. I then had a talk with his father, old Toby, who "wished I had shot him and stopped the confusion," and with Alex, both of whom I enjoined to hold their tongues in future. When halfway home Cato stood waiting for me in the road, opening a gate as I approached, touched his hat and said he was very sorry for what he had done and was willing to go with me. I told him to follow me to the house and I would talk with him. I found him very humble. I reasoned with him, telling him I was sure Rose's child was his and that he had done her great wrong, that he ought not to listen to such scandal after living peaceably with her for eight or nine years. Cato said he hoped he should never do so again. I told him that if I ever found him making any more trouble here I should send him to work on Fort Pulaski.

Mr. Philbrick's next letter shows him trying to arouse the slothful by "sharing out" a bale of white cotton cloth, in bonus form, to the industrious.

Sept. 27. I gave one yard for every task of cotton hoed in July, requiring about 600 yards. The Coffin people all got some, but about half the people on the Fripp plantations had to go without, having neglected the last hoeing. The people who were too lazy to hoe their cotton in July looked rather glum, and those who got their cloth laughed and looked exultant. Some people here got twenty-two yards, and many got only two or three, but all took it thankfully and seemed content that they got any. Those who got so little will have to buy more, which they are doing already. I sell it at about half the price that is asked by our own quartermaster, so I shall be liberally patronized. In dividing up this cotton cloth I deducted from the shares of those people to whom clothing was given last spring the value of that clothing. The only cases were those of Martha, Amaritta, and Rosetta, to each of whom Mr. G. gave a dress. Rosetta's cotton was only *one* acre and her share of cloth was therefore but four yards, which was fully paid for last spring. So she got nothing now. She did n't take it very kindly, and growled about the dress being too small for her, so she could n't wear it, whereupon I offered to take it back, but I have n't heard anything more about it. The more I see of these people, the more I am opposed to the practice of *giving* them anything except in payment for services actu-

ally performed. The cases of destitution are comparatively very few.

At this time some of the superintendents were trying hard to instruct the negroes in military drill. A
young enthusiast on one of the Fripp places was very
proud of his little squad of black recruits, but found
their attendance on the daily drill amazingly irregular.
Apropos of his own efforts in this direction, Mr. Philbrick pursues his letter as follows:

I have tried in vain to get my young men together
to drill for self-defense; my twenty-five guns are lying
useless. One might as well think of a combination
among the Boston kittens to scratch the eyes out of all
the Boston dogs as to look for an insurrection in this
State, if the negroes on these islands are a fair sample
of those on the main. If there should be any insurrection in the South, it will not be in this State. The
negroes in the sugar plantation districts are different,
I suppose, being, a larger portion of them, Kentucky
and Virginia born, torn from their old homes or sent
South for bad behavior, and therefore more revenge-
ful. But you know the people here are too timid to do
any fighting unless driven to it. If General Hunter had
not *forced* them into his regiment last May, we might
do more at drilling now. As it is, my men won't listen
to me when I talk about it; they only suspect me of
wanting to press them into service by stealth, and lose
what little confidence they have in my sincerity.

C. P. W. opens the next letter with a melancholy
comparison between the autumnal glories of " home "
and the absence thereof on the Sea Islands of South
Carolina.

FROM C. P. W.

Oct. 3. Here there are no stones but grindstones, no elevation that can be called a hill except one mound, forty feet long and ten feet high, and that is artificial. The roads are sandy, the fields are broad and flat and full of weeds, the water stands about in great pools, not running off, but absorbing into the sandy soil.

I find myself often using nigger idioms, especially in conversation with them. It is often very difficult to make them understand English, and one slips into the form of speech which they can most easily comprehend. O how deliciously obtuse they are on occasions! A boy came to me for a curry-comb for a Government mule this morning, which I was to send to the driver on his place. While scratching my name on it, I asked him if Jim had sent for some tobacco, as he said he should. "Yes, sarr." "Did he send the money?" "Sarr?" Repeated. "No, Sarr." "How much does he want?" "Don't know, Sarr." "How can I send the tobacco, if I don't know how much he wants?" "He send for him, Sarr." "Did he send you for it?" "No, Sarr." "Whom did he send?" "I dunno, Sarr." "How will he get his tobacco?" "He come himself, Sarr." "Where is he?" "Him at home, Sarr." "He is coming to get it himself, is he?" "Sarr?" Repeated, in nigger phrase. "Yes, Sarr." "Did Bruce send you for anything beside the curry-comb?" "Yes, Sarr." "What else?" "Sarr?" "Did Bruce tell you fetch anything beside this?" "No, Sarr." "Is this all Bruce told you to get?" "Yes, Sarr," with intelligence. "Go home, then, and give that to Bruce. Good-morning."

This delay in payments is outrageous. It was bad enough to pay for May and June work the second week in August; but here is the work of July and August unpaid for yet, and with no prospect of its being paid for for six weeks to come.

Sunday morning, Oct. 5. The President's proclamation [1] does not seem to have made a great deal of stir anywhere. Here the people don't take the slightest interest in it. They have been free already for nearly a year, as far as they could see, and have so little comprehension about the magnitude of our country and are so supremely selfish that you can't beat it into their heads that any one else is to be provided for beyond St. Helena Island. After telling them of the proclamation and its probable effects, they all ask if they would be given up to their masters in case South Carolina comes back to the Union. I tell them there is little chance of such a thing, but a strong probability that there will be a long, bloody war, and that they ought to prepare to do their share of the fighting. I can't get one man to come up and drill yet. They say they would like to have guns to shoot with, but are afraid of being sent off into the "big fight," though willing to fight any one who comes onto this island to molest them. Of course their defense would amount to nothing unless they were organized and drilled. I do not, however, feel any uneasiness about the rebels coming here. If they came at all they would attack our forces at Beau-

[1] The preliminary proclamation of emancipation, dated September 22, 1862.

fort or Hilton Head, where I am confident they would
be whipped. Refugees continue to come in from the
mainland every week. They all agree in saying that
there are no troops left about here but boys, and that
it would be an easy matter to take Charleston now.

I am anxious to get the winter clothing here before
next pay-day, so the people may buy it in preference
to the trash they see in the shops at Beaufort, etc. Nothing is heard of our money yet. Some say that General
Saxton will probably bring it. I only wish he would
come; his picket-guard at St. Helena amuses itself
hunting cattle on the Fripp Point Plantation. As I have
no positive proof against them I can't do anything but
watch the cattle to prevent a repetition of it.

October 7. I received on Sunday a copy of President Lincoln's proclamation. I now feel more than
ever the importance of our mission here, not so much
for the sake of the few hundreds under my own eyes
as for the sake of the success of the experiment we are
now trying. It is, you know, a question even with our
good President whether negroes can be made avail-
able as free laborers on this soil. I, for one, believe
they can, and I am more than ever in earnest to show it,
for the importance of this question is greater than ever,
now that we are so near a general crash of the whole
social fabric in the Southern States. I don't think the
old masters will ever be successful in employing the
blacks, but I do believe that Yankees can be.

Our people are picking the cotton very industriously,
and though they have only about one third of last year's
crop to gather, they are determined to make the most
of it, and allow none to waste. It is interesting to see

how much more economical of food they are this year than formerly. Every family now feels the responsibility of providing food for itself. The same rule should be followed with all tools. I would make the men pay a low price for every tool they want to use, and pay wages enough to enable them to do so.[1]

Oct. 8. I succeeded day before yesterday in getting thirteen of the young men on this plantation to come up and drill, but they did not come again yesterday. I don't believe there is sufficient zeal among them to enable them to go through the tedious routine of drill with any regularity, unless held together by some stronger motive than now exists. I find them rather stupid. About half did n't know which their right foot was, and kept facing to the left when I told them to face to the right. They seemed to enjoy it, however.

FROM C. P. W.

Oct. 9. We need people at headquarters who understand the details of plantation work. There is no one now who knows anything about the plantations except Hooper,[2] and he knows very little. He confesses and mourns at it himself; but he has done nothing but go back and forth between the Oaks and Beaufort ever since he came down. There is a general want of concerted system on all the places. Each superintendent has to do as he thinks best in all cases himself. General plans are usually determined on just too late.

[1] It will be seen that this excellent idea was not adopted by the authorities.

[2] Edward W. Hooper served on Saxton's staff, with the rank of Captain.

Oct. 14. The steamer which brought your letter brought also the General. It is said that he comes with additional powers.[1] This question will probably be settled soon, as a difficulty has already arisen between him and his old antagonist, Brannan, on a point of authority, and our General has gone to Hilton Head, probably to see Mitchel about it. This interference of the military authorities with our work and our privileges is going to make trouble. One of Mitchel's first acts was to send to Judd, as Superintendent of Port Royal Island, for 10,000 bushels of corn for army purposes. Poor Judd had been rationing his people for some time, owing to a lack of provisions occasioned by the depredations of the soldiers. We have none too much provision now, and any considerable drain must throw the plantations, sooner or later, upon the Government for support.

In the next letter (October 21) Mr. Philbrick says that the corn harvest, which is so light on St. Helena as a whole that it will hardly feed the people in the interval between old and new potatoes, will nevertheless amount to a surplus at Coffin's, adding:

I attribute the greater comparative success ón my plantations to my having abandoned the system of working a common field early in the season.[2] I now measure the yield of each family's corn-patch separately, with a view to pay them for it, if they have enough for their support in their private fields, or to regulate their allowance, if they need any, by the quantity they raise.

[1] He came with authority to raise negro troops.
[2] See p. 58.

We had a case of imprisonment here last week. I learned that old Nat's boy, Antony, who wanted to marry Phillis, had given her up and taken Mary Ann, July's daughter, without saying a word to me or any other white man. I called him up to me one afternoon when I was there and told him he must go to church and be married by the minister according to law. He flatly refused, with a good deal of impertinence, using some profane language learned in camp. I thereupon told him he must go home with me, showing him I had a pistol, which I put in my outside pocket. He came along, swearing all the way and muttering his determination not to comply. I gave him lodging in the dark hole under the stairs, with nothing to eat. Next morning old Nat came and expostulated with him, joined by old Ben and Uncle Sam, all of whom pitched into him and told him he was very foolish and ought to be proud of such a chance. He finally gave up and promised to go. So I let him off with an apology. Next Sunday he appeared and was married before a whole church full of people. The wedding took place between the regular church service and the funeral, allowing an hour of interval, however.

Cato never went back to Rose as he promised. 'Siah tells me he is afraid of his father, old Toby, who has been in a state of chronic feud with Rose's father, old Alex, and does all in his power to make trouble. Cato has gone over to Pine Grove and begun to build a house. I daresay he will take Rose into it bye and bye, when it is done.

I have been very busy lately weighing pease and cotton and measuring corn. The latter is not very pleasant, for I have to stay in the corn-house and keep tally from nine to three o'clock, and the weevils are more numerous than were the fleas the first week we came here to live. Mosquitoes are about gone, but we have sand-flies again. No fleas yet that I am aware of.

FROM C. P. W.

Oct. 23. General Saxton returned, as you know, with full powers from the President to raise one or if possible five negro regiments. I think it will be difficult to induce the men to enlist. Their treatment in the spring and summer was such as to prejudice them against military duty under any circumstances. They were forcibly drafted, were ill-treated by at least one officer, — who is a terror to the whole black population, — have never been paid a cent; they suffered from the change of diet, and quite as much from home-sickness. I think if their treatment in the spring had been different, it would be possible to raise a regiment on these islands; as it is, I think it will be surprising if they fill a company from St. Helena. I think, too, that it would be very difficult, under any circumstances, to train them into fighting condition under six months, and if they had at the first the prospect of coming into actual conflict with the Secesh, the number who would be willing to enlist would be extremely small. They have not, generally speaking, the pluck to look in the face the prospect of actual fighting, nor have they the character to enlist for their own defense. They can understand the necessity of their knowing how to defend themselves, they acknowledge their obligations to help the Yankees, and do their part in keeping the

islands against their old masters; a good many of them
express their willingness to fight under white officers,
and some have intimated a desire to know something
of drill and how to handle a musket. But they are very
timid and cautious. They fear that when they have
learned their drill they will be drafted. They are very
reluctant to leave their homes to go and live on Hilton
Head or Port Royal, in camp, away from their families
and crops. The mere mention of "Captain Tobey,"
with a hint that "General Saxton wants the black people to help the white soldiers keep the Secesh off the
islands," sends them in panic into the woods. Mr. Philbrick saw the General this morning, and was told that
if the regiment were not raised we should have to give
up the whole enterprise; that the President and the
people of the North were looking to the raising of this
regiment as a test experiment. That if it succeeded and
it was found that the negroes could and would aid the
Government, then the Government would be encouraged to hold the islands, trusting not only that the
negroes could aid in defending them, but that as fast
as negroes were freed, they could be used effectively
against the rebels. Moreover, that the success of one
regiment here would make the President's proclamation a more terribly effective weapon against the South-
erners. (There is no doubt that in many parts of the
South, especially on the Mississippi, the negroes are
much more intelligent than here. Those from the main
seem a superior class to those who have always lived
on the islands. The success of armed negroes of this
inferior class would indicate the danger of the masters
of other slaves of a higher class, when they learn that

"all slaves of rebel masters who enter into the service of the United States are forever free," with their families.)

If, on the other hand, no black troops can be raised, the General says that the Government will be discouraged from attempting any longer to protect at such an expense a people who cannot or will not aid in defending themselves. I hope that General Saxton has not held out too grand hopes of the success of this undertaking to the President and to others at the North, and I hope he is exaggerating the importance of the movement. Perhaps the President wants to try his colonization scheme on these people. He had better lose a campaign than evacuate these islands and give up this experiment. This experiment and the war must go on side by side. I hope that before the war is done we shall have furnished the Government with sufficient facts to enable them to form a policy for the treatment of the millions whom the conclusion of the war, if not its continuance, must throw into our hands.

I am very much afraid that the Government will look too much to the material results of the year's occupation for determining the success of free labor among the slaves. They will neglect to take into account the discouragements and drawbacks of the year. The sudden reaction consequent upon the change from slavery to what they hardly knew as freedom; the confusion incident upon military occupation (and the contradictory directions given concerning the year's crops); the abundance of money where the cotton-agents and officers were stationed, and the high wages promised and often obtained, at Hilton Head and Beaufort; the

lateness of the cotton crop, the poorness of the seed,
the uncertainty and doubt and want of system in regard to the management of the crops; the drafting of
the able-bodied men at a critical period, their hardships and subsequent distrust and fear, or idleness
and insubordination; the changing of superintendents,
the fewness of both superintendents and teachers; and
lastly, the shameful delay in the payments, causing
distrust, carelessness, neglect of plantation work, and
in some few cases, suffering for want of the means to
purchase clothing. It is too bad to treat people so, and
it is wonderful how much they have done and in what
an excellent state they are, under these discouraging
circumstances. If they were assured of a market at
the end of the year, and sufficient money advanced
them to enable them to get "sweetening" and clothes
through the year, I would trust my plantations to go
right ahead, put their crops into the ground, and
insure to the Government a handsome surplus next
November.

The cheerfulness and hopefulness of the people in
regard to next year's crops, and the interest they take
in their success, is surprising. "If we live to see," "if
God spare life," they say, "we will plant early, and
begin in time, and then you will see. O — yes, sar."

Mr. Philbrick is appointed cotton-agent for this crop.
He is going to have the cotton ginned here, not at New
York. Good seed is scarce. The improved seed, the
result of many years' cultivation and selection, was
lost to the island by the policy of ginning last year's
crop in New York.

FROM E. S. P.

Oct. 27. When in Beaufort last Wednesday, I got leave to pay off my people with my own funds, through the paymaster, Mr. Lee. So he came here next day, and I advanced the funds, $649. I sent Joe out to tell the people to come and get their money, but they did n't come with the usual promptness; bye and bye two men came to sound the way, the rest held back. I laughed at them and sent them off with the chink in their pockets, after which the rest came fast enough. They were evidently afraid of some trap to press them into United States service as General Hunter did. I did n't have the slightest difficulty in collecting what I had advanced last September. Every one paid it cheerfully and thanked us for what they got. This payment was all in specie. I don't think I shall be refunded in coin, and shall probably lose the difference, which is now about $120, but I don't grudge them this. I had rather let it go than see them paid in the paper currency which they can't read or judge of. It will come to that bye and bye, however, for I can't get any more coin here, and half of this money may not come back again into my hands.

General Saxton is striving earnestly to fill up his brigade with negroes, but finds it very slow work. The people are so well off on the plantations they don't see why they should go and expose themselves. Moreover, the way they were treated last summer is not very attractive to them. Many of their officers abused them, and they were very generally insulted by every white man they met. It will now require a good deal of time and very judicious, careful treatment to get rid of these impressions, particularly as some of the very officers who abused and maltreated the men are still in General Saxton's confidence and have places in his new organization.

I took this place [1] more because I want to see the work properly done and to keep it out of the hands of speculators and sharks than because I wanted the position. It is a useful position, however, and I mean to make it so.

A meeting of superintendents [2] is to be held at the Episcopal Church next Wednesday, which I shall attend, and employ the occasion by trying to start some more methodical system of employing the negroes than heretofore.

Nov. 2. At the meeting we discussed several methods of dealing with the corn crop, and several of the superintendents reported that the negroes had raised hardly enough corn to feed the plantation horses and mules on when at work. The small yield of cotton was also talked over and its causes discussed. I do not think it will pay expenses even on this island. My own plantations will yield about $5000 worth, when I expected $15,000, a good share of my crop having rotted in the pods during the rains in the early part of October and another share having dropped off the plant before filling, probably from lack of drainage after the heavy July rains.

After returning from the meeting I found a large box of woolen goods forwarded by Edward Atkinson.

[1] As Saxton's agent to collect and ship the cotton crop. See p. 99.
[2] The superintendents of the Second Division of the Sea Islands.

I sold $100 worth the next day. Though providing for their wants quite freely, the people seem more frugal with their money than last summer, and I am glad to see them so.

As far as I can learn now there are very few gins able to work [1] in the department. I have some very good seed here and at Pine Grove which I think I can gin on the spot. Mr. S.[2] came and spent a night here. He came to hire some men to go with him to pick up a lot of stray timber on commission for the Government. So my plans for ginning cotton here are postponed for a while. I had flattered myself that we were fairly rid of him, and the men were beginning to take an interest in plantation work in his absence, but he turns up again just as disagreeable as ever.

There have been great exertions made the week past to fill the ranks of the first negro regiment. A Rev. Mr. Fowler has been appointed chaplain and is at work recruiting, appealing to their religious feelings. He spent two nights here and talked in the praise-house, both evenings. The women came to hear him, but the young men were shy. Not one came near him, nor would they come near me when he was present.

The last time I saw General Saxton he seemed to think our whole destiny depended on the success of this negro recruitment. It *is* certainly a very important matter, but I think as before that it is doomed to fail here at present, from the imbecile character of the people. I thought while at work with Mr. Fowler that if I were

[1] The negroes had broken the cotton-gins by way of putting their slavery more completely behind them.

[2] Again the cotton-agent.

to go as Captain I might get a company without trouble, but I failed to get a single man when seriously proposing it to them. If I had been able to raise a company to follow me and the same men would not have gone without me, I think I should have accepted General Saxton's offer,[1] but although I consider the arming of the negroes the most important question of the day, I don't feel bound to take hold unless I can give an impetus to the undertaking. I think it would have been attended with some degree of success a year ago at this place, directly after the masters left, when the negroes had more spite in them and had seen less of their facilities for making money which they have enjoyed this summer, and if General Hunter had not made his lamentable blunder, the men would not have been disgusted with camp-life at least, but it is difficult enough to get any one of them to feel any pluck. We succeeded in getting Ranty to promise to go, and he seemed quite earnest, but when he came to start next morning he suddenly found he had a pain in his chest! his heart failed him and he backed square out. Next day he came over here and, after begging some time for me to give him a shirt, without success, offered me in payment for it a counterfeit half-dollar which I had told him a week ago was such, but which he had meantime polished up and hoped to pass. So you see when a man's heart fails him he will stoop to almost anything.

We had four couples married after church to-day, Andrew and Phœbe of Pine Grove among the rest. Mr. Phillips tried to tie all four knots at one twitch, but found he had his hands full with two couples at

[1] Evidently the offer of a captaincy.

once and concluded to take them in detail. They all
behaved very well and seemed impressed with the ceremony, so it certainly has an excellent effect. We also
had an address from Prince Rivers,[1] a black coachman from Beaufort, who has been in General Hunter's
regiment all summer, and is of sufficient intelligence
to take a lively interest in the cause of enlistment. He
has been to Philadelphia lately and comes back duly
impressed with the magnitude of the country and the
importance of the "negro question," but has not sufficient eloquence to get many recruits. Of course the
young men kept away from church and will keep away,
so long as the subject is discussed. They have made
up their silly minds and don't want to be convinced
or persuaded to any change.

[1] Of Prince Rivers, who became color-sergeant and provost-ser-
geant in the First South Carolina Volunteers, Thomas Wentworth
Higginson, its colonel, writes: " There is not a white officer in this
regiment who has more administrative ability, or more absolute authority over the men; they do not love him, but his mere presence
has controlling power over them. He writes well enough to prepare
for me a daily report of his duties in the camp; if his education
reached a higher point, I see no reason why he should not command
the Army of the Potomac. He is jet-black, or rather, I should say,
wine-black; his complexion, like that of others of my darkest men,
having a sort of rich, clear depth, without a trace of sootiness, and
to my eye very handsome. His features are tolerably regular, and
full of command, and his figure superior to that of any of our white
officers, being six feet high, perfectly proportioned, and of apparently
inexhaustible strength and activity. His gait is like a panther's; I
never saw such a tread. No anti-slavery novel has described a man of
such marked ability. He makes Toussaint perfectly intelligible; and if
there should ever be a black monarchy in South Carolina, he will be
its king." (*Army Life in a Black Regiment,* pp. 57, 58.)

You can imagine what a comfort it is to see Mr. G. again and looking so well.

W. C. G., he who in June spoke so lightly of the dangers of the Sea Island climate, had been dangerously ill during the summer and had been obliged to go North for some weeks. In a letter written October 30 he refers to the death of one of the superintendents, adding, "It greatly startled me." A month later another of the superintendents died in the same house, which later proved fatal to still a third white man. These three were cases of typhoid, but the malarial fever of the district not infrequently was as deadly; on October 30 General Mitchel himself died of it. The fact as to the climate is expressed in one of the letters by the statement that fevers were "common among the negroes" and "universal among the whites." A letter of Mr. Philbrick's, written early in October, speaks of Captain Hooper's "indisposition" as having cut down "the trio of tough ones" to himself and Mr. Soule.

FROM E. S. P.

Nov. 7. Everybody has been at work this week digging their winter crop of sweet potatoes, planted with slips in July. They bear famously on all three of my plantations, yielding in some cases two hundred bushels per acre. You know I told every man to plant for his own family separately, so that each one takes the potatoes home to his own yard and buries them, for winter use. They dig a hole about four or five feet in diameter and one foot deep, in which they pack the potatoes and pile them up above ground in a conical heap about four feet high. So when done they look like a sort of overgrown muskrat's nest, or small wigwam.[1]

[1] "These heaps are, *lucus a non*, called holes." C. P. W.

Large families have in some cases seven or eight of these conical heaps in their back yards.

The mellowing effect of the potato harvest upon the hearts of the people is manifest. Yesterday was a rainy day and the women kept straggling up here in squads all day. Each one brought a basket of potatoes on her head, from a peck to half a bushel, as a present to me. Uncle Sam and Joe are making a cone of them in the yard. Many of the children bring ground-nuts, of which I now have half a bushel. They have raised a good crop of them this year, and we amuse ourselves evenings by roasting them in the ashes of our open fire and munching them at leisure. I endeavor to acknowledge all these good-will offerings in kind, by making deposits of sugar or coffee in the baskets after emptying the nuts.

We live in the dining-room now, that being the only room without broken glass, and even there I can't get the thermometer above 60° with all the fire I can build.

FROM C. P. W.

Nov. 8. The only interesting event the day that I was in Beaufort I was obliged to leave without beholding, viz.: the mustering in of the first full company of the new regiment,[1] Captain James! They marched through the streets just before I came away, making a fine appearance. Many of them were in the first regiment,[2] and the regularity and steadiness of their marching was very creditable. They are a fine body of

[1] The First South Carolina Volunteers (colored), Thomas Wentworth Higginson, colonel.

[2] Usually referred to as the "Hunter Regiment."

men. The regiment is filling fast, its friends are much encouraged. A number of men from the regiment (now numbering about four hundred) have been allowed to return home for a few days, and I think they will carry back quite a number with them.

We have been in occupation just a year. The future, with the prospect of sale, or removal, or renewed blunders and mismanagement, is not very cheerful.

FROM W. C. G.

Nov. 15. Our island work is acquiring a little more system, but I 'm not sure that the people are as good as they were six months ago. Great mistakes have been made, and I 'm afraid the experiment so far only shows the absolute necessity of avoiding errors which common sense pointed out before any experience. Still, my belief is n't altered that the slaves would speedily become a self-supporting people, either by a system of wise and humane care, or by the opposite method of letting them alone to feel the misery consequent on idleness and the comfort that with very many would at once result from industry.

FROM E. S. P.

Nov. 16. I had a talk with General Saxton. He was feeling very blue, had just been to Hilton Head to get some tents for his new recruits of which he enlisted about a hundred on his recent expedition to St. Mary's.[1] There are some 3000 tents in warehouse there, but

[1] A town very near the extreme southern point of the Georgia coast.

General Brannan [1] refused to open it for him, alleging the advice of the Medical Department, which closed it because yellow fever had been near it. Now it is notorious that whenever one of General Brannan's men wants anything from the same warehouse, he gives a special order and it is opened for him, but not for General Saxton, the *Abolitionist*. So the new recruits have to sleep in open air these frosty nights, dampening their ardor somewhat. General Saxton agreed with me that if there is no more earnestness and sincerity among other army officers than among the specimens we have had here, we should all go to the dogs. His expedition was so successful that he was in good spirits till balked by General Brannan. The best item in it was that one of the rebel prisoners taken was marched to Beaufort jail guarded by one of his former slaves! The conduct of the negro troops was very well spoken of by their officers, but is the subject of a good deal of ribaldry among the white soldiers at Beaufort, who exhibit a degree of hatred really fiendish towards the black regiment, taking their cue from their commanding officer, of course.

We had a very interesting discussion on Wednesday about the future management of the plantations. I advocated the subdivision of the land, allotting to each family what it could cultivate and measuring their crops separately. Mr. Bryant, who came from Edisto last June,[2] preferred working the people in a gang with a foreman, and paying them by the month. His people had worked very well in that way, but it would

---

[1] After Mitchel's death, Brannan again acted as head of the Department, till General Hunter's return in January, 1863.

[2] To the Dr. Jenkins plantation.

be impossible to work the people on this island in that way. They are too independent and too ignorant to see the advantages of it, and too deceitful to enable any foreman to discriminate between the lazy and industrious. Such a system, with the insufficient force of white foremen we could supply, would be only a premium on deceit and laziness, and would fail to call out the individual exertions of the people.

The cotton crop will be worth, on this and Ladies Island, about $40,000. I have stored twenty-five thousand pounds stone cotton[1] on my plantations which will be worth at least $4000. The Pine Grove people have done picking and commenced ginning this week. All the men take hold of it readily. I can't find foot-gins enough here to gin more than one fourth the crop, and I don't think it worth while to gin by steam or horse-power, so remote as we are from mechanical repair-shops. There are several power-gins which might be readily fitted up in time of peace, but now it would cost too much. The engines have been appropriated to sawmills in some cases, and worn out in others, while the belting and other movable parts have all been stolen by the negroes.

I have not yet decided whether or not to take care of these plantations another year. General Saxton says he don't think our relations with the people will be disturbed by the tax-commissioners, but, if the estates are offered for sale [2] as they expect to do, I don't see how he is to help it. I think I should like to buy this

---

[1] Stone or seed-cotton is unginned cotton.

[2] Of course on almost all the plantations no taxes had been paid, so that the Government was at liberty to sell them at auction.

one and see what could be done with the people. I
should not expect to make anything out of it. I don't
believe much can be made out of this generation by
free labor, nor out of the next without teaching them
to read, and am sorry so little has been done as yet in
the teaching department. It is difficult to get people
to stick to it, especially in summer and during the un-
healthy season.

I have already started ginning on nine plantations
along this seaside road and shall succeed in saving on
the spot sufficient seed to plant this island, I think.
General Saxton has given me *carte blanche* as to ginning and general management of the crop. It seems to
be his way to leave all details to his subordinates, whom
he holds responsible for a proper result. If I had the
same authority in New York I could save something
as compared with last year's crop, which was nearly
all eaten up by the brokers and agents and contract-
ors, through whose hands it passed, leaving but $200,-
000 net proceeds from a shipment of about a million
dollars' worth.

Mr. Lee has paid me the amount I advanced on my
plantation pay-rolls for July and August. I have finished up my pay-rolls for September and October and
intend to get him to go and pay off my people for these
months with my funds when paying the other plantations for June and July.

In the prolonged absence of window-glass, I have
resorted to other expedients known to Irishmen, etc.,
but can't keep the wind out of my chamber these frosty
nights by any amount of ingenuity. Shingles might
do it, but they are as difficult to obtain as the win-

dow-glass, and the towels won't stay put in a high wind.

We are very sorry to hear of Captain Hooper's serious illness. He had kept up his strength so long on quinine during the summer, that a break-down must be danger-ous now. I imagine that General Saxton misses his indefatigable zeal and straightforward gentleness.

I want to see what is to be done at the tax-sale and what sort of a title is to be given. For I don't think I shall stay here another year unless I can control my men better than I have done, and I don't believe a better control can be had with the long-delayed pay-ments rendered almost necessary by the lumbering machinery of the Quartermaster's department.

The next letter is from C. P. W., and sets forth the result of his cogitations on plantation methods.

FROM C. P. W.

Nov. 16. The slip-potato crop is the only crop by which to judge of the negroes' capacity to take care of themselves. This crop they have, as a general rule, raised entirely by themselves, and for their own con-sumption; they found their own manure, and received no help except the use (small) of the Government teams on the place. The crop exceeds, on the average, one hun-dred per cent. that raised by their masters, — I mean that each man gets twice as much as he used to when they worked and shared in common; and in some cases the tasks bear twice as much. "They beer uncom-mon." "If we live to see," all the crops next year, under a management that will encourage and stimu-

late, will be proportionally as good as this 'tater crop.
One thing the people are universally opposed to. They
all swear that they will not work in gang, *i. e.*, all working the whole, and all sharing alike. On those places
where the root 'taters were thus worked this year, the
crop did very poorly, and gave out long before its time.
Where the Government corn was thus worked, the
yield averages, I suppose, six to ten bushels, the nig-
ger-field, meantime, bearing twice as much, where
they had manure.

Wherever the people have been able to look forward
to the result of the crop as beneficial to them, they have
shown industry, care, and energy in putting it through.
There is much laziness to be overcome in them, however; even in tending their own crops they sometimes
neglect well-known precautions because they cost too
much trouble. But the best of them have carried their
own crops well, and their example is beneficial in stimu-
lating the lazier ones to exertion. There is a good deal
of emulation among them; they will not sit quietly
and see another earning all the money. And it is far
better to adapt the system to the intelligence of the
best than to treat them all, as one occasionally has to
treat one or two, in special matters, like mere children.
I am sure a large number of them could get through
the year without any pecuniary aid from Government,
on the simple assurance that they should be paid for
their crop when they had picked it. I am often urged
by the best of the people not to trouble myself about
the means of doing work, but just to tell them to do
the work, and expect to see it done, and not encourage
them to ask for help to do everything. "They kin do

it, sir; don't you worry yerself, sir; they kin find
herself, sir." They have not been working cotton for
nothing for so many years under their masters. They
recollect how their masters used to treat the land and
crops, and what treatment proved most successful. They
need supervision and direction constantly, if only to
prevent fighting when one says "I free," "I as much
right to ole missus' things as you," etc., and more than
all, they need the presence and conversation of a white
man, not only to elevate them, but to encourage and
stimulate them.

There is but one opinion expressed. "We won't be
driven by nobody;" "I don't want no driving, either
by black man or white man." "We don't want de
whole valler of de cotton. De land belongs to de Gov-
er*ment*, de mule and ting on de place belong to de Gov-
er*ment*, and we have to 'spect to pay somef'n for um.
But you just pay us our share, accordin' as we make
crop, and if you live to see, Marsa Charlie, and God
spare life, you 'll *see a crop on dis place next year*."
"There will be a difference in de land, sir, but we can't
help dat; each one work his own and do as well as he
kin." It is mere fortune that one is on one soil, another
on another, kept in better order, perhaps, by the
Secesh master.

The negroes ought not to bear the burden of the loss
of their crop through any external cause, as the caterpillar, drought, etc. The Government ought to stand
in the gap and bear the loss. But I should not tell the
negroes anything about such atonement before it is
made, else one would be overwhelmed with applications from those who had become tired of cotton-hoe-

ing, and a thousand plausible stories would be fabricated, to show that this man or that was peculiarly afflicted in his crop.

Nov. 25. The people have begun ginning cotton on several places. The gins are of the rudest construction. Two rollers, about the size of a spool of thread, one above the other, horizontal, just touching, are turned in opposite directions by two upright fly-wheels, moved by a single treadle. The cotton, with the seed in it, is presented to these rollers, which catch it and draw it through, leaving the seed behind. Ginning is considered "light work." Thirty pounds of the clean cotton is considered a good day's work. It is pretty severe for the knees. Women gin with the men. The movement of "jump and change feet" when one knee gets tired should be introduced into the ballet; it is very elegant.

We have been reduced to the old system of rationing.[1] For the last two months we have had liberty to draw the value of the soldier's ration which is allowed us, in any kind of food. Consequently everybody has rushed for sugar, rice, candles, and molasses, disdaining hard bread, salt beef, and such low fare. Of course there was soon a deficiency of the better articles in the Department, the Army Commissary at Hilton Head declaring that we used up more candles and sugar than any regiment; so we have got to draw soldier's rations again, a few candles, a little dab of sugar, a big hunk of salt food, and hard biscuit. They can be swapped for duck and chickens, but what a bother to get them.

[1] That is, of drawing their own rations.

Nov. 26. I hear that Hunter's reappointment [1] causes some dissatisfaction among the pro-slavery army officers here, as might be expected.

Dec. 2. It is now rumored that we are likely to receive but little help from Congress this winter, and that the Cotton Fund [2] is getting low. It is said that the taking of Charleston would benefit us more than anything else could; that any way we must take some place on the main to attract attention and inspire confidence. The black regiment may do something for our interests. General Saxton is going to send a report of the year's work to Headquarters, and it will doubtless be laid before Congress. Commissioners, if appointed to investigate the matter, would probably have their notions of the character, ability, and prospects of the "Universal Nigger" much revised, with additions and corrections, before their investigations were completed. You at the North know nothing about niggers, nothing at all. When more is known of their powers and capacity and character more attention will be paid to the cultivation of free black labor.

The next letter again focuses attention on the white population.

FROM W. C. G.

Nov. 29. The wives are multiplying on St. Helena. Since Mrs. Bryant came, two other superintendents have made their houses homes, — one our Baptist par-

---

[1] General Hunter did not actually arrive until January. See note 1, p. 108.

[2] The $200,000 (mentioned on page 110) received by the Government for the crop of 1861.

son, and the other a young fellow who went home
shortly before me to marry his betrothed on our salary
of $50 a month. Brave youth — in these times! One
man has brought his sister and established her as
the beauty of the island; one his mother; and one an
older sister, a perfect New England housekeeper, who
makes his home the paradise of mince-pies and family
bread.

FROM E. S. P.

Dec. 10. (At the Oaks.) I like the General [1] ever
so much. He is so simple — straightforward, and earnest, so evidently pure and unselfish and so kind in his
manner.

I rode down to Dr. Jenkins' with Mr. G., but found
all the "white folks" gone to Hilton Head. I visited
the cotton-house, where about a dozen of the people
were ginning cotton. They had just packed two bales
of it, which I ripped open to inspect, and found, as I
had feared, that it was n't half cleaned. I left a note
for Mr. Bryant telling him I did n't want to send the
cotton off so and told his driver. Mr. B. was not acquainted with the way the staple is usually prepared
for market, concerning which I had taken pains to inform myself before leaving home, and the negroes had
taken the chance to shirk. I started off to take the tour
of Ladies Island and see their cotton. I visited about
a dozen cotton-houses during the day along the east
side of the island, and rode on to Cuthbert's Point to
sleep with Joe Reed and Mr. Hull. I found them
delightfully situated in a small house on Beaufort

[1] Saxton.

River surrounded by a superb grove of live-oaks, clear
of brush and nicely kept. It is the finest situation that
I have found in the State, but the greater part of the
plantations on Ladies Island are miserably poor, being the property of small proprietors who had not sufficient capital to make planting profitable. The soil
is poor and the negroes for the most part have not sufficient food on hand for the coming year. The cotton
crop is proportionally small and poor. No ginning
apparatus being found there, I shall have it all taken
to Beaufort for the steam-gins.

Leaving Cuthbert's Point this morning, I rode with
Mr. Hull to the superintendents' meeting at the Episcopal Church, about eighteen miles, and back here to
sleep. We have matured a plan of operations for the
employment of the negroes next year, at these meetings, and it is to be presented to General Saxton for his
approval this week.[1]

I have made some further inquiries of Dr. Brisbane,
one of the tax-commissioners, about the sale of lands,
which is to take place on the first of February next.
He tells me it is to be a free sale and that the Government warrants the title, subject, however, to redemption by such proprietors as can prove themselves loyal
within one year. I think it highly important that the
welfare of these negroes should not be intrusted to
speculators, and have written to Dr. Russell [2] to see
if Boston people can't be interested, individually or
collectively, in buying these lands and employing the

---

[1] This plan of operations was adopted by General Saxton.

[2] Dr. LeBaron Russell, of the Committee on Teachers of the Educational Commission.

laborers. I am ready to go into it as far as I am able alone, and have offered my time in Boston to carry out any plan they think best. If I can't get any coöperation, I mean to buy some of the estates alone, if they don't go very high, and carry them on by means of such agents as I can get. I can find several first-rate men among the superintendents here who would work for me and do well, but I don't think I should care to stay here next summer, for sanitary reasons if nothing more. My experience here will enable me to act to good advantage in carrying on any such undertaking, and I hope to be of use in a permanent way to these people with whom I have been thrown in contact this year. I have given [to Dr. Russell] an exact statement, in dollars and cents, of the expenses and products of my three plantations this year, showing a profit to the Government of about $2000,[1] besides providing a year's supply of food to a population of four hundred and fifty blacks, "big and little." This island is very much more favorably placed than Ladies, Port Royal, or Hilton Head Islands, which are all much exposed to the depredations of the Union soldiers. I find on the north end of Ladies Island the pickets are changed every little while, and have killed nearly all the negroes' poultry. The people don't dare to leave their houses, and take all their hens into their houses every night. They shoot their pigs and in one case have shot two working mules! All these things are duly reported to General Saxton, but it does no good. Two regiments have come to encamp

[1] Taking the plantations as a whole, the Government lost in 1862 the whole $200,000 which it had cleared from the planters' big cotton crop of 1861.

at Land's End on St. Helena, and Mr. Hammond says they have burnt up a mile of his fences, and burn the new rails just split out in the woods; they burn the heaps of pine leaves raked up for manure and take possession of all his cotton and corn houses. It is certainly of no use to try to carry on any planting near these fellows. They would steal all the crops if any grew near them,[1] and if the whole military establishment is to be transferred to this side the harbour, it is of little use to try to do much on that end of the island. Coffin's Point is, however, remote from all these disturbances, and I hope it will remain so. I am anxious to continue this free-labor experiment through a term of years and under circumstances more favorable than those under which we have this year been placed. I do not see how I can do much good in any other way.

The next letter is the first from H. W. on her return to Port Royal after spending the summer at home.

FROM H. W.

Coffin's Point, Dec. 14.   As we drew near the Fripp Point place at last, the people began to gather on the shore to watch us, and when the boat stopped the people were all on the banks, pressing forward, and Sammy rushed into the water and took me ashore in his arms. Then they got my trunks in the same manner, and such a shaking of hands! "So glad for see you! Glad for see you come back." Boys were sent off at once to catch the mules to take me over, while I went into 'Siah's house to wait, and had some hominy and chicken,

---

[1] On Port Royal Island "whole fields of corn, fifty acres in extent, have been stripped of every ear before hard enough to be stored."

as I was very hungry. Everything was as neat as a pin here — the children were kept out of the house while I was eating, and then the hominy and chicken were mixed and passed round among the women when I had finished. Mr. Philbrick's sulky happened to be over there to be mended, and as it was finished I drove off in it, Sammy, Peter, and Tony on the mule-cart with all my traps, and Chester following me. The children all asked about school at once, and as I was waiting I drew words for them to spell in the sand to see how much they remembered.

FROM C. P. W.

Dec. 14. I am glad H. came, for Mr. Philbrick has decided that he cannot attend to his plantations and his cotton-agency at the same time, and needs some one to take his place here. He thinks of buying the place in the spring, when the lands are sold (Feb. 1), and I have agreed to work it for him part of the time. So that, as some one must take Mr. Philbrick's place, and as the people had better have me than a stranger, and as I had better become acquainted with them at once, if I am to have charge of them in the spring, I have decided to take the places off his hands, stay here with H., and let my own plantations go to as good a person as I can find. H. is most welcome and much needed here; I am thankful to have her here, if only for the children's sakes. The only difficulty is that she may be devoured on her first visit to Pine Grove.

FROM H. W.

Dec. 16. Had the children sent for to school. They brought eggs, and were pleased enough to begin school again.

Dec. 18. Told the children yesterday that I wanted them to bring me some corn "shucks," as they call them, which are all left on the stalks in the fields. Mr. Philbrick thought I could get enough to stuff a bed with. I thought so too when the children all appeared with sheets and bags full on their heads, some containing two or three bushels!

Dec. 20. C. managed to get the piano downstairs this morning before he went off. I went with him in the double sulky as far as the cotton-house and then made an expedition to the quarters, where I shook hands with every man and woman to be seen, inspected every new baby (there have been a dozen born since I went away), visited Bacchus in his school, was kindly greeted, though the people hardly knew me and I don't know their names at all, was told that I looked "more hearty" than when I went away, and returned with two dozen eggs and the morning school at my heels.

Two dozen eggs at fifty cents a dozen was no mean proof of affection!

Dec. 21. We started for church. C. rode his largest horse and preceded or followed me in the double sulky, an unpainted box with a seat in it, of Mr. Philbrick's manufacture and quite "tasty" for these parts, on a single pair of wheels; and though it is on springs the exercise is not slight which one gets in driving over these sandy, uneven roads.

FROM E. S. P.

Sunday evg. Dec. 21. The cotton on this island is nearly all ginned. I have not been able to start the steam-gins in Beaufort yet — am waiting for authority to use the steam, which comes from the condensing boiler under the control of General Brannan's quartermaster. I asked General Saxton about it the other day, but he said he did n't know as they would let him have it. The General feels very blue about his position here, and I don't wonder. He declares he will not stay if he is not sustained, and says that General Halleck [1] sympathizes with Brannan and don't mean to let him be removed.

Wednesday evg. I looked over the Coffin people's cotton Monday and found it was not yet clean enough to pack, so refused to weigh it, and set the women at work picking over the whole of it again. Each woman keeps her own pile — the same that she and her husband raised.

I find rumors here that General Saxton and staff are to be relieved. General Saxton believes in his being relieved, but no mail has come yet to confirm it.

I want to keep R., G., C. P. W. and Bryant on plantations which I may buy, and they are all anxious to stay.

FROM H. W.

Dec. 22. Joe doubled up and went off into convulsions when C. mentioned to me at table that he had

---

[1] Henry W. Halleck, since July 11 General-in-Chief of the Army, with headquarters at Washington.

been to call on Mrs. Jenkins (Wil'by) and did not find
her at home! I gave Joe a piece of gingerbread for
her the other day, and he informed me this morning
that she found it very "palatiable"! He inquired
how my "palate was satisfy" with some oysters he fried
for me the other day.

Christmas. C. took me in his double sulky to see
the Pine Grove people, driving first to the quarters
here, where I went into Bacchus' school and distributed toys. I had also armed myself with a hundred
cents and several pounds of candy. At Pine Grove the
people crowded about to shake hands, and as I went
through the street, stopping at every house, they were
pleased as possible that I remembered their names.
They were very eager to know if I was not going to
teach school, the children all rushing home to wash
face and hands and dress themselves in their best,
after the old fashion, when I told them I wanted to
have them go to the praise-house. Flora followed me
about, as usual. I saw York for the first time. He is a
very fine-looking specimen of a thorough black, large,
manly, courteous, and straightforward.

Once more in the old praise-house, I heard the children spell, and then distributed toys among them,
with candy to the babies and grown people! and gave
to each of the girls who have been married since I left
a Bible with her name in it. All seemed honestly glad
to see me there — there was no mistaking their shining faces. I was there two hours and then went to
Fripp Point, where I gave candy to all the grown people and children, and a toy to each child. I do not know
all names and faces anywhere except at Pine Grove.

Dec. 26. I was in the midst of school when Joe announced two strangers on horseback. They were the Quartermaster and Adjutant of the 1st S. C. V., come for a dozen cattle to be roasted on New Year's Day at General Saxton's grand celebration. C. and the officers went off to select the cattle. They had a very long tramp of it and did not get back till some time after dark. They are very pleasant and gentlemanly and give a charming impression of their intercourse with Colonel Higginson, and of his with the regiment. They had no "taps" Christmas Eve or night, and the men kept their "shout" up all night. One of the Captains heard a negro praying most fervently, contrasting their "lasty Christymas and thisty Christymas," greatly to the advantage of that in the "Yankee Camp" with "too much for eat."

FROM E. S. P.

Dec. 26. The preparation of the cotton for ginning goes on very slowly. I am out of all patience with some of the superintendents. They are slower than the negroes. I don't believe in putting Reverends in places where prompt business men are required. Some of them don't get through morning prayers and get about their business till nearly noon, and then depend entirely upon their black drivers for their information in regard to plantation matters. I saw Captain Hooper for a few minutes last evening and he relieved my mind about General Saxton's removal. It seems it was all a false report got up for a sensation by the *Herald*.

Dec. 28. I was in the midst of school when it was announced that Mr. G. was coming. The children's eyes glistened and they audibly expressed their delight, but kept their seats very well till he was fairly in the room and had shaken hands with one or two near him; then their impatience could resist no longer and they crowded about him with great delight, tumbling over the benches in their eagerness to shake hands with him. It was a very pretty sight.

Mr. Philbrick has been entertaining us with an account of his week's experience, which ended at church to-day in a funny way. A couple came forward to be married after church, as often happens, when Sarah from this place got up and remarked that was her husband! Whereupon Mr. Philbrick was called in from the yard and promised to investigate and report. Jack said he had nothing against Sarah, but he did not live on the plantation now, and wanted a wife at Hilton Head.

General Saxton was at church to-day to invite the people to camp Thursday, telling them that they need not be afraid to go, as no one would be kept there against their will. They are afraid of a trap, as they were at the Fourth of July Celebration, but I hope a good many will have the sense to go.

Mr. Philbrick and C. are having an amiable comparison of relative plantation work and which has raised the most cotton. The cotton raised on these places and C.'s and R.'s is more than half of that raised on all the islands.

The Pine Grove house has been broken into and the furniture we left there carried off. The way in which those people have degenerated and these improved since we moved here is a proof of how necessary it is that they should have the care and oversight of white people in this transition state. When we lived there, that plantation was the best behaved and this the worst; now the reverse is the case. The Point Plantation has not been affected so much any way, as they never had a "white house" and have the same excellent driver.

Finding that Maria, the old nurse, and some babies were sick, I made a pilgrimage to the quarters, visited the invalids and also Bacchus' school, and told the people I hoped they would go to the Celebration at camp. As I went through the long street, women were washing outside their doors, sitting on their doorsteps sewing or tending babies, while the smaller children were rolling in the dirt. In one of the cabins I accidentally encountered Sarah, the deserted wife, and coming out found Grace, Jack's mother, holding forth in her dignified way upon the subject, condemning her son, quietly but earnestly. She turned to Sarah as she came out and, gesticulating with her hands respectively, said, "I take Becca in dis han' and carry her to punishment, an' Sarah in dis right han' and carry her to Christ." She is a "fine figure of a woman" — I wish I could have drawn her as she stood. She did more work than any one on the plantation on cotton this year. Her husband was coachman and was taken off by the overseer the day after the "gun was fire at Hilton Head."

Minda gave me an amusing account of a conversation she heard between Mr. Cockloft, the overseer, and his niece, Miss "Arnie," about the prospect of the Yankees coming here, she telling him, when he was expressing his gratification at the very large crop raised last year, that he did not talk sense, — he was just raising it for the Yankees. And when they had to run off, in the midst of all the crying and dismay, she could not resist telling him she was glad of it, to prove her right. Minda said that she knew more than her uncle because she had been to school, and had "high edicate." They sent Henry to the other end of the island to see if the forts were really taken, and he came back and told them that they had better be off, for all the Yankee ships were "going in procession up to Beaufort, solemn as a funeral."

Dec. 30. My occupation was interrupted by the arrival of William Hall,[1] bag and baggage. You can think of us as a household of three [2] pursuing our several occupations, of which more hereafter.

[1] Another young Harvard graduate, cousin of H. W., come to teach the two Fripp schools.

[2] Mr. Philbrick had changed his residence to the Oaks.

1863

Celebration of Lincoln's Emancipation Proclamation — The land-sales of 1863, Mr. Philbrick's purchase of plantations — "Shop" — Visit to Camp — Arrest of General Stevenson — Difficulties with army officers — More drafting by Hunter — Encouraging signs among the negroes — "The black draft" — The siege of Charleston — Assault on Fort Wagner — Care of the wounded — Depredations of the soldiers on the plantations — Interest in the former owners of plantations — The "Plantation Commission," an informal civil court — Negro speech and negro ways — Attacks on Mr. Philbrick as a "speculator" — Discouraging signs among the negroes — Plans of the Government for selling land to the negroes — The cotton crop of 1863 — The black draft again.

THE first letter of 1863 gives an account of the cere-monies with which the Sea Islands celebrated the Emancipation Proclamation. The place was the Smith Plantation, on Port Royal Island, where the First South Carolina had its camp.

FROM H. W.

Jan. 1, 1863. We started [from R.'s] at ten o'clock with four oarsmen, under a cloudless sky, which remained undimmed through the day. The men sang and we sang, as we wound our way through the marsh-bound creek, reaching the Smith Plantation just as the *Flora* was landing her first load from the Ferry. We followed the crowd up to the grove of live-oaks with their moss trimmings, which did not look so dreary under a winter's sun, but very summer-like and beautiful. The regiment, which had been drawn up at the wharf to receive the guests from Beaufort, escorted

them to the platform in the middle of the grove, where
we found it — the regiment — in a circle round the
stand, where .they remained quiet and orderly as possible through the whole proceedings, which lasted about
three hours. Guests, white and colored, were admitted
within the line, and as ladies we were shown seats on
the platform. The general arrived in his carriage with
the Mission House [1] ladies.

It is simply impossible to give you any adequate
idea of the next three hours. Picture the scene to yourself if you can, — I will tell you all the facts, — but if
I could transcribe every word that was uttered, still
nothing could convey to you any conception of the
solemnity and interest of the occasion. Mr. Judd, General Superintendent of the Island, was master of cere-
monies, and first introduced Mr. Fowler, the Chaplain,
who made a prayer, — then he announced that the
President's Proclamation would be read, and General
Saxton's also, by a gentleman who would be introduced by Colonel Higginson. And he rose amid perfect
silence, his clear rich voice falling most deliciously on
the ear as he began to speak. He said that the Proclamation would be read "by a South Carolinian to
South Carolinians" — a man who many years before
had carried the same glad tidings to his own slaves now
brought them to them, and with a few most pertinent
words introduced Dr. Brisbane, one of the tax-commissioners here now, who read both proclamations
extremely well. They cheered most heartily at the
President's name, and at the close gave nine with a

[1] An institution situated in Beaufort, managed by the New York
Commission.

will for General "Saxby," as they call him. Mr. Zachos then read an ode he had written for the occasion, which was sung by the white people (printed copies being distributed, he did not line it as is the fashion in these parts) — to "Scots wha hae." I forgot to mention that there was a band on the platform which discoursed excellent music from time to time. At this stage of the proceedings Mr. French rose and, in a short address, presented to Colonel Higginson from friends in New York a beautiful silk flag, on which was embroidered the name of the regiment and "The Year of Jubilee has come!"

Just as Colonel Higginson had taken the flag and was opening his lips to answer (his face while Mr. French was speaking was a beautiful sight), a single woman's voice below us near the corner of the platform began singing "My Country, 'tis of thee." It was very sweet and low — gradually other voices about her joined in and it began to spread up to the platform, till Colonel Higginson turned and said, "Leave it to them," when the negroes sang it to the end. He stood with the flag in one hand looking down at them, and when the song ceased, his own words flowed as musically, saying that he could give no answer so appropriate and touching as had just been made. In all the singing he had heard from them, that song he had never heard before — they never could have truly sung "my country" till that day. He talked in the most charming manner for over half an hour, keeping every one's attention, the negroes' upturned faces as interested as any, if not quite as comprehending. Then he called Sergeant Rivers and delivered the flag to his

keeping, with the most solemn words, telling him that
his life was chained to it and he must die to defend it.
Prince Rivers looked him in the eye while he spoke,
and when he ended with a "Do you understand?"
which must have thrilled through every one, answered
most earnestly, "Yas, Sar." The Colonel then, with
the same solemnity, gave into the charge of Corporal
Robert Sutton [1] a bunting flag of the same size; then
stepping back stood with folded arms and bare head
while the two men spoke in turn to their countrymen.
Rivers is a very smart fellow, has been North and is
heart and soul in the regiment and against the "Se-
ceshky." He spoke well; but Sutton with his plain common sense and simpler language spoke better. He made
telling points; told them there was not one in that crowd
but had sister, brother, or some relation among the
rebels still; that all was not done because they were so
happily off, that they should not be content till all their

[1] Of Corporal Sutton Colonel Higginson says: "If not in all respects
the ablest, he was the wisest man in our ranks. As large, as powerful,
and as black as our good-looking Color-sergeant, but more heavily
built and with less personal beauty, he had a more massive brain and
a far more meditative and systematic intellect. Not yet grounded
even in the spelling-book, his modes of thought were nevertheless
strong, lucid, and accurate; and he yearned and pined for intellectual
companionship beyond all ignorant men whom I have ever met. I
believe that he would have talked all day and all night, for days together, to any officer who could instruct him, until his companion,
at least, fell asleep exhausted. His comprehension of the whole problem of slavery was more thorough and far-reaching than that of any
Abolitionist, so far as its social and military aspects went; in that
direction I could teach him nothing, and he taught me much. But
it was his methods of thought which always impressed me chiefly;
superficial brilliancy he left to others, and grasped at the solid truth."
(*Army Life in a Black Regiment*, p. 62.)

people were as well off, if they died in helping them; and when he ended with an appeal to them to above all follow after their Great Captain, Jesus, who never was defeated, there were many moist eyes in the crowd.

General Saxton then said a few words, regretting that his flag had not arrived as he intended, and introduced Mrs. Gage, who spoke to them of her visit to St. Croix and how the negroes on that island had freed themselves, and telling them that her own sons were in the army; she might any day hear of their death, but that she was willing they should die in the cause and she hoped they were ready to die too. Quartermaster Bingham led the regiment in singing "Marching Along." Mr. Judd had written a hymn which he and a few friends sang. Judge Stickney spoke. The whole regiment then sang "John Brown," and was dismissed in a few words from the Colonel to the tables for the twelve roasted oxen,[1] hard bread, and molasses and water, except one company and certain corporals whom he mentioned, who came to the foot of the steps to escort the colors.

Lieutenant Duhurst was waiting to escort us to dinner at his mess-table. We walked into the old fort, part of the walls of which are still standing, made of oyster-shells and cement, very hard still. It was built, say the authorities, in 1562, half a century before the Pilgrims landed.

---

[1] Mr. Philbrick describes the feast: "I walked about for a half hour watching the carving, which was done mostly with *axes*, and the eager pressing of the hungry crowds about the rough board tables, by which each ox was surrounded. The meat did n't look very inviting."

Miss Forten [1] had a letter from Whittier enclosing a song he had written for the Jubilee and which they have been teaching the children to sing at church next Sunday.

After dinner we went up to the camp, and a very nice-looking place it was. The tents only hold five, so that there were a great many of them, making the camp look very large. The officers' tents are in a row opposite the ends of the streets, but with only a narrow street between. The Adjutant took us into his, which is a double one with two apartments like the Colonel's, as his wife is coming out to live there and teach the first sergeants to read, write, and keep their accounts. As dress-parade was to come off at once, we stayed to see that. Only the commissioned officers are white; the uniform of the privates is the same as any others, except that the pantaloons are red, [2] faces and hands black! The parade was excellent, — they went through

[1] Miss Forten was of partly negro blood. H. W. says of her elsewhere: "She has one of the sweetest voices I ever heard. The negroes all knew the instant they saw her what she was, but she has been treated by them with universal respect. She is an educated lady."

[2] When General Hunter, bent on raising his negro troops, asked the Secretary of War for 50,000 muskets, "with authority to arm such loyal men as I find in the country, whenever, in my opinion, they can be used advantageously against the enemy," he added: "It is important that I should be able to know and distinguish these men at once, and for this purpose I respectfully request that 50,000 pairs of scarlet pantaloons may be sent me; and this is all the clothing I shall require for these people." (Hunter to Stanton, April 3, 1862.) Of the privates of the First S. C. V., when clothed in these trousers, Colonel Higginson writes: "Their coloring suited me, all but the legs, which were clad in a lively scarlet, as intolerable to my eyes as if I had been a turkey." (*Army Life in a Black Regiment*, p. 7.)

the manual, including, "load in nine times." There
were eighteen men absent without leave, a circumstance
not to be wondered at, as they had kept no guard all
day, and a negro thinks to go and see his family the
height of happiness. Colonel Higginson said, "Think
of a camp where there is no swearing, drinking, or card-
playing among the men, — where the evenings are spent
praying and singing psalms, and it is the first sound you
hear in the morning!" He is a strong anti-tobacconist,
but he lets the men have all they can get, and helps them
get it.

We started just after sunset, and at the same time
with the band, who were rowed up to Beaufort as we
went across the river. They played "Sweet Home," and
the music sounded delightfully, but made Mr. Williams
exclaim, "Now that's too bad, when a fellow is going
to an old South Carolina whitewashed house, with a
broken table and chair in it!" Nevertheless, he was
very merry, and we had a fine row. The sunset was
perfectly clear, the sky retained its brightness for a long
time, and the moon was so bright that it did not grow
dark. Our delay made us against tide for the second
hour, so the negroes turned out of the main creek into
the narrow creeks among the grass, which at high tide
are deep enough, though very narrow. Our oars were
often in the "mash" on one side, but the men knew
their way and brought us safely through. They grew
very much excited as they rowed and sung, shouting
with all their might, and singing song after song the
whole way home. The singing while they row always
sounds differently from [that] at any other time to me,
though they always sing the same, religious songs.

In the following letter Mr. Philbrick begins by defending himself against the charge of rashness in proposing
to buy land of which the legal title was so insecure as to
make it a most unsafe investment, and the geographical
situation such as to make it unfit for habitation by Northerners.   The point of view of his critic is amusingly different from that of the good people who subsequently
accused him of buying with the expectation of making
large profits.

FROM E. S. P.

Jan. 2. As to the title, the right of redemption ex-
pires at the end of two years in all cases, and fifteen per
cent. interest must be paid by the redeemer before he
can take possession.   Now I never thought of paying
more for these lands than the net value of two good
crops, and don't undertake it for the sake of making
money at all, but for the sake of carrying out to a
more satisfactory issue the present short-lived and un-
fairly judged experiment of free labor, and for the sake
of keeping the people out of the hands of bad men.
You will of course admit that such an enterprise is
worthy of my assistance and worthy of the time of such
men as are now engaged in it.   The health of every
white man who has lived on the seaward side of St.
Helena, from Coffin's Point to Land's End, has been
perfectly good, and that is where I intend to buy, if at
all, including perhaps the places under R.'s charge which
he wishes to retain, and those of Captain John Fripp
and Thomas B. Fripp, which could easily be managed
by a person living on Cherry Hill or Mulberry Hill,
directly adjoining them on the south.

We had a flare-up with Ranty about the furniture left

in the big house [at Pine Grove]. The people broke in on Christmas and took out what we left there, appropriating it to their private uses. I found Frank had the sideboard in his new house (the old carriage-house). I told him to give it up and asked where the rest was. Mily had taken the desk, for safe-keeping, and offered to deliver it when wanted, but the bedsteads are not reported. Ranty had locked up the large dining-table in the peasehouse. I blew him up for not reporting such things instanter, and hired June to sleep in the big house nights and be responsible for its safe-keeping. Otherwise the doors and windows would soon disappear.

The future of our country looks darker than ever. I can't see much prospect of an improvement in the conduct of the war, so long as the mass of our people do not see in slavery the great cause of all the trouble. Neither do I believe that the war will terminate slavery unless the blacks will voluntarily take a part in it. The 1st Regiment is at length filled here, by means of a great deal of coaxing and the abandonment of St. Simon's Island,[1] taking all the men for recruits. They have made two raids upon the Florida coast, where they met with little resistance and accomplished but little. If they can once gain a footing on the mainland and add to their numbers as they advance, they could easily carry all before them. Any other race of men under the sun would do it, but I doubt yet whether there is the requisite amount of pluck in them to fall into such a scheme even when we are ready to lead them. I feel as if this winter were the turning-point of the whole question.

[1] On the Georgia coast.

FROM W. C. G.

Captain Oliver's, Jan. 4. Mr. Philbrick has very generously offered to assist three or four of us poorer superintendents in buying plantations. If we do not buy, the occupation of most of us is probably gone. Government will probably retain possession of many plantations from the lack of purchasers,— but they will be the poorer ones and those where the people will be subject to such influences that our purposes will meet with little success. For such plantations superintendents may be needed, but, besides doing little good, their own position I think will be very unpleasant. Nor do I think it unmanly to withdraw from such plantations. The irregular wayward life which the people on such places would probably lead undoubtedly will help to develop their self-reliance, but our style of development — that of regular, persistent industry — is so wholly different, that I doubt the wisdom of attempting to yoke the two styles together. In one point experience confirms what theory would suggest, — that their own increasing comfort or *misery* will be a far stronger agent in the development of these people than any amount of outside human effort.

I think I shall accept Mr. Philbrick's offer. I wish to stay down here, and I see no satisfactory way of so doing, except by this arrangement. It may turn out disastrously, — so be it; the Government will probably refund the purchase-money in case the lands return to the Confederate States either by capture or compromise. But with success, I doubt if I should realize the amount of my present salary and support. If the lands sell at a nominal price, however, they are worth that risk. To stay in the work is my object.

I am having a pretty hard time at present. The people are very wayward, — now they work and then they stop, — and some stop before they begin. Several men have been acting badly, too; I actually knocked a man down the other day, — and think I did right, — for the first time in my life. It very much hurts one's popularity to be often severe, — and one's reputation with higher authorities also, I fear. My places have the disadvantage — to me — of being very near headquarters, and my people have learned through a very unwise act — the removal of a superintendent on the complaint of the negroes — the benefit of appealing from me. I have always been sustained — otherwise I should probably have resigned; but it very much weakens my authority, and, as I said, probably my reputation. But the worst is that it discourages and dulls one for the work.

FROM H. W.

Jan. 7. I went into Ellen's house to see her sick children. It was her children who were so sick last summer, and Nancy died. They had swollen throats and I promised red flannel — then went all through the quarters talking and giving to all the old women some of our ration coffee and sugar. The women went on talking, Louisa winding up with an attempt to solve the to them great mystery — "Miss Hayiat, you not married? when you going to be married? What, and you so smairt?" C. says they are constantly asking him the same question. "Oh, Mass' Charlie," said a woman to him the other day, "if I was as pretty a woman as you are a man I should be so glad!" I find I shall have to give up going to the quarters if they insist upon giving me so many eggs — I had two dozen and a half given to-day — I can't use them up so fast! I found C. in collo-quy with a man who came down to see if he could not move here so as to be under him. "But how do you know you shall like me ? " said C., "and get along with me ? " "See it in your countenance, sar, first time I eber see you!" Nat talked some time (he was a sort of Major Domo here and kept the keys) about the necessity of some white people's staying here, and of the people's confidence in Mr. Philbrick and C. They are very desirous that Mr. Philbrick should buy. "You see, sar; you won't have no trouble 'bout cotton dis year — Mr. Philbrick pay more money than any other man — de people know now you here to see justice. People all work cotton dis year. I don't care if you neber go 'way — like you much."

Jan. 8. General Saxton said he was here on the Coast Survey seven years ago, cut that gap through the trees for his triangles, which caused us so much speculation last spring,[1] and landing at the Point one day dined here with Mr. Coffin.

Jan. 12. Just as we were going to sit down to lunch, Tim came running up with a line from C. for his revolver, which I sent. Tim said two of the men were fighting, so Mr. Philbrick [2] took his pistol and went to see what was the row, and soon came back to say that a former hus-band of the woman who had been married the day be-fore at church had turned up, and C. had ordered him off the place. It is a complicated story and I do not know its merits and demerits. I wish C. would write it out as

[1] See p. 60.
[2] Mr. Philbrick was staying at Coffin's for a few days.

a specimen of that part of his business. It is equal to
Indian Cutchery.

Jan 16. Woke to find it very blowy and cold. The
changes seem to be as great here as in New England, of
their kind. It is funny to see how the people feel the cold.
I got no milk, because they could not milk in such weather, and it was so warm the day before that all we had
soured. The children wore sheets over their shoulders
and handkerchiefs on their heads to school.

Jan 17. Went to the quarters to see the people, who
wondered to see me out such a cold day! Found those
who were out of doors on the sunny side of the street
against the houses to keep warm.

This afternoon I had to sew up a bad cut in Hester's
arm. She sat all through school without a word to me,
and then I could not close the wound with sticking-
plaster, so there was no alternative. She behaved like a
Spartan — her black skin made it easier for me, but not
for her, I fancy. So much for my first attempt at surgery.
It was an ugly job.

FROM E. S. P. TO C. P. W.

The Oaks, Jan. 21. I got a letter from Mr. Forbes,
who says he can raise $12,000 for land, etc., to put in my
hands, with the understanding that when I get tired of
managing the thing I shall close up and divide what shall
be left.[1] So I shall certainly buy that end of the island,

[1] The agreement made on April 8, between Mr. Philbrick and
fourteen gentlemen, all but one of Boston, provided that Mr. Philbrick, in whose name the land should be bought and who should have
complete responsibility for managing it, should, after paying the sub-
scribers six per cent. interest, receive one fourth of the net profits.
Mr. Philbrick was to be liable for losses and without the right to call

provided the lands are sold, which in Boston they feel very sure they will *not* be, and provided nobody else bids over one dollar an acre or so.

FROM H. W.

Jan. 21. C. was gone all day tramping over the Pine Grove plantation to see and map out the land so as to allot it for corn and cotton to the people for this year's crop, — Flora's York for guide, who was much amused at his maps. He brought me home as a present from Susan half a dozen delicious sausages and a piece of fresh pork, which is very nice here, as the pigs run wild and feed on the potatoes left in the field, and other roots. Having had to wait for my washing for over a week, as Judy went first to Beaufort to see " him niece," a man grown, who was sick and died, and then was too sick herself, I hunted up some one else and had our washing done. Housekeeping with such young things to look after as Robert and Rose [1] only is not an easy or thoroughly satisfactory proceeding, with so much else to see to in this great house.

Jan. 22. Sam sent word that buckra and white lady were coming. I went to the door. There stood Miss R., Mrs. Clark, and Mr. De la Croix, and coming up the path were the rest of their party, Mrs. Bundy, Mrs. Williams, Mr. R., and, still on the beach, Mr. Williams and

for further contribution; on the other hand, no subscription was to be withdrawn unless he ceased to superintend the enterprise. On his closing the business, the net proceeds were to be divided *pro rata*.

[1] Joe having gone back to his trade of carpenter, the domestic force now included a boy and a girl (daughter of Abel and sister of Hester), marvelously ignorant, even for a Sea Island field-hand. Uncle Sam, Robert's father, was acting as cook.

Dr. Bundy shooting. I flew down to Uncle Sam to give him potatoes, white and sweet, and rice and hominy, telling him to have the tea-kettle boiling so that I could give them a cup of coffee. We had eaten our last loaf of bread that morning, so I mixed some griddle-cakes, and Robert, who enjoyed the fun of so many people, set the table and did very nicely, Rose running up and down stairs with the hot flap-jacks. I don't wonder that country-people eat " griddles " so much, — they are so much easier and more quickly prepared than anything else. But nothing is done quickly in this region, and all this was a work of time, during which I entertained my guests and they entertained themselves in the " shop," and they became great purchasers. Then the boatmen who had brought them came up for sugar and tobacco, and Mr. De la Croix opened the new box for me, and they were very much amused to see me diving into the depths of the sugar-barrel and handling the tobacco at " eight cents a plug! " They were very merry and jolly and seemed to enjoy themselves, — certainly Mrs. Bundy did at our piano, and we in hearing her. Robert and Rose could not put the things on the table — they were fixed, as soon as they entered the room, with delight. It was funny work getting together dishes enough, but I made out. My table was full and my guests hungry, though they protested they only came for a call and did not want any luncheon. We got up from table about three, I got Dr. Bundy to take the stitches from Hester's arm and dress it, and then they said they must be off, — they had stayed too long already. And so it proved, for the tide had gone out and the boat was high and dry on an oyster-bank! They did not seem much distressed, and all betook themselves to a walk towards the quarters, which they visited in a body, to the delight of the people. I was informed, " Miss Hayut, buckra-man on hos-bahck," and Mr. Thorpe appeared on business with C.; as it never rains but it pours, two officers from our blockading vessel now landed, to see the pickets they were told were here. They did not stay long, and then I went to find Dr. Bundy and see what time they would get off. I found they could not get away till seven, so began to make preparations for tea. I knew my table would not be large enough, and was quietly taking all the books and papers off the big round one in the corner, when the ladies discovered what I was about; they rose in a body and protested they would not have any tea. But the gentlemen equally protested I should do just as I chose, and set them to work if I would, so they wheeled out the table and Mr. De la Croix went with me to the milk-closet to take down the shelves, which were the leaves. The table is a monstrous great round one, solid mahogany, and with its leaves in made my table-cloth look like a towel on the grass, so we took to the bare boards. We sat down twelve to a repetition of the lunch, with the addition of Susan's pork and sausages, as our boys had had no dinner. I could not persuade any of them to stay all night, though I showed them that I had bed accommodations for four, and sofas for nore, to say nothing of a floor! There was a little moon and they all got home safely — we had a suspicion we might see them about midnight!

Jan. 23. In the midst of all the fun and frolic yesterday there came a sudden pause, when Mrs. Williams drew down the corners of her mouth and remarked, " And this is a band of Missionaries! "

I had the room in the basement cleaned to-day by Samson's Betty. She is the woman whose old husband turned up and gave C. so much trouble. This thing is happening a good deal now, and must. A man who was sold six years ago to Georgia came up from St. Simon's with the troops not long ago to find his wife here married again. He gave her leave to do so, however, when he was sold off, so had nothing to say. To go back to Betty. I gave her as careful directions as I could and left her to her own devices. When I went to her once I found her in the middle of the room with two great tubs of water, her skirts all tied up to her knees, the floor swimming in water which she was flinging about with a handful of shucks *i. e.*, corn-husks! It would be easier to keep house in a small country house at home and do my own work (minus the washing) and live better than we do here. However, I am very philosophical, and ignore dirt and irregularity.

Jan. 24. I had promised to go to the quarters and rode down, C. walking by my side to take down the amount of cotton and corn land each hand wished to work this year. He stood with his back against a fence, the "gang" collected in front of him, book in hand, taking down the number of tasks each agreed to work, talking to them about the crop, laughing with them and at them. A not less unique picture certainly was his sister riding his little horse whose back her large shawl nearly covered behind, in her ordinary dress and hoops, stopping at door after door to look at this sick baby, talk to that old woman; give a comb out of one pocket and put an egg into another; dismount to show Amaritta how to make yeast and raise bread, examine some sore throats, go to Louisa's house and repeat the

yeast operation there, then remount and proceed through
the street in the same style, only that now the flour and
warm water are brought to the door and she stirs on
horseback! Sunday is the "Quarter meeting-day" —
over a hundred are to be baptized and they want some
bread to carry, as they will have to stay all day. I ride
back through the overseer's yard, stop at her door to
speak to Judy, then have a talk with Abel, who wants
to know how I find Rose, says he knows character is
better than all the riches of this world, and that he was
taught and teaches his children not to lay hand on anything that does not belong to them. I took her partly
because I knew it was a good family. Demus [1] attends
me, and I ride home followed by half a dozen little
boys who are coming up to school and run races by my
side. The wind has turned east, and a thick fog is driving in visible clouds over the dreary cotton-fields, raw,
chilly, and disagreeable enough. I come out of school
wondering what I am going to have for dinner and what
for Sunday, knowing that Uncle Sam, whose daughter
Katrine is "going in the water," will probably be away
all day and that the R.'s are coming to spend Sunday.
You know there was trouble last summer about the
superintendents who were not Baptists remaining to
the Communion Service — there has been more since,
and the negro elders have become so excited about it
that they will not allow them to stay, so the R.'s did
not wish to go to church, and planned when we were
there at New Year's to come down here to spend that
Sunday. They told me when they were here Thursday

---

[1] A boy lately added to the corps of house-servants at Coffin's
Point.

that they were coming, so I ought to have been ready, but except my three loaves of bread I had made no preparation, and was expecting them momentarily. The Fates were propitious, however, for Minda sent me a piece of fresh pork, and a note from Mr. Philbrick said he would send us a piece of fresh beef for our rations Sunday. I had just time to wash my hands when my guests arrived. That is a process, by the way, which I have to go through with, at the least, twice in an hour — sometimes oftener than that in fifteen minutes — with sand-soap and brush!

There was a great church-going from this place, as fourteen people were to be baptized, and Sam when he was rigged was a sight, with his beaver over his head-hankercher. Carts were in requisition to bring home the wet clothes — Louisa told C. that she could n't wear hoops into the water and should be so cold she should wear eight coats (they drop the petti-) and she could n't bring them all home. It was foggy and chilly, though the sun came out at noon when the proceedings must have been at their height, as the tide was high then. There were one hundred and forty-nine dipped on this occasion.

The next two letters are largely occupied with the beginnings of the new workir ; year.

C. P. W. TO E. S. P.

Jan. 25. I went down to this nigger-house yesterday morning, called the people up and told them what they were going to get on their cotton besides the pay for picking already paid, and then, after talking over plantation matters a little, got their acres for next year.

They seemed "well satisfy" with the additional payment, fully appreciated the pay according to crop and
according to acre combined, and started on this year's
work with "good encourage." I suppose Mr. Forbes
and you are two bricks, serving as the beginning of a
good foundation for these people's prosperity.

FROM W. C. G.

Captain Oliver Fripp's, Jan. 26. We are very busy
now on the plantations. A new system of labor to
inaugurate, — lands to allot, — grumbling to pacify
and idleness to check, — my hands — with nine plantations — are perfectly overrunning. The worst of it
is that my people are in pretty bad disposition, — the
new system has been received with joy and thankful-
ness in most parts of the island, — here with suspicion,
grumbling, and aversion. How far it is the fault of their
past and present superintendents, I cannot tell, — it
has been known as a hard district ever since we came
here, — but it must be our failing in some degree. I
devoutly hope that by the middle of February it will
be over as far as I am concerned. It is a little remarkable that while the Abolitionists and negroes' friends up
North are striving so hard to have the sale postponed,[1]
we superintendents, without exception that I have
heard, are very desirous to have it effected. This
"superintendence" is a most unsatisfactory system, —
temporary and unprogressive in every element. Of
course, nothing else could well have been tried this last
year, and perhaps the time has not yet come to abandon
it. But we all think it has. I am satisfied that the sooner

---

[1] From unwillingness to see the land owned by any one but negroes.

the people are thrown upon themselves, the speedier will be their salvation. Let all the natural laws of labor, wages, competition, etc., come into play, — and the sooner will habits of responsibility, industry, self-dependence, and manliness be developed. Very little, very little, should be given them: now, in the first moments of freedom, is the time to influence their notion of it. To receive has been their natural condition. They are constantly comparing the time when they used to obtain shoes, dresses, coats, flannels, food, etc., from their masters, with the present when little or nothing is given them. I think it would be *most unwise and injurious* to *give* them *lands*, — negro allotments; they should be made to *buy* before they can feel themselves possessors of a rod. There are some who are now able to buy their houses and two or three acres of land, — by the end of the year their number will probably be greatly increased. These will be the more intelligent, the more industrious and persistent. But *give* them land, and a house, — and the ease of gaining as good a livelihood as they have been accustomed to would keep many contented with the smallest exertion. I pity some of them very much, for I see that nothing will rouse and maintain their energy but suffering.

In regard to the immediate sale, — even should speculators buy some plantations, I don't think the people would suffer much oppression during the years of their possession. It would be for their interest to continue or increase the wages which Government offers, — and probably many would let the places almost alone. Should oppression occur, the negroes will probably have an opportunity to move, — such cases would be closely watched and loudly reported, — and the people would be all the more dependent on their own exertions. I should think the great injury would come at the end of the war, or whenever the speculators sell the lands: then, instead of selling at low prices and in small lots or of consulting the people's interest in any way, they will simply realize the greatest advantage for themselves. Other places, however, will be bought by friends and by the Government, — on the whole, great good would result to the people. Moreover, the work will then have very much more value as a test of their capacity and ambition, — as an experiment in American emancipation.

I feel that outside of directly spiritual labor, this emancipation work is the noblest and holiest in the country.

FROM H. W.

Jan. 27. Both schools were very satisfactory. If any one could have looked in, without the children's seeing them, they would have thought we presented quite an ordinary school-like appearance. I have a blackboard with numerals and figures and the second line of the Multiplication Table written on it, all of which the oldest school know tolerably, but they make sorry work trying to copy the figures on their slates. I let them use them every day now, however, for they must learn, by gradually growing familiar with the use of a pencil, not to use it like a hoe. There are furrows in the slates made by their digging in which you might plant benny-seed, if not cotton!

Jan. 29. Am trying to teach the children how to tell

time on the dial-plate of an old English clock, "Presented by Sir Isaac Coffin, Bart.," as its face informs you — one of the many valuable things demolished.

Jan. 31. Started directly after breakfast to spend the day and night with H. We broke down, as usual, had to stop and be tinkered up, so that William was late for the ferry, and when we got to the Oaks avenue I got out with my bag and basket and let him go on. I trusted to fate to find some one to carry my traps for me the mile up to the house. The drive was lovely, and I found some people waiting by the roadside for Mr. Soule, to get passes to go to Beaufort. A boy readily took my things for me without promise of any payment. On the walk I found he was one of the Edisto refugees who are quartered at the village and supplied with rations by Government, but he had left home with only two pieces of hardtack in his pocket and without breakfast. "Think we'll go back to Edisto, Missy?" he asked most earnestly, hoping that a stranger would give him some hope that he should see his home again. He was a nice boy; as a general thing the Edisto people are a better class of blacks, more intelligent and cultivated, so to speak, but those brought from there were then refugees from many other places.

Mr. Philbrick brought word that the North Carolina army [1] had arrived at Hilton Head, and we were excited to know who of our friends had come.

Feb. 1. A message came back from Mr. Philbrick that General "Saxby" was coming to dinner. The

[1] A detachment from the Eighteenth Army Corps, under Major-General John G. Foster, had come to help in the operations against Charleston.

General was decidedly blue about affairs here at present. He wants to stop the sale of lands very much, though, as he can control the sale so as to keep it out of the hands of speculators, I hope the sale will take place. You cannot understand how much we long to have the sale over. If it could only have taken place a month sooner it would have been all the better, as then the purchasers could have stocked their places by the time work began. As it is, the people have gone into the fields without the necessary number of cattle or mules, and with only their worn-out hoes; the Edisto people who are now being distributed onto the plantations have nothing. With the chance of giving up the control so soon, Government has not supplied all that is necessary and work bids fair to be as behindhand here as it was last year. Where the people have gone to work at all — at this end of the island — they have started with "good encourage," but at other places it has been impossible to get them to start any cotton, though they work corn. This is partly due to the fact that this end of the island is removed from the demoralizing effects of the camps, and partly, too, to the confidence the people have in the superintendents here, who have mostly been with them steadily now for nearly a year. It seems to us on the spot as if things could not go on another year as they are now, and we long for February eleventh and things to be settled. The auctioneer is at Washington trying, not to have the sale postponed, but to have lands set apart and given the blacks beforehand, and we dread lest any day we should hear that it has been delayed. Some of the blacks mean to buy — we don't wish them to till the war is over, as our tenure here is too uncertain for them to sink their money.

C. on horseback, I in the double sulky started home-
ward, reaching home — and we agreed that it was certainly homelike — by half past six. Rose came up
from her house acknowledging that though she wanted
to see me she could have waited till to-morrow, but her
mother made her come!

FROM C. P. W.

Feb. 2. The sale is a week from Wednesday. General
Saxton (proclaim it not from the house-top) says he
shall take the liberty to use the Cotton Fund to outbid
any troublesome speculators. Glory Hallelujah!

FROM H. W.

Feb. 4. Cold as ever again — can do nothing but try
to keep warm. Have a good fire in the school-room,
and quite a full school — those who stay away for the
cold being jeered at as not wishing to learn by the
others. I think they have done well for a year with
the amount of teaching they have had.

Feb. 7. Found C. was going to Pine Grove, so thought
I would go too, as I have not been to see them since
Christmas. I went round to see the people who were at
home; many of them had gone into the field, where C.
went to deal out the land to them. Then I followed him
in the sulky to bring him home, but when I reached the
field, Flora, who came running out to see me, crying
out, "my ole missus!" informed me that "Mass'
Charlie have much long jawing, people in confusion."
Mr. S.,[1] it seemed, had disturbed them about the land-
sale, and York vowed if anybody but Mr. Philbrick

---

[1] The new postmaster for Beaufort.

or C. had the place he would pack up and go to New York with his family. Went home alone, forced to leave C. to walk. Found some of his old people waiting for him — they are very much attached to him and he to them — it is hard for him to give them up. One man met him at church last Sunday, took off his hat, rolled up his eyes, and remarked pathetically, "I goes to sleep and dreams of you, Boss!"

Feb. 8. Dr. Russell sends me word that after March 1st my salary will be $20 instead of $25.

We all went up to church this morning for the chance of finding John L.[1] there. We go to church to see our friends, and generally manage to get there just as service is over. If it were any good to the people we could bear it, but they get stones, not bread, I am sorry to say. We did not find any friends from the Twenty-Fourth.

I shall hope to send you Colonel Higginson's report of his expedition [2] with the Black Regiment, which was a great success. Oh, if the formation of the regiment last spring had only been differently managed! we should have had a brigade by this time. January, who I wrote you was taken from here one night as a deserter, and who was found up his chimney, almost frightened to death at going back, he was so badly treated before, came for a day or two since he got back from the expedition and told C. he would not take a thousand dollars to leave now, he had such a good time.

On February 10, the very eve of the eagerly awaited

[1] A cousin in the 24th Massachusetts, which had come to Land's End as part of the "North Carolina army."

[2] For lumber up the St. Mary's River, which separates Georgia from Florida.

day set for the land-sale, H. W. writes: "The cart went up for rations, so I sent some sausages for H. and got some cake at night, with a note saying the sale was stopped." True to his extreme record as friend of the negro, General Hunter had been the means of postponing the sales, in the hope, as has been said, of eventually turning most of the plantations into negro holdings, by gift or the next thing to it. More will be heard of all this shortly.

FROM C. P. W.

Feb. 14. It is supposed that the postponement of the land-sales till the allotment of lands is made will be for a year at least. I expect to find the people, though they are all members, will become profane immediately. They are depending on a chance to buy or hire land.

W. C. G. writes the next letter after having had a talk with a friend in the Twenty-Fourth Massachusetts.

FROM W. C. G.

Feb. 17. He seemed very well, more contented than most of the soldiers and talking more rationally and humanely than four fifths of those with whom I have conversed. The troops will probably be here a month or two at least, before any attempt is made in any direction. The commanding generals have quarreled,[1] and one has gone North; the troops are insufficient, the enemy on the alert and strongly defended. The history of the Department so far might read: the forts were taken, one thousand-odd children were taught to read, and one negro regiment was formed.[2] Hunter seems

[1] See p. 162.
[2] The history of the Department had been defined as "a military picnic."

to be a narrow, self-willed man — to me — who don't
know much about his affairs. At first the soldiers were
allowed to go wherever they pleased; consequently
they poured over our end of the island, confusion
coming with them. They cheated, they plundered,
they threatened lives, they stole boats, poultry, hogs,
money, and other property, they paid for dinners with
worthless Richmond money, taking good bills in
exchange. They behaved like marauders in an enemy's
country, and disgraced the name of man, American, or
soldier. The houses of one whole plantation they burnt
to the ground in the night. For three whole days and
far into the night I did nothing but chase soldiers and
ride about to protect the people. The consequence of
it all is that the soldiers are now tied up in camp pretty
firmly.

The sales have been postponed to my and many
persons' great disappointment. And yet it does seem
absurd, in view of the increasing uncertainties of the
moment here, to sell land. But I am so heartily sick
and weary of this system! What I shall do if the lands
are not sold within a month or two, I don't know.

FROM H. W.

Feb. 19. You will see by this copy of the *Free South* [1]
the outrages that have been committed by the troops
who were landed at Land's End, but it can give you
but little idea of the outrages that have been committed
or the mischief done. Besides the actual loss to the
people, — and in many cases it has been their all, —
the loss of confidence in Yankees is an incalculable

---

[1] A paper published at Beaufort.

injury. The scenes some of the superintendents have
had to go through with are beyond description. Sumner
had a pistol put at his breast for trying to stop the
soldiers and protect the negroes, and Mr. Hammond,
when he went with General Saxton to tell Hunter of
what had been done under his very eyes on his own
plantations, burst into tears. It is disgusting that any
Massachusetts regiment should be mixed up with such
savage treatment, and that the Twenty-Fourth should
be is shameful in the extreme.

Feb. 20. To-day all the people were on the Bay
"drawing seine" when I came out of morning school,
and as that is a process I have wished to see I ran down
to the beach myself between whiles. Here was a droll
enough scene indeed. They had made one "drawing"
and were just casting the seine again as I walked along
for half a mile towards the drum-hole.[1] The shell-
banks, which are exposed at low tide, were fringed with
small children with baskets and bags which they were
filling with oysters and conchs. Rose followed me as
guide and protector, jabbering away in her outlandish
fashion to my great entertainment, and was very much
afraid that the oyster-shells, over which she walked with
impunity with bare feet, would cut up my heavy leather
boots. I could go out to the very edge of one of these
curious shell-banks, and the seine was drawn up almost
at my feet. The net was laid on a boat which was hauled
out into the water by the men, who were up to their
waists, then dropped along its full length, which is very
great, and gradually hauled in shore again with two or
three bushels of fish in it, and any number of crabs,

[1] Haunt of the drum-fish.

which the children pick up very carefully and fling
ashore. There were about thirty men, and you would
have thought from the noise and talking that it was a
great fire in the country, with no head to the engine
companies and every man giving orders. They were
good-natured as possible, but sometimes their gibber-
ish sounds as if they were scolding. The boys, with
their pantaloons, or what answer for sich, rolled up to
their knees, were hauling at the rope or picking up the
crabs and making them catch hold of each other till
they had a long string of them. Another mode of proceeding with them — for a crab-bite is a pretty serious
thing — is to hold an oyster-shell out, which they grab,
and then with a quick shake the claw is broken off, and
they are harmless. A large bass having been taken in
the haul I witnessed, it was laid at my feet for my
acceptance, and then, the girls following, most of the
boys staying to see the third drawing, I wended my
way back to school.

Feb. 21. Such steady shop that C. could not get off
very early and sold a barrel of flour before he departed.
Shop is a great nuisance, but I don't know what the
people would do without it and don't see how it can be
given up for a long time. They can't get things as cheap
anywhere else, but they cannot understand that it is
of no advantage to us. When I told them yesterday
they must not hurry me, for I had to put everything
down so as to keep a correct account to send to the
Quartermaster and people who sent the things, they
were quite surprised, and when in explaining the state
of the case to them I remarked that I was not even paid
for the trouble, Binah said she would not take the

trouble then; and they can't understand that any one should.

Other comments on this laborious shop-keeping are: [Feb. 23]. What with sugar and dry goods upstairs, and flour, pork, and salt down, it's busy, not to say nasty work. [Apr. 9.] Mr. P.'s molasses fell short about $5.00 on the barrel! Yet you can't convince the people he is not making heaps of money, and I, too, for the matter of that. [June 6.] A stranger the other day asked me for a looking-glass that he might see how his new hat looked, and then informed me that I ought to keep lemonade for my friends! But such things are rare, and so ludicrous that one does n't mind.

FROM H. W.

Feb. 22. I heard Uncle Sam read the first three chapters of Genesis, which he translated into his own lingo as he went along, calling the subtile serpent the most "amiable" of beasts, and ignoring gender, person, and number in an astonishing manner. He says "Lamb books of Life," and calls the real old Southern aristocracy the gentiles! His vocabulary is an extensive one — I wish his knowledge of the art of cooking were as great!

Feb. 25. I was in full tide with my A B C's when I saw two mounted officers pass the window. They presently appeared at the door of the school-room, one of them with a General's stars, addressing me and asking about the school. But he did not introduce himself, and I was in profound ignorance as to who it might be. They came, apparently, to see the place, and while they walked on the beach I got up what lunch I could. The itle had an immense effect upon Robert; when I told

Sam I must have the water boiled to give the General some coffee, he opened his eyes as wide as the gate, and Rose, who came to ask for the key of the corn-room for him to feed the horses, was such a comical sight, as she stared with mouth and eyes and then dropped a curtsey in the middle of the room, that if any one had been here I think I should have disgraced myself and snickered! Unfortunately the dignitary did not see her.

Feb. 26. I had scarcely done breakfast when I was called upon to serve in the shop for half a dozen men from the blockading vessel off Otter Island, all negroes. They come every once in a while and buy large amounts of sugar and other little things. They evidently think their patronage of great advantage to us.

Five grown men have come in to swell the evening school. I can't do much for them, as they don't all know their letters, but they have books and I hope the children will help them on out of school.

Have I told you that the path to the beach has been bordered with flowers for several weeks, jonquils and narcissus, so far as I can make out, though unlike any I ever saw before? They are in great profusion, and there are a few snow-drops, very pretty, but a foot or more high, and losing their charm in the height and strength. The jasmine and hawthorn are just coming into blossom, and I see what looks like a peach-tree in full bloom in Sam's yard.

Feb. 27. C. came home before night, with the news that the sales had begun [1] and that our fate would be

---

[1] The War Department ordered the sales to go forward, leaving the restrictions to be arranged by Hunter, Saxton, and the Commissioners in charge. See p. 165.

decided by next week probably. He brought no other
news of importance except that my unknown guest was
probably a General Potter [1] on Foster's staff. When I
came out of school this morning I found Rose asleep on
the rug in front of the parlor fire! She is quite a Topsy
in some things, playing all sorts of tricks with her voice
and actions, but I have never had reason to doubt her
truth or honesty in the smallest particular, since the
first, and I have been very watchful.

Feb. 28. Before I was up I heard a perfect babel of
tongues, a magpie chattering, which, on looking out
of the window, I found came from about twenty women
at work in our new garden getting out the "jint-grass,"
swinging their great, heavy hoes above their heads. Dr.
Dio Lewis should have seen their gymnastics and the
physical development therefrom. It was a droll sight —
red, blue, and bright yellow in their costume, and such
a gabbling! Hindustanee is as intelligible as their talk
among themselves. How C. astonished a man who
was muttering away to himself the other day at the
Oaks by laughing at him and telling him he understood
Nigger as well as he!

Old Deborah walked from Cherry Hill this morning,
— she has lately moved there from here, — and came
into the early school, which greatly delighted her. She
is Rose's grandmother, and heard her great-grandchild
reading to me, yet she is a smart old body and carries
on her own cotton this year. Her delight over Raphael's
angels — we have Mr. Philbrick's photographs of
them here — was really touching. "If a body have
any consider, 't would melt their hairt," — and she

[1] Brigadier-General Edward E. Potter, Foster's Chief of Staff.

tried to impress it upon Rose that she was a greatly privileged person to be able to see them every day.

In the next letter is described a visit to the camp of the "North Carolina army" at Land's End.

Sunday, March 1. We started off in time to reach church before the sermon was over, I in the sulky with my things to stay all night, — if it should prove practicable for me to go to camp, by staying at G.'s or the Oaks. H. got into my sulky and we drove off, the question to be decided after dinner. The road to-day was lined with the jasmine in full bloom running over everything. I was too late to see it last spring and as I had not been out of the house for a fortnight the change was very marked. Some trees are putting out fresh, green leaves, the peach and wild plum-trees are all in blossom. Our large field, too, had been "listed" [1] since I passed through it last, and altogether things had a very spring-like look. After dinner it was decided to take the carriage and Northern horses, with Harry, and make our expedition to the camp in style, escorted by Mr. Sumner on horseback.

Behold us, then, starting about ten in the morning, Monday, March 2, driving for fifteen miles through the woods, a perfect spring day, till, as we reached our journey's end, we found the woods cut down and fields cleared for the camps over an immense space. Tents in every direction and masts beyond, looking very busy and thriving. Real war camps, not such as we see at Readville, for most of the regiments coming on such an expedition, from which they expected to return

[1] That is, hoed over again and new furrows made for the next crop.

before this time, had only shelter tents, as few things
as they could possibly get along with, and their worst
clothes. There were men washing (with a bit of board
in a half of a barrel with a horse-brush!), cutting wood,
mending the road very much cut up with the army-
wagons, sticking down trees in front of their tents, and
in almost every camp we saw some men playing ball.
Horses and wagons, rough stables, and the carpenters
at work with plane and saw getting up comforts. The
Twenty-Fourth was at Land's End indeed, so we
passed through all the others before we came to it, each
additional one causing a louder and more wondering
exclamation from Harry at the sight of so many men, till
the oxen, evidently waiting to be slaughtered, and of a
size so vastly superior to those indigenous to these
regions, quite dumbfounded him.

The Twenty-Fourth reached at last, we went at once to
James's tent, where he greeted us very kindly, and inviting
us in, went off for John. Glad as I was to see them at last,
it only made me doubly sorry that they should have
been so near us and unable to come down to the few
home comforts we could have offered them; but they
have both tried to get away in vain. We found the Twenty-
Fourth was in a very excited state over General Stevenson's arrest; [1] and speaking of his release and return to
camp the day before, James said — "We gave him such a
reception as the Twenty-Fourth *can* give." The whole
North Carolina division were feeling very sore over the
quarrel between Hunter and Foster which has so unjustly,

[1] Brigadier-General Thomas G. Stevenson, originally colonel of
the Twenty-Fourth Massachusetts, was arrested by General Hunter
and soon after released.

as they feel, deprived them of going under Foster on this
expedition, and over ιne general treatment of them and
their officers which they have received ever since they
came into this Department.[1] This I heard from James
first, but more at length and in detail from the surgeon
afterwards. For as we drove home a gentleman passed
us on horseback, and we presently saw him racing
with Mr. Sumner, and then riding by his side. They
soon turned. Mr. Sumner introduced to me S. A. Green.
Mr. Sumner had never seen him before, but asked him
to join us at lunch at Mr. G.'s, where we were to stop
on our way.

G. was expecting us, and such a dinner as he spread
before us! A little roasted pig, over which Mr. Sumner
grew pathetic as he described its baby-like appearance
before it was cooked, when Tamah, their invaluable
cook, brought it in to show them — potatoes, rice, etc.,
and for dessert, trifle, cake, muffins, waffles of a most
excellent variety, and I don't know what. But the spice
of the dinner was a long and animated discussion over
the cause of General Stevenson's arrest and other matters appertaining thereto. Dr. Green was present at
the time Stevenson had his discussion with Major Bar-

[1] The immediate cause of this trouble was a disagreement about
the extent of Hunter's authority over Foster and his command while
they were in the Department of the South, but the underlying difficulty was that Foster and his officers distrusted Hunter as an anti-
slavery zealot.

Finding that the operations against Charleston could not go forward immediately, Foster returned to North Carolina within a few
days after his arrival in the Department of the South. His troops remained, so restive under Hunter's command that Foster's whole staff
was presently sent back to North Carolina for alleged insubordination

stow and is reported to have said that he would rather
be defeated than gain a victory with the aid of black
soldiers, — and says that he said no such thing. The
question was asked as a leading one, and before General
Stevenson replied, Major Barstow exclaimed, "You
hear that declaration?" and went off and reported.
Pretty small business, anyway, though the General and
most of his officers apparently are not at all waked up
to the question, and oppose the idea of negro soldiers
very strongly. They seem to have been living for a
year with their old prejudices quietly slumbering —
without coming in contact with the subject and its
practical working as we have here, and so are not prepared for the change of opinion which has been silently
advancing here. We did not think a year ago that these
people would make soldiers, though it might be a wise
measure to organize them for garrison duty to save the
lives of our men in a climate they could not bear well
and where no fighting would be necessary. Now it is
a matter of fact, not opinion, as Colonel Higginson's
report shows, that they will fight in open warfare, and
will succeed in a certain sort of expedition when white
men would fail, thus being too valuable an aid in
putting down the Rebellion for us to give way to the
prejudices of the mass of the soldiers. But I do not
think it strange those prejudices exist, and they can
only be removed by degrees.

The sales are to go on — how glad I shall be when
the whole thing is settled! Dr. Brisbane thinks he has
proof that Mr. Coffin is in jail in Charleston for Union
sentiments,[1] so that he shall reserve his plantations for

[1] This report turned out to be a mistake.

him. Mr. Philbrick may be able to lease them till the
war is over, but if we take Charleston and if Mr. Coffin
claims his own again, behold us! I don't know what the
negroes would do, at first, if they thought Mr. Coffin
was coming back to take possession of the lands —
though they all acknowledge that when he was here
there was no "confusion" — "that was all along de
overseer." I suppose, if they were not taken by surprise
and could understand matters, they would work for
him as well as any one else; but a great deal would
depend upon whom they had over them — they would
not work under Cockloft again "first." They will be
disappointed if Mr. Philbrick does not get this place.

FROM W. C. G.

March 1. The sale of lands, which was arrested by
General Hunter's order, has recommenced by authority
obtained from Washington. The generals commanding
— Hunter and Saxton — are both interested in terms
and regulations which will favor the negroes. I hear
they are both added as, in some way, joint commissioners to those who have been acting in that capacity,
with full powers to retain all lands in Government
possession which may be wanted for military or educational purposes.[1] What plan they may adopt is not
yet known; but we have already been called on for a
complete census of the population, with a view to a
land allotment of some kind. I pray it may not be by
gift. I used to dread the effects of immediate emanci-

---

[1] That is, the revenue from the cotton on certain plantations was
used for these purposes. A plantation thus devoted to the educational needs of the people was called a School Farm.

pation and think it was the duty of a Christian nation
to ease the passage from slavery to freedom with all
kinds of assistance; but I am nearly satisfied that the
best thing our Government can do, for the good of these
people themselves, is simply to offer and enforce their
acceptance of the advantages of civil law and education.
I should hope that for a time the relations of employer
and employed might be also watched and determined
by law, — but more than this, anything in the form of
gifts and *charity* will, I'm pretty sure, only relieve
momentary distress at the expense of their development
in manliness and independence. Very few will take a
responsibility which they can in any way avoid, and not
one in a thousand will refuse charity if offered, even
when there is no slightest need of it. At the same time,
they perfectly understand the rights of property, almost
superstitiously appreciate the advantages of education,
and will eagerly seize any opportunity they may have
of acquiring the one or the other. As to these island
people I feel no doubt that at least three out of five
of the present children will be able to read and write
when men and women, and that of the present generation of grown people, half a plantation at least would
own land in their own right before four years had past,
— if they were permitted to buy. Then how much better to throw them on themselves, to leave them to their
own ambition and intelligence, when they have so
much of both. Their inveterate suspicion of white
kindness, too, joined to their ignorance, so clog the
wheels of any system of charity like this of superintendence that for this reason alone I think it should cease.
But they only too thoroughly comprehend the idea of

law, — and are therefore well able to understand and be grateful for beneficent law, which at once protects and leaves them to themselves. "Let us alone" — the cry of their masters — really belongs to them and is their wisest demand.

I am anxiously hoping to be freed from this place by the sales and to return to my old neighborhood, and there to be able to accomplish something. This is but a stand-still experience, compared to our wishes. The people advance in spite of it. I believe almost the only real good I've done was to partially protect these people for three days from the soldiers.

FROM H. W.

March 5. C. came home at night with the news that the First South Carolina Volunteers started on an expedition [1] to-day which Colonel Higginson considers of very great importance, which will have very great results, or from which they will probably never return. Also that drafting has begun in Beaufort by Hunter's orders.

General Saxton has *passed his word* to the people here that they shall not be forced into the army — I don't see what is to be the upshot of it — they will lose all confidence in us. Anywhere but here! Saxton himself gave Colonel Montgomery [2] leave to draft in Florida and Key West, but he had no need to — more recruits offered than he could bring away with him. I don't wish to find fault with my commanding general, but I have yet to be shown the first thing Hunter has done

---

[1] To capture Jacksonville, on the St. John's River, Florida.

[2] Of the Second South Carolina Volunteers (colored).

which I consider wise or fine. Saxton has had to go
down more than once and persuade him not to execute
his orders.

In the following letter the reference to Mrs. Wolcott
and McClellan has to do with that visit to Boston of
the deposed general which was made such a triumphal
progress for him by the conservatives of the town. The
reference to Hallowell, who had a commission in the
Fifty-Fourth Massachusetts, the first colored regiment
raised by a state government, is interesting as further
evidence of the prejudice against negro troops.

March 6. C. brought me last night a long letter from
S. descriptive of Mrs. Wolcott's party, McClellan, the
fashions, and Hallowell's feeling at the position in
which he places himself in going into a negro regiment.
I wish he could see Colonel Higginson and his, but a
Northern black regiment will be a very different thing
from a Southern one — the men will have the vices of
civilization from which these are free. Colonel Higginson is an enthusiast, but I do not see that he exaggerates
or states anything but facts.

Then follow specimens of the conversation of Robert
and Rose, with which may be put here two others,
really of later date.

"Miss Hayiut, that your home?" Robert asked me
this morning, looking at some colored pictures of the
Crystal Palace I found in a *London News* and nailed
up in the entry yesterday! He's bound to go North
with Mass' Charlie. If he expects to live in such a man-
sion I don't wonder he wishes to.

Saturday, March 7. If you could have seen Rose's as-
tonishment this morning when she comprehended that

the clock was not alive! I made her tell me what time it was, which she did successfully, and then, as she stood gazing at the minute-hand "move so fast," I said, "Yes, it is going all the time — it never stops." "No rest for eat?" she said with the utmost innocence; and when I told her it was not alive and did not need to eat, she was quite sure the pendulum must be if the hands were not.

[*March* 10.[1]] Some instructions about cleaning up led me to ask Rose if she liked dirt, to which she replied, like a true Yankee, with the question, "Miss Hay't, you like um? You no like um, I no like um." A little while after, she got talking about "Maussa" and Cockloft; when I asked what she would do if she should see Mr. Coffin come here, she said, "I run," "dey bad." Oh, no, not bad, I guess. "Miss Hay't" (you have no idea how short it is, almost "Hat"), "you shum? [see 'em] Well, you do'no; I shum, I know."

[*Nov.* 1.] "I say praise for you, 'cause I mind you," said Rose to me in her affectionate way this morning. She tames slowly, as Mr. Soule and I thought when we came home from riding this morning and saw her waiting for us at the entrance of the path on the beach turning somersaults on the sand! Her hands would appear high in the air, when suddenly her heels would be in their place! Yesterday morning she said: "Miss Hayiut, you gwine let me go home to-day for wash?" Yes, Rose, if you are a good girl. "Yes, *Ma'am*, me gwine be good girl, my contans [conscience] say, 'Rose, you be good girl, not make Miss Hayiut talk.'"

To return to H. W.'s letter of March 7:

---

[1] The bracket is used for unimportant dates which are out of their chronological place.

We drove up to church and heard the text read for
the first time! H. was not there, so we went there to
dinner again, probably for the last time, as we found
the places are really to be sold to-morrow. Mr. Philbrick hopes to be through with collecting the cotton
in a fortnight, and then they will be able to come down
here, as he can go to Beaufort once a week for a night
or two until it is all ginned and shipped, and then they
will go home.

The next letters return to the all-absorbing matter
of the land-sales. The opening paragraph refers to
them and the way they were being managed, as well
as to the old question of negro character and negro
labor.

FROM C. P. W.

March 8. I should like to come home and make inquiries among my friends concerning Port Royal matters. I should like to take the part of an intelligent for-
eigner desiring to obtain information concerning this
interesting experiment of free black labor. And when
I had heard and written down their description of this
enterprise, I should return to my friends here and read
for their entertainment. How we should laugh; I must
try it some day.

When the lands are finally sold, a great many entertaining questions will arise. Only the real estate will
be sold; what is to be done with the cattle, the mules,
the boats, the furniture, the carriages? How is the
Government to be repaid for what it has spent on this
year's crop? How are the reserved plantations to be
worked by the Government?

The sale having taken place at last on March 9, the list with which C. P. W. begins his next letter is of plantations reserved from sale by the Government.

March 10.   The Oaks, Oakland, where Mr. Hunn's Philadelphia Commission store is, Eddings Point, T. B. Fripp, my two McTureous places, the Hope Place, and a few others on the Sea Side road, about four at Land's End, etc., etc.   Mr. Eustis and a Mr. Pritchard, living on Pritchard's Island, near Land's End, paid taxes before the sale.   (Most of the places reserved were selected for the purpose of selling land to the negroes next year, after this crop is in.)

The General [Saxton] is afraid that some speculators may interfere with the plan for this year which has been started.[1]   He has made certain promises to the people in regard to this year's crop, and he feels that he ought to be able to impose some conditions on purchasers. Of course he could not impose conditions under which the lands should be sold, but he still may, as Military Governor, enforce justice toward the people.

FROM H. W.

March 10.   C. and Mr. Philbrick stopped at the nigger-house to see and tell the people of the result of the sale.   At Fripp Point, which he also bought, the people were as usual unmoved and apparently apathetic, but here they were somewhat more demonstrative, and slightly expressed their pleasure.   All the places he most cared for Mr. Philbrick was able to bid off, and two of C.'s old places, which he wanted but did not expect to get.   So much is settled; but there is a great deal besides

See p. 147.

that it will take a long time and a deal of trouble to arrange — we don't know yet how much goes with the plantations, or when possession will be given.

The confirmation of the report that Hunter is going to draft these people causes a great deal of feeling, as Saxton has publicly promised them that they shall not be forced to join the army. They seem to understand that Hunter is in authority and Saxton can't help himself, C. says, and so have no ill feeling towards the latter; but they will hide, if possible, and it is hard to feel that they have been so treated as to make them as suspicious of a Yankee's word as they have always been of a white man's. I think it right they should go if they are needed, — the war is of more importance even than the experiment of free labor, — but to have them lied to so! Why was Hunter ever sent back here?

FROM C. P. W.

March 14. Mr. Philbrick has bought in all thirteen plantations,[1] at an expense of about $7000: three places for R., two for Wells, two for Hull on Ladies Island, six places within five miles of this place. I remain here, and shall probably assume Cherry Hill and Mulberry Hill, my old places; G. comes to Pine Grove, and takes that, the Point, and Captain John Fripp Homestead. The people are all starting well, we are in excellent spirits, and are in proper season for the crops; and "if God spare life," "if nothing strange happens," "if we live to see," we shall "*see* crop make, sir."

This drafting business is simply folly. Hunter is an

---

[1] Two of the thirteen were merely leased.

ignorant, obstinate fool.[1] General Saxton is very much
opposed to the measure, especially after promising the
men again and again that they would not be taken
unless they were willing to go; but he says he has done
all he can to dissuade Hunter without any effect, and
if he should go further in the matter, either he or Hunter
would have to go home, and he is not willing at this
crisis to raise this additional difficulty. Hunter's order
was published in the *New South*[2] last Monday. For
a full week before the negroes had been anxiously ques-
tioning us about this strange news that "they want to
take we to make soldiers." Up to Monday I was able
to tell them that I had heard such stories, but did not
believe them; but Tuesday night, when I got home, I
told them how matters stood, and they confessed that
for a full week before hardly a man on the plantation
under sixty years of age had slept in his bed. A strange
white face drives them from the field into the woods like
so many quails; they will not go to church, they will
not go to the Ferry. Two Sundays ago I happened to
ask one of the elders at church, to make talk merely,
how soon the next Society meeting took place at Pine
Grove. It was last Saturday evening. My question to
Demus was reported at the meeting, they immediately
became suspicious of some trap to catch them, they

[1] H. W., commenting more mildly, says (Mar. 18): "He certainly
has not a clear idea of what the superintendents and teachers are doing,
and unfortunately classes them as in opposition to himself, — as preferring the agricultural to the military department. This I do not think
is the case, but they most of them feel his want of wisdom in dealing
with the subject, which has made his own especial object as well as
theirs harder to accomplish."

[2] A short-lived newspaper published in the Department.

grew anxious, a cry arose that there were soldiers out
on the plantation, the men left the praise-house, and
the meeting, instead of continuing all night, broke up
about midnight with some confusion.[1] They were
caught last year, they will not be caught again. They
cannot understand how it is that the Government, for
whom they have been working, and in whom they have
learned to place confidence as a protection, should wish
to interrupt their work here. It is a terrible discouragement to them, just as they are starting their first fair
trial for themselves, to be forced, I do not say into the
military service, for very few will be caught, but forced
to abandon their crops, and skulk and hide and lead
the life of hunted beasts during all this precious planting
season. The women would be physically able to carry
on for some time the men's share with their own, but they
would be very much disheartened, and would need
constant encouragement.   Under this terrible uncertainty and fear, the work has begun to slacken. Even
the head men on the plantations are losing courage.
I make as light of the evil as I can, but I am always
met by the remark: "We are a year older than we was
last year, sir." Their trust in me is a little surprising.
They converse in my presence about their dodging life,
and I could easily take any ten of them I chose alone;
or, with the aid of one other, I could take the whole
plantation.   "If we did n't trust to you, sir, we should

[1] H. W. describes another service that was broken up by this fear
of the draft: "[May 2.] At church yesterday a squad of soldiers with
their officer came from Land's End to the service, when a general
stampede took place among the men, and women too, jumping from
the windows and one man even from the gallery into the midst of the
congregation."

have to leave the plantation entirely; you are the only person to protect we now, sir." It is hardly necessary to remark that their confidence is not misplaced. Help catch them? "I would n't do it first."

In accordance with Hunter's order, referred to above, Saxton issued a general order to superintendents, which bade them send to Captain Hooper a list of all able-bodied freedmen between eighteen and fifty on the plantations, and instructed them to urge the negroes to enlist by appealing to "their reason, sense of right, their love of liberty and their dread of returning to the rule of their late masters," adding : "The General Commanding expects to form a pretty correct judgment of the comparative efficiency of the different superintendents and the amount of influence for good they are capable of exerting over their people, by the proportion of the whole number subject to draft which they are able to bring in without the aid of physical force." Referring to this last sentence as a "mean insinuation," C. P. W. goes on:

For my people, I know there is about as much use in asking them to enlist as in requesting my horse, a very intelligent animal, to drink salt water. I hope they will draft, they may possibly enlist, the loafers at Hilton Head and Beaufort, and those whose proximity to camps, or general worthless character, prevents them from taking much interest in their crops. But these men, who have been paid up in full for last year's crop, and have seen that their crop, slim as it was, brought them a fair compensation, are bound to show *a crop* this year. Crop-raising is their business, their trade, and they intend to show what they can do at it this year for the Government, which protects them, for me, who "see them justice" (they have a vague idea that

I reap a certain percentage from their crop — they say,
"You will have a bigger crop of cotton than Mr. Philbrick, sir" — they also think that if I "overlook" four
hundred hands, I ought to get more pay than a man who
only sees to two hundred), and last, and principally, for
themselves.   They have not been learning cotton-
raising, perforce, all these years for nothing. Now their
enforced knowledge comes out in tending a crop of
which they are to own a share, and the little tricks of the
trade, which had to be watchfully enforced in the old
time, are now skillfully produced, especially in the food
crops, which are more evidently their own. I let them
go ahead very much as they choose; I make regulations for the good of all, as in the matter of carts, oxen,
etc., but the minutiæ I do not meddle with, except as
a matter of curiosity and acquirement of knowledge.
They work well, some of them harder than in the old
time; the lazy ones are stimulated to exertion for their
own benefit, the energetic ones *race like sixty*.

FROM H. W.

March 13. I had the sick people to visit, and C. was
going over to the *Kingfisher*, our blockader, for coal-tar
to plant corn with, so he went to the field and I was to
make my professional calls for the Doctor, and meet
him at the Creek at the nigger-house to take the row
with him. Just as I came out of school, however, two
officers of an Illinois regiment rode up to look about and
see what they could see, and asked if they could have
food for man and beast. So I left orders for some lunch,
dressed, and started on my tour. I went through the
quarters — not a man was to be seen. There lay the

boat, and the women were coming in from their work, but said the men would not come till the officers had gone — they were afraid of being taken. C. had to beg the officers to go off the plantation, for he could not get his crew. Not a man sleeps at night in the houses, except those too old to be taken. They have made a camp somewhere and mean never to be caught. There is no question that they can hide; a slave here hid himself for two years on one of the little islands, though the whole district was after him; he finally came out himself.

FROM W. C. G.

March 14. On March 9th the estates were at last offered for sale. On our island two thirds were bidden in by the Government and I presume they will remain under the system of superintendence. The other third was bought by Mr. Philbrick and two or three sutlers. No agents of Southern owners and no dangerous speculators made their appearance, to my knowledge. Where any person evinced a desire to buy, the commissioners, by their bids, forced an offer of one dollar per acre and let the place go for that price. Several plantations, perhaps one in five or six, were bidden in for the special purpose of negro reservations; but in what way they will be offered to the people is undecided. Indeed, nothing is certain except that the sales have been made and titles given. I should have bought only two of my places in any case, — and that for the benefit of the people, — but it happened that both were among the number reserved. So I own none of the sacred soil.

In regard to your questions concerning the condition

and capabilities of the blacks, I hardly feel like writing anything at length, my opinion, as far as it is made up, is so short and decided. Every one says that these island negroes are more ignorant and degraded than the great majority of the slaves, and I feel no doubt that, under conditions of peace, three years would find these people, with but very few exceptions, a self-respecting, self-supporting population. Almost everything about them, even to their distrust and occasional turbulence, has that in it which suggests to me the idea of capacity and power of development. Their principal vices, — dishonesty, indolence, unchastity, their dislike of responsibility, and unmanly willingness to be dependent on others for what their own effort might bring, — their want of forethought and inability to organize and combine operations for mutual benefit, — nearly all their mental and moral weaknesses can be traced naturally and directly to slavery, — while on the other hand, the fact that at my close view I cannot make them out to be characteristic traits confirms that opinion as to their origin. Industry is very certainly the *rule;* there is much idleness, but apply the spurs of which you think a white man worthy, and you are sure to obtain earnest and persistent exertion. Manliness and self-respect are sufficiently strong and common to excite an expectation of finding them. Instances of plan, contrivance, forethought are very numerous; you are constantly meeting "smart" fellows. Their eagerness and aptitude in learning to read surprises every one. Their memories are usually excellent, their power of observation pretty keen, and their general intelligence is in most striking contrast to the idea of chattel and

wonderfully harmonizes with that of man. I am only
stating the grounds on which I have hopes of their
development, not trying to describe their characteristics
or the course or limit of that development. The discussion whether they will ever be equal to the white race
in anything seems to me to be entirely irrelevant to
everything. The only question of importance is whether
they can become a moral, self-supporting, and useful
part of our population, and of this I cannot feel the
slightest doubt. That they ever can leave the country I
regard as impossible, that they ever ought to leave it, as
ill-advised. That the period of transition will be one of
great difficulty and considerable suffering is certain.
The best heads and hearts in the country will find work
in it. As I think now, I would recommend no gradual
system of preparation and training. Strike the fetters
off at a blow and let them jump, or lie down, as they
please, in the first impulse of freedom, and let them at
once see the natural effects of jumping and lying down.
Then if the Government would simply provide or enforce education, and with few laws but very many eyes
would watch over the new relations of laborer and
employer, I should trust that in ten years America
would again raise her head proudly among the nations.
But all this supposes that we gain our end and have the
work to do. Till the common head of the people understands and the common heart of the people feels that
this *is* the work of the war, that Emancipation should be
the means, and not only the best means but the holy
end of the war, — I tremble, and fear neither our
strength nor God's help will give us the victory.

FROM H. W.

March 20. C. amused himself and us by making two
or three of my children who were waiting for school
read to him upside down, which they did as readily as
the right way.

Just a year to-night since Mr. Philbrick spent his
first night in this house. He has been telling us about
it: a file of soldiers were drawn up at the gate and
refused him admittance till his credentials were examined; now he is lord of the manor. I reminded the
children to-night that a year ago they did not know
their letters; now they are reading Hillard's Second
Reader for the second time.

The feat of reading upside down might seem to suggest that they were reading Hillard's Second Reader
for the second time chiefly by the aid of memory!

The next letter, written by Mr. Philbrick to a Northern correspondent, was printed at the time on a broad-
side, for distribution.

FROM E. S. P.

Coffin's Point, March 20. Just a year ago to-night
I entered this house for the first time. If our Northern
croakers could only be made to realize as we do here
the ease with which we have reduced a comparative
degree of order out of the chaos we found, and see how
ready this degraded and half-civilized race are to become
an industrious and useful laboring class, there would
not be so much gabble about the danger of immediate
emancipation, or of a stampede of negro labor to the
North.

We found them a herd of suspicious savages who regarded their change of condition with fear and trembling, looking at the cotton-field as a life-long scene of unrequited toil, and hailing with delight the prospect of "no more driver, no more cotton, no more lickin'." They had broken up the cotton-gins and hidden the iron-work, and nothing was more remote from their shallow pates than the idea of planting cotton for "white folks" again.

Now they have, without the least urging, prepared for planting some two hundred acres of cotton-land upon this plantation, having spread on it sixteen hundred ox-cart-loads of manure, and worked up every inch of the ground with their hoes. They have also planted one hundred and thirty acres of corn, and have begun ploughing to-day, banking up into ridges with the ploughs the cotton-land into which the manure had been first hoed. The ploughs run over twenty acres per day on this place. They were made at Groton, Mass., and astonish the negroes by their efficiency.

As a sample of the change of feeling in regard to working on cotton, I will relate how I got the cotton ginned on this and the various other plantations in this neighborhood. I walked through the negro quarters one day in December and told the people I would pay them three cents per pound of clean cotton if they would gin, assort, clean, and pack their cotton ready for market. They said in reply their gins were all broken up. I told them that was their own fault, and that, if they wanted other people to gin their cotton and get their seed away from the place, they would do so, and so get all the money and leave them no good seed to

plant. "Dat' so, Massa," said they, and I passed along.
The next time I came they had hunted up the broken
pieces of twenty-five gins, and patched them up, and
had ginned and packed all their cotton, in two weeks,
wanting to know what I would have them do next,
for they did not want to lie still and do nothing.

So you see there is some satisfaction in being among
these people, although they are not exactly companions
for us.

FROM H. W.

March 23. C. came home to-night, having resigned
his position under the Government.

H. W.'s next letter, after describing a drive towards
Land's End, narrates the events of her return trip as
follows.

March 25. I opened the first gate myself, then met a
man coming from his work, who took off his hat with
rather a surprised look at seeing a lady alone, and an
"Evening, Missus, how far you come from?" "From
Coffin's Point, and am going back again — Mr. Charlie's
sister." Whereupon another bow and a pleased grin
as I go on. Soon I met another man coming out into
the road with a piece of paper, which he asked me to
read to him. I took the precaution to ask him his name
before opening it, to be sure he had not another man's
pass, and then read him an autograph pass from General Hunter for him to go to St. Helena and back to
Hilton Head, to see his wife. He was a servant of Hunter's
and *afraid of some trick.* He seemed satisfied, and
thanked me. When I asked him where his wife lived
and if he had seen her, he said, "Shum dere?" point-

ing to a woman hoeing, towards whom he made his
way again. At the next gate I was cutting cherokee-
roses before opening it, when a slight sound behind
me attracted my attention to a boy on a mule who had
come noiselessly up, so I got into the sulky again, and
as he followed me along and I questioned him, found
he was coming here to see his "aunty." In a few minutes a loud whistle attracted my attention and Sharper[1]
announced Mass' Charlie, who came cantering up behind me. He had sent the boy with a note to me and
exemption-papers for the old and feeble on his places,
as he could not go home and had met the black soldiers out taking the men for the draft. With Sharper
for attendant I drove on to Pine Grove, where I gave
C.'s note to William and the papers to distribute on both
the Fripp places while I went on to deliver those here.
Heard one man say to William that he wished his old
master was back, — he was at peace then. Poor fellows!

By the time I reached our quarters it was bright
moonlight, and in that light I drove through the street,
read the names on C.'s papers and the contents to the
men named as they came out at Primus' knock. A
little group gathered about to hear what I had to say
as I explained to the men, — a sober, disturbed set, saying nothing, but receiving the explanation with a sad
silence that went to my heart.

FROM W. C. G.

Coffin's Point, March 31. You see I write from my first
home. In truth it seems like a home. Mrs. Philbrick

---

[1] The boy.

and Miss W., Mr. Philbrick, and Mr. Hall are here, besides Mr. Folsom — of '62, Harvard — who is to be my future house-mate. A week ago, after settling up all business at Captain Oliver's, I resigned my place of Government Superintendent, and last Friday came down here. To-morrow we shall take up our quarters at the "Pine Grove." I am going to take charge of the two William Fripp places. The people are old friends. I used to teach school for them. I think I shall like the work here much better; the people are far better and the locality less exposed to outside influences. It is a much better opportunity for trying the experiment of free black labor. I manage the places, Mr. Philbrick supplies money to carry them on, and at the end of the year, after deducting all expenses, we share the profits, if any.

The draft is either taking or frightening off most of the men, but it should be made, I think.

FROM H. W.

April 3. Cæsar came home on a furlough, and it was fun to see him in the street afterwards, surrounded by a great gang, talking away as eagerly as possible. I should like to have heard him, if I could have understood him; he had had a "firs' rate time" and he and January have been trying to get some of the men to go back with them, but they can't succeed any better than C. or Mr. Philbrick.

The next few letters are entirely occupied with incidents of the draft.

E. S. P. TO C. P. W. (IN BOSTON)

April 7. Nothing has been done yet about enforcing the draft on our island, but Captain Bryant[1] told me yesterday he should probably strike the last of this week, taking every point at once as near as may be. Colonel Montgomery's regiment[2] are given him for the purpose, with orders not to *shoot* except in self defense!

FROM H. W.

April 14. The soldiers had been there [at Fripp Point] in the night, but had only caught old Simon and Mike, a boy of about fifteen, though one of them had shot at Dan's Peter, about seventeen, and wounded him in the head slightly. They went in squads all over this end of the island except Pine Grove and here. They got sixty men in all, most of them old, a waste of Uncle Sam's money. Of course our people here are warned and all off again. The white officer said they took what men they could get without reference to the superintendents' lists.

April 15. Hamlet's wife, Betsey, came to buy salt, said her husband was carried off the other night and she left with ten children and a "heart most broke, shan't live long, no way, oh my Jesus!" My new cook's husband was shot (and killed) as he ran away when the Secesh tried to make him go with them — how are they to understand the difference? Captain Dutch[3]

---

[1] Captain J. E. Bryant, of the Eighth Maine.

[2] The Second South Carolina Volunteers (colored).

[3] Of the *Kingfisher*, the blockader.

says he thinks that six or eight have gone onto the Main from this island; they openly say, some of them, that they wish the old times were back again.

April 23. The men at Fripp Point are said to have fired on the soldiers from their houses. They are very bitter that negroes should be sent against them. They would not mind white men, they say. R. has persuaded all his men to go up to Beaufort,[1] and only a few were retained. The rest have come back as happy as kings — no more bush for them! I wish all would do the same.

April 29. Mr. Philbrick went off to the wharf before breakfast, and as he was coming back met Phillis on her way to tell the men who were at work on it that the soldiers had come. As we sat down to lunch we could see the gleaming of the bayonets as they came through the first gate, and Primus sent up to say that he was taken and wanted Mr. Philbrick to come down. Mr. G. appeared from Pine Grove, where they had taken only two men, who will probably be let off. Soon William appeared, saying they had been at the Point, too, but had got no one. Mr. Philbrick rowed down to the [Fripp Point] quarters and presently returned with Captain Hoyt and Captain Thompson, who were very tired, to lunch. They all received him very crustily and coldly at first, but they were prejudiced against him and vexed at their want of success, and I think it did something towards removing ill feelings to see him. When they reached the nigger-house here, where the men [the soldiers], about fifty, had been waiting, they

[1] To be examined, adjudged not "able-bodied," and given exemption-papers.

found they had tracked two men down through the marsh from Fripp Point and caught them just here, after shooting one. The people were in a wild state of confusion. The soldiers had been telling our people all sorts of stories — that they had orders to shoot because Mr. Philbrick had said in Beaufort that he had a battery here to defend his people, etc. They came flocking round him, all women of course, and all talking at once to try and get at the truth of things, and Mr. Philbrick had to quiet them before he could make out a word. Then Amaritta naturally stood forward as spokeswoman to get "satisfaction," and they were easily made to understand that the soldiers had been telling lies, and their confidence in Mr. Philbrick quieted them.

E. S. P. TO C. P. W.

Beaufort, May 1.   We are led to admire more than ever the cool discrimination of the General commanding the Department. The other day some officer conceived the idea that the superintendents of St. Helena in general, and W. C. G. in particular, were opposing the draft, *employing* able-bodied men, etc.; also that shots had been fired at the black soldiers on his plantation. It was so represented to General Hunter, and he ordered on the spot that he should be arrested and sent out of the Department. Fortunately Captain Bryant, who was to have executed the order, was a man of sense and consulted Captain Hooper, who told him that General Saxton did n't want to spare Mr. G., and that as he had no written orders he had better hold on. The editor of the *Free South* has been amusing him-

self by throwing out owlish insinuations to the effect
that speculators and others on St. Helena had better
take heed of General Hunter's orders, for the prospect-
ive profits of a speedy fortune would hardly warrant
the risk, etc., etc.

The next paragraph gives another version of the
search for black recruits.

Captain Thompson came to Coffin's on Wednesday
with about fifty men. They caught no one but Primus,
who felt safe and did n't hide. If he had behaved himself he would n't have been taken, but got into a passion and talked so wild that he was taken out of punishment for his impudence, and then held on the ground
that his influence must be against the draft, and as he
was foreman, his power must be considerable! Captain
Thompson pretended to have orders to shoot men running, and scoured the Fripp Point place through Lieutenant O. E. Bryant and some black soldiers. They
met no young men except Sancho and Josh, whom
they chased down into the marsh opposite Coffin
nigger-house, and then shot Josh. He was taken with a
bullet in his leg and a buckshot in his head, carried
to the village, and placed under Dr. Bundy's care.
Of course, Sancho was taken, too, and brought up to
camp. He had an Enfield rifle with him, and admits
that he fired it to "scare away the soldiers," after
Josh was hit, but not before. The black soldiers all say
he fired first, and no white man was present to see.
I came up to lay the matter before the General, but
he is not well. Captain Hooper has taken it in hand and
promises to investigate it. The Major of the Second

Regiment [1] was down here, but I could n't see him. He may have given such orders to Thompson as he pretends. They seem to have got enraged because they could n't find any men on those three plantations after having been quartered at the village for two weeks, and imputed their want of success to G. and myself. I should n't be surprised if I am ordered out of the Department at any moment.

Then comes the sequel.

FROM H. W.

May 17. Primus has come home. He deserted a week ago and has been all that time getting here. He says that he has not drilled but once since he was taken to camp, that he has been sick all the time, but that he has not been in the hospital. Of course, not being volunteers, there is a great deal of shamming, and they have to be very strict; in short, they pursue the old masters' system of believing they lie until it is proved they have spoken the truth, — a most elevating process! and he had a large blister put on the back of his neck and was kept in his tent. Finally Captain Hoyt took him to Colonel Montgomery and told him that he thought the man was really sick and not fit to be kept, but the Colonel was very short with him and said drill was the best cure for him. Then Primus ran away, and is now in his bed here. Mr. Philbrick has seen him and says it is impossible to tell whether he is sick or not, but he understands fully the consequences of desertion, and that Mr. Philbrick and C. cannot employ him again. Mr. Philbrick told him that he should not inform

[1] Second South Carolina Volunteers.

against him, but that if the officers asked him if he had
come home he should have to tell them that he had.
" I know dat, massa, but I won't stay dere." He understands that we are helpless. He says, and we have
learned in other ways, that all who were drafted have
been deserting. One day they brought in fourteen, and
the next day twelve of them had gone, and the next
the other two. They can't pretend to get them back
again, and of course the demoralization must be great.
It will be very bad for Primus now, if they do not take
him, to live on here an outlaw, working his wife's cotton
but not able to resume his plow or his old position in
any way — yet if he is taken again he will never make
a good soldier. The whole thing is wrong from the
foundation, and should be given up, and all those who
did not volunteer sent to their homes — if any are then
left in the regiments. Yet I don't see how that could
be done unless Hunter went off, and some other Major
General repealed his orders.

To return to matters of plantation management.
C. P. W. had recently been sent home by Mr. Philbrick to buy and send a schooner-load of provisions,
merchandise, etc., for the "store." He found himself
" an object of regard and curiosity," "engaged out
to dinner and tea to ' talk Port Royal ' many days
ahead." Apropos of the things he bought for Coffin's
Point, he wrote:

C. P. W. TO E. S. P.

Boston, [April 27.] I received permission from the
Secretary of the Treasury to ship the powder, shot,
saddle, bridle, tar, pitch, and rope, but I had to consign
these, with the hats, to General Saxton, from whom

you will have to obtain an order for them. The tobacco, shoes, rice, and buggy are not contraband. They were going to stop the hats, on the ground that they were "adapted for military uniforms," and I had to get a "character" from one of my friends, a clerk in the Custom House, and then assure the crusty old Collector that the hats were not to be used for any illegal purpose, before he would let them pass.

FROM W. C. G.

Pine Grove, May 17. The schooner has but just come round to Coffin's, and the rain has prevented our plundering her with energy. But Friday I got up my molasses and gave some out yesterday. You ought to have seen the little ones dance as the mothers came home with their piggins full. We are going to give some molasses and bacon monthly for the present, — in lieu of an increase of wages. Most of the proprietors are offering rather better terms than the Government, — some in money, others in a larger share of the crop. We keep the Government scale of prices, but give them the " poke " and " sweet'ning," and I think have touched their sensibilities much more certainly thereby.

This same day Mr. and Mrs. Philbrick left Port Royal and went home. The next extracts are from two of H. W.'s letters, full of details about the home life and the wonderful ways of the "people."

FROM H. W.

June 10. As we drove up under the shade of a button-wood-tree [at Fripp Point] we found a group of children under it, three or four boys and girls washing at washtubs, others sitting round taking care of younger children. They were just like children all over the world,[1] playing and teasing each other, but very good-naturedly, and as happy as you please. This weather the children wear nothing but a shift or shirt, and the other day Lewis and Cicero appeared in the yard entirely naked. Aunt Sally, from Eddings Point, amused us with her queer, wild talk a long time. The story is that she was made crazy by her master's whipping her daughter to death, and very sad it was to hear her talk, though it was funny. She knows any number of hymns and parts of the Bible, and jumbles scraps and lines from the one with Genesis and Revelation in the most extraordinary manner, talking about Mr. Adam and Madam Eve, who brought her and her race all their woe, whom she knows but will never forgive. She stands and reads everything out of her "heart-book," which she says tells her everything, looking all the time at her left hand, which she holds out like a book. Her epithets against her old master and the rebels were voluble and denunciatory in the extreme, and she left us with many warnings to remember "Det and de Jugment." I had sent for the "Widow Bedotte," to whom I presented some tobacco and who was very funny indeed. She is in her right mind and delights in making herself agreeable. I wish I could describe to you this extraordinary specimen of humanity — a short little old body with an intelligent face — all her wool carefully concealed by an enormous turban, from beneath each side of which hung four black strings, looking like an imitation

[1] A noticeable thing about the children of slaves was that they had no games.

frisette of false curls, her odd figure enveloped in shawl and cape, rubbing her hands nervously and sinking into the floor, as it seemed, as she curtseyed to us lower than I ever saw anybody go and get up again straight. And then her conversation and manner were as comical as her appearance.

Another characteristic of the "Widow Bedotte" H. W. describes elsewhere.

She prides herself upon her good manners, which she says she gets because she belongs to the church, which every now and then she joins again. She has just done so here, so is full of extra flourishes.

On June 12 Hunter was replaced by Brigadier-General Quincy A. Gillmore.[1] Here follow comments on Hunter's last acts before leaving, as well as on the impression made by his successor.

FROM H. W.

May 28. Mr. Williams brought word that Hunter has issued an order to all civilians to enter the army or leave the Department! Twenty days' notice. You need not be afraid of C.'s enlisting here; he would n't do it "first." I don't think many of the superintendents would now like to serve under Hunter. He imprisoned two of them upon the evidence of their people without inquiring into the matter, and ignored Saxton in the most insulting manner. Mr. Hammond was released by a court-martial with honor.

May 30. In the evening came a note from R. saying

---

[1] In the words of the order the command of the Department was taken from Hunter and given to Gillmore "temporarily."

that there was no danger from the draft for the superintendents, but they would probably have to get exemption-papers.

June 20. C. came home after church Sunday with the information that General Gillmore had given out that he should carry out Hunter's orders, but that he took the liberty of believing a white man as well as a negro!

June 24. We hear but little about the new General. He is General Saxton's junior in rank, but a fine engineer, so it is supposed he was sent to conduct the siege of Charleston.

The siege of Charleston, — another attempt, "prompted more by sentiment than military sagacity," to capture "the city in which the secession had begun," [1] — is the subject of the next dozen extracts. The expedition failed to justify the high hopes that accompanied it, yet one event in it has attained undying fame.

When, in the first week of July, all the troops left Hilton Head, Land's End, and Port Royal Island, the regiment followed with the keenest interest by the writers of these letters was the Fifty-Fourth Massachusetts (colored), Colonel Robert G. Shaw.

July 10. It was strange to be waked this morning by the incessant, thundering roar of heavy guns. It was just at sunrise, and as I gradually woke to the full realization of what it must be — though as it mingled in my dreams, I was conscious that our masked batteries had opened at last — it was very exciting to feel my

[1] Rhodes' *History of the United States from the Compromise of* 1850, vol. iv, p. 332.

bed shake under me from such a cause. I could hear the people talking excitedly in the yard. About seven o'clock the heavy firing ceased, and we hoped that Morris Island was ours. C. went to the beach and reported a very heavy cloud of smoke resting in the direction of " Town."

The following extract is a good specimen of the groundless rumors, all with copious circumstantial evidence, that infested the islands.

FROM H. W.

July 11. About ten o'clock came Juno's daughter Fanny from " Pope's " to spend Sunday, bringing us the apparently reliable intelligence that " Town taken." It seemed too much to believe, but her story was this: her aunt, Juno's sister, and one of Dr. Whitredge's servants, is washing at Hilton Head and was there yesterday, when a vessel came from Charleston with the news and many people (prisoners, we infer), and the first who came ashore were Mass' Alonso and Mass' John, Whitredge, who said to her, "How d' ye!" She says that five boat-loads put off to the Yankees and gave themselves up. "Mass' John know too much to fight 'gainst de Yankee — him get college at de Nort' — him say him got no nigger — him no gwine fight." It is preposterous to write you all this. You will know everything with certainty before this reaches you.

July 12. The good news was most welcome from Vicksburg and Pennsylvania, and our attack on Morris Island was successful, if Town was not taken; but Colonel Higginson's attempt to reach the railroad was a failure,[1] and he was wounded, thought not, it is said, badly.

The successful attack on Morris Island on July 10 had resulted in the occupation of all the ground south of Fort Wagner. On July 18 was made the famous assault on the fort itself, — an assault hopeless from the start, — in which the attacking column was led by the Massachusetts negro regiment, its colonel at its head.

July 20. C. came back with the terrible accounts of the Charleston fight and the almost total destruction of the Fifty-Fourth. Beaufort[2] is in amaze at the spirit of "that little fellow, Colonel Shaw." Certainly it is one of the most splendid things ever known in the annals of warfare. I long to be doing, and not living so at our ease here. C. offered everything, and Mr. Eustis has been with Hallowell and James[3] all day. The greatest want is of physicians — there is no proper medical staff for the Department, and surgeons are scarce. Drs. Bundy and Wakefield were sent for yesterday. The officers are in the Fripp house, where the Forbeses were.

There has been very heavy firing again to-day. You see we hear it all, though sometimes very faintly.

July 24. William took farewell of his schools and came home, having received six dozen eggs as tokens of regret — an ovation at his departure.[4] He left them

---

[1] Colonel Higginson had been sent up the South Edisto River, to cut the railroad at Jacksonboro.

[2] Whither the wounded had been brought.

[3] Edward N. Hallowell and Garth Wilkinson James, Major and Adjutant of the Fifty-Fourth.

[4] For the North.

to go up to the sick and wounded to-morrow with contributions from the people. All vegetables, etc., are seized by the Provost and paid for, for the use of the sick, and there is some one on this side the ferry to receive the gifts. We send all we can, but it is unsatisfactory not to be on the spot.

July 25. William is just off for Beaufort. He will stay to watch to-night, if needed. But "no ladies" is the cry.

[Later.] William went to the hospital for the officers, of which Dr. Bundy has charge, where he was set to watch and administer to a very badly wounded captain of the Forty-Eighth New York, Paxton by name. He cannot live, and knows it, but bears his terrible wounds with the utmost fortitude. William was with him Saturday and Sunday, parts of the day, and G. and Wells divided the night between them. Everything seems to be well conducted, and the hospitals in good order. I suppose the *Fulton*, which is expected daily, will bring supplies and surgeons. Captain Hooper is invaluable — busy as possible, as he always is — I don't know what the Department would be without him. Yet he found time to write me a long note to tell me about the wounded, and that there was no doubt of Colonel Shaw's death.

FROM W. C. G.

Beaufort, July 26. Last night several of us passed in Beaufort at the hospitals. The wounded have been brought down and all the hospitals in Beaufort are full. Wednesday we heard at the superintendents' meeting that there was a great scarcity of fresh fruits and vege-

tables; so at the Thursday night praise I told the
people about it, and yesterday came up with nearly
two cartloads of provisions, most of it contributed by
the people. Another gentleman had done the same and
between us we supplied five hospitals. It is my first
experience in such work. It's surprising to see how
cheerful and jolly all the wounded are — all who have
any strength. A wound means home and a vacation to
many of them, and with few exceptions these men with
holes in them lie on their beds like boys waiting for the
word which gives them recess. To-night I shall try
to go to one of the colored hospitals.

A boat is just in from Charleston. A cartel of exchange had been agreed upon, by which all the wounded
on our side were to be exchanged for all the wounded
upon the other, so that reference to negro soldiers is
avoided. The negro soldiers appear to have received
the same care as the white; on the other hand, some
of the rebel officers told with much gusto how Colonel
Shaw's body had been thrown into a common pit and
those of two of his men tossed on top of him.

FROM H. W.

July 31. In at our open door walked Captain Hooper,
and with him Captain Rand of the First Cavalry, now
on General Saxton's staff. Captain Rand told us
that our wounded who came down from Charleston
had been miserably cared for — the rebels acknow-
ledged that they could not take care of them. The
surgeon said but one man had been properly operated
upon, and his wound had been dressed by one of the
navy surgeons, a prisoner. No men or officers of the

Fifty-Fourth among them: they said the officers we should hear of by way of Richmond; the men, I suspect, are not. No one knows who are among the dead or living — only that Colonel Shaw is dead, and probably Cabot Russel. It is said to have been a very imposing sight, when, in the midst of heavy firing from every fort, battery, and gunboat on each side, the *Cosmopolitan*, with the rebel wounded on board, her hospital flag and flag of truce flying, steamed up toward the city. Instantly every gun ceased, and white flags appeared from each fort and ship till she had passed, met the rebel steamer (a very fine one, which had run the blockade in the morning!), exchanged her wounded cargo, and returned.

To give complete the story of the siege of Charleston as seen from St. Helena Island, some letters have been included in advance of their chronological place in the series. Therefore the next letter goes back to an earlier date.

FROM H. W.

July 3. We were all standing at the back door when a small crowd became visible at the first gate. We watched to discover what it meant, as it was an unmistakable "gang" drawing nearer. 'Siah's boy had come over from the Point to tell C. that some white soldiers were there from the village stealing corn, etc., after the manner of the soldiers in this region, but so far our plantations have been very free from such depredations C. had just told Tony that he did not feel well enough to go over, and that the men would be gone before he could get there — and turning to Mr.

Soule he said that those Point men were just the men
to catch white soldiers, if they could do it, and he should
not be surprised if they did. The words were hardly
out of his mouth before the "gang" appeared, so you
may imagine we watched it with great curiosity as it
drew near. On they came, a compact body of people,
among whom we tried to discover some white faces.
Presently the gleaming of muskets was distinctly visible, and as one of the men stepped forward and threw
the gate wide open for the company to pass through,
three white soldiers appeared in the front ranks. They
were all perfectly quiet, not a word was said; and as
C. ran down the steps to receive them and they came
to a halt, the men brought the muskets to the ground
and the women emptied their aprons of corn-shucks at
his feet, waiting quietly for him to do what he thought
right. I did not hear one loud or angry tone while I
stood listening as C. heard their story and then questioned the soldiers. They were perfectly quiet, too, —
young fellows from the One Hundred and Fourth
Pennsylvania Volunteers, a new regiment, — and they
evidently thought that C. was a person of authority or
the blacks would not have marched them three miles
to him. He took from them their dirks and pistols,
and the musket which one of them had, and they
made no resistance — nor did they say a word when
he called to me for "three pair of hand-cuffs" (all
he brought down), and asked the three men from the
Point who had guns, if they would stay and guard
them all night. It was rather a troublesome elephant
and he did not quite know what to do with it now
it was in his possession. It was a good chance to

do something if he would be sustained, but General Saxton has not conferred any magisterial powers [1] on the superintendents yet, and if he undertook too much and was not sustained, it would be worse than nothing. At any rate, he would have to take them to the village in the morning, so he decided to do so that night, and went off with his prisoners and their guard, driving his light sulky, and carrying the light arms, one of the men taking the musket again. He did not use the hand-cuffs.

It was strange to see how very quiet and apparently unexcited the people were. After the first few minutes they came up to me to buy, and then all went off when C. did, as quickly as possible.

July 5. When two buckra were reported as approaching while we were at breakfast it turned out to be two men from the village picket with a note from the Lieutenant to C. I did not find out the sequel to the story the other night, but it seems that C. and William crossed the creek with the soldiers, only taking two men to row. The blacks certainly behaved extremely well, and Moll told the men they might have the corn, which of course they refused to take. And as they went into

[1] A few weeks later (July 15) General Saxton authorized the general superintendents to appoint plantation commissions, or courts for the administration of justice. The people eligible for these commissions were Government plantation superintendents and Mr. Philbrick's six plantation superintendents, and they were instructed "that in cases where immediate arrest is in their opinion necessary, the plantation superintendents, and the persons above named, are hereby authorized themselves to make arrests of civilians upon the plantations. But they must exercise this power with great discretion, and will be held responsible for any abuse of it."

the boat a boy put in the watermelon they had taken, saying, "B'longs to you, sah," but the man sent it ashore. The coals were rather hot, I guess, and the men were heartily ashamed of themselves and thoroughly penitent. C. went with them to the mess-room and saw the sergeant, who expressed great regret and said it was the first time any of their men had been guilty of such acts. The Lieutenant was away, and as C. drew paper towards him to report the case in writing, they looked very blank and begged him not to report. After some consideration he concluded not to report them, as he could not see the Lieutenant and they had behaved so well about it, and told them he would not unless some further acts of the kind were perpetrated by their men. They were very grateful, but C. did not feel sure that the Lieutenant would not hear of it. And so he did, in some way; investigated the affair and sent the men to Beaufort to be punished by the Commander of the post, who is now not General Saxton but, as it happens, is their own Colonel,[1] who is not likely to be lenient towards them. The Lieutenant sent a note to this effect to C. this morning, and also wished to know what would repay the negroes for the damage done. (The soldiers had already promised to make it good to them, and were to have been paid off yesterday, but their pay was stopped in consequence of this very occurrence.) So the whole affair has ended very satisfactorily. I am sorry for the poor fellows, for they will probably suffer not so much for what they actually did themselves, but to serve as an example to all other offenders.

[1] Colonel W. W. H. Davis was in command of the post at Beaufort during Saxton's temporary absence.

July 7. Mr. Wells was to come at nine o'clock to the wharf to take Mr. Soule [1] to Morgan Island, one of his plantations. Mr. Wells appeared at the door to say that he had a large sail-boat — it was only a half-hour's sail to the island, and would not I go too. So I put up a little lunch and C. had his horse saddled and down to the wharf we went, and were soon at our destination. The only white-house on the island now occupied is on quite a bluff looking directly out to sea, pleasantly shaded, with a fresh breeze all the time up the Sound, and is a very healthy situation. But the house is of the roughest description, without paint inside or out, very much like a New Hampshire farmhouse in the back-woods a quarter of a century ago, but not so large, clean, or thrifty-looking, by any means. Here we stopped to see an old man who was brought from Africa when he was over twenty, and remembers his life in his own country, from which he was sold by his brother to pay a debt. Mr. Soule said he was bright and talkative when he last saw him, but now he is very much broken; and after sitting a few minutes we went on to the driver's house, a great contrast in neatness, and the gentleman left me in a rocking-chair under the shade of the large Asia-berry tree in front of the house, while they went off with Bacchus, the foreman, to see the cotton-fields. Here I stayed for a couple of hours, I should think, talking with Elsie, Bacchus' wife, who was not in the field because she had a headache, and very neat and nice she looked in

---

[1] R. Soule, Jr., now one of Mr. Philbrick's superintendents, who, upon the departure of the Philbricks, had come to live at Coffin's Point.

her calico gown. She has no children, but made up for the want as far as she could by the number of chickens and ducks she had round. By and bye she got up, and picking up a piece of brick, pounded it up with an axe, and began to clean a large knife, which I knew meant watermelon. And when the gentlemen came back, Bacchus brought out a. small table and put a melon on it which was almost large enough for a table-cloth; then he produced plates, and Mr. Wells carved the huge monster, which we nearly devoured. The air and grace with which one of the men, who came up to clear off the table for Mr. Wells to pay the people, touched his hat with a bow and a scrape would not have misbecome a Commencement Dinner or Wedding Party.

The keen interest which these Northern interlopers took in everything that concerned the people into whose shoes they had stepped, and their constant sense of the strangeness and romance of their situation appear in the extracts that follow. Again the chronology of the letters has been somewhat disregarded.

FROM H. W.

July 14. G. came over here and spent the day. He told us that a man who belonged on his place came back with the troops on one of their late expeditions, and told him that his master, T. J. Fripp, was killed at Darien. He said he (Fripp) had been past here in a boat and came back with his hands all blistered from rowing; they had been hailed by the *Kingfisher*, but told some story of having come from here, and escaped. He said his master swore the Yankees were everywhere, and that there was a light in every window of Tom Coffin's house.

E. S. P. TO C. P. W.

Boston, Sept. 30. I heard the other day that Captain Boutelle of the Coast Survey, who used to enjoy the hospitality of the planters of St. Helena, Edisto, etc., was dining at Cambridge, Mass., with a classmate of T. A. C.'s. The host inquired what had become of the Captain's former friends, the South Carolina planters. "Oh, they are all scattered and their property ruined." "Well, what has become of my classmate, Thomas A. Coffin?" "Oh, he is gone with the rest, and his fine plantation is in the hands of that confounded Abolitionist, Philbrick."

FROM H. W.

July 10. William has been overhauling the old letters and papers in the garret and has come across many very interesting bits of information among them. They are mostly very old. Old plantation books of Mr. Eben Coffin, the first proprietor of the name of this estate, dated 1800, containing lists of the slaves of former generations, in which some of the oldest here now, like Uncle Sam, are mentioned as two years old; estimates for this house and the building in the yard, etc.

Aug. 5. C. has found a spike of papers in the old overseer house, on which he and Mr. Soule are now expending their eyesight. Letters from Mr. Coffin to Cockloft, etc. They have found out how much he was paid for the year — also some references to an exciting time on Frogmore where the overseer seems to have mismanaged — somebody was shot and there was a trial! We shall ask the negroes about it all.

Aug. 6. I entertained myself to-day reading over these same letters. It made me feel very queerly — they were mostly written during the summer of 1860, from Charleston and Newport. It seemed so short a time ago, and every thing and person spoken of about the plantation was so familiar. It seems that the over-seer of Frogmore, Benjarola Chaplin, was a bad man, and, suspecting a boy and girl there of poisoning him, had them tried and sentenced to be hung without let-ting Mr. Coffin know anything about it. We find that the sentence was not executed, — for Peter and Katy are still living, — but don't know why they were par-doned, though apparently there was no proof of their guilt.

Sept. 22. This morning I had a call from Henry, Mr. Coffin's old cook, a very intelligent mulatto who wanted me to read some letters to him and then talked a little while about Mrs. Coffin, to whom he seems very much attached, and says he would serve her to the end of his days. He and his wife would like to go North to her, and he was very glad to hear from Captain Bou-telle that she was safe there; he says she suffered so the last part of the time she was here, he could not bear to look at her. "The first Mrs. Coffin was a very nice lady, but she *succeed* her" He talks very well. He was much pleased that I offered to write to her for him sometime, and said he had not liked to ask any one to do so for fear they should not think it right to have anything to do with the old people — "but she's a

Nort' lady, you know, Ma'am, a beautiful lady, I would serve her all my life."

Sept. 27. Have I told you of an interesting talk we had from one Pompey, who said that it was the poor whites in Beaufort who made the negroes "sensible" about the war? That if it had not been for them he should have believed his master and gone away with him, but that they let him into the secret.[1] He says that [the poor whites] wished to stay, but were driven off by the rich men, whom they hate, and are now in the ranks fighting the rich men's battles. He has heard several times from the Main, through his old fellow servants who have run off, and mentioned two or three of the old proprietors here who are now in jail for trying to escape, among them Dr. Clarence Fripp, of whom they all speak with great affection. He never wanted to go, but was carried off by his brothers, one of whom, Eddings, has since died.

Oct. 15. As soon after breakfast as Robert had finished his regular work we mounted two pair of stairs "to clear up the attic." Do you think you know what that means? You have not the least idea. So far as we can make out, this house was built in 1809, and I think Robert dragged out from under the eaves the original shavings. It was melancholy to see the spoiled and demolished furniture which would be of so much use to us now, bureaus without drawers, sofas with only the frames, and those all broken, pieces of washstands and bedsteads, etc.

---

[1] The rebel masters had told their slaves that the Yankees intended to sell them "South," — that is, to Cuba or the Gulf.

It seems that such wonders were afterwards performed in renovating this broken furniture that the parlor became almost a parody of its ancient splendor. The letters now return to chronological order.

July 18. The cotton-fields are quite full of yellow and pink blossoms. We rode through many cotton-fields, and a pretty sight they were, some good, some poor, — those belonging to the Government as a general thing showing marked inferiority to those of the "Concern."

C. has been in the field all day, and has come home with a strong feeling of how much the people in general have gained and improved in the last year. There are poor ones among them, of course, — some he says he should like to send off the place, another year ; but the majority of the people are very much ashamed of them, and for some time have been very anxious he should go over the fields to see who "work for deir money and who shirk." To-night he has been distributing the pork and molasses and has refused the bonus to those who have not done their work properly, preferring to make the distinction here rather than in the pay, and most of the delinquents have appreciated the justice of the proceeding, only one or two making any fuss at all, and the others were very much ashamed of them. C. says he thinks that school has improved the children, too, their manners are improved, as have the grown people's, — less cringing and subservient, but more respectful and manly. Tim does not pull his forelock at every word he speaks, as he did last year, looking like a whipped dog, but looks you full in the face and speaks out as if he were not ashamed of himself, and is perfectly respectful withal.

The names of the people have often puzzled me as to what they were originally intended for, and in taking down the names of the children "Rode" puzzled me completely, until old Maria, in talking of her "crop" the other day, told me that one child was born in the *road* on the way from the field the day "gun fire at Bay Point, and I give him name o' Road"!

I don't think any of the heirs will find that these people are deteriorated when they redeem this property. I only hope young Mass' Julian, who is in Europe, will be glad to find them so far in training for free laborers and be grateful that they are not ruined, as some of the people are!

FROM C. P. W.

Aug. 3. The people say, all in good earnest, that the best of the [cotton] crop (including nine tenths of it) equals and excels the "Secesh own." There are a few lazy, who have allowed their crop to grow grassy, and some young ones, who need careful instruction or severe admonition from the elder ones. But the large majority are careful, faithful, honest, enthusiastic, and are doing much better for themselves than they would have for their "obershere." The people anxiously inquire for cotton sheets to pick in. They are hiring hands now to pick for them; some of them will be tight pushed to save all their crop.

Pine Grove, Aug. 22. We are all very busy, all day and every day. And it is well that it is so, for in this climate the only way to keep one's faculties from rust is to keep them constantly in use. It is encouraging, however, to find the good results of our labor so apparent. I think our people are improving very fast, and they are very contented and happy. (Next week don't be surprised, however, to find the thermometer lower.)

A great step has lately been taken. On the whole the people have been growing more lawless this year; to remedy the evil, civil law has just been introduced. The first Commission [1] was appointed a few days ago, and as I am one of its members, it gives occupation for another day or two days of a week. I hope it will be able to do much good; at all events it will be abundantly supplied with cases. This life is very narrowing, — we talk nothing but negro, we think nothing but negro; and yet it develops a man at almost every point. From house-carpenter to Chief Justice is a long way. And in one who uses the opportunity aright it develops patience and faith marvelously, but through many failures.

Aug. 15. Just as we got up from the dinner-table, a woman came running up for C. because the people were fighting. Poor thing! she was dreadfully frightened and had run the whole way with her baby in her

[1] See note, p. 201.

arms and looked as if she had just stepped out of the river. I don't know what the trouble was — it was the tongues of the women, and they fired shells and tore each other's clothes in a most disgraceful way, much to the mortification of the better part of the community. Jealousy is the foundation of a great deal of trouble among them, and there is often too much foundation for it.

Aug. 31. Mr. Soule had planned to go to Beaufort and see the General, and C. wished especially to get permission to turn all the young men from outlaws into private citizens by employing them and paying them regularly, for he could not help their aiding their wives and being employed by each other, a species of evasion which was eminently calculated to give them high ideas of the power and value of the law in the hands of the present authorities — C. helpless, and they doing as they pleased! It looked like rain, however, and they gave it up for that day.

Sept. 1. We had breakfast very early, and Mr. Soule and C. went off, to discover as usual that our clock was about an hour fast! I thought I would go out and dine and see how Mr. G. was, as he had had a fever turn. So I mounted and started alone on my expedition, after carefully locking the house. It was cloudy and cool, but I found my beast beastly hard, so had to content myself with a walk. It was very pleasant, as I rode along, to see how brightly the people looked up to bow and speak. First old Richard in the overseer-yard, watching the arbors, as they are called — the frames where the cotton is spread out to dry; then men and women coming from the field with great sheets of cotton on their heads which made them almost unrecognizable, little Susie staggering under such a pile that I saw she never could get it onto her head again alone as she was, if I asked her to put it down and run back to open the gate for me, so after more than one trial I succeeded in opening it for myself. Then I took my sack off and rode in my white jacket, putting the sack round the pummel and fastening it there by the extra stirrup which, as the only saddle we had for a long time, was rigged onto it for Mr. Philbrick and still remains, a relic of our early, barbarous days. But in a canter I lost it off, and had to call a child to pick it up for me. Then Miller came along, going out to help his "old woman" pick cotton, and walked by my side talking of the fine crop, and that next year there would not be land enough for the people — "dey work better nor Secesh time — encouragement so good!" He was as bright and jolly as you ever saw any honest farmer when his crops were in fine condition, and as we came in sight of Phillis and Katy, his wife and daughter, and Amaritta in a task just behind them, the latter called out to him, "Hi! Hi! bru' Miller, where you go? my back mos' broke!" as if it were the pleasantest news in the world. He answered, "Oh, I go walk, I got people pick my cotton," with such a hearty ha! ha! as did me good to hear. Many of the men laugh just like little children — Abel does. Next came Nancy, Peg, and Doll, Demus' mother and sisters, and such a nice family — the bright, smiling faces they raised to me and the cheerful "Hahdy, Missus," was worth seeing and hearing, and when Nancy sent Peg running after me to open the gate I was "fighting" with, she looked

so bright, strong, and handsome as she strode along
so splendidly, her dress caught up at the waist and let
down from the shoulders, that I wished I could daguer-
reotype her on the spot.

I found Mr. G. in a very decided chill on the sofa in
front of the parlor fire. I stayed an hour or two, and
then, the fever coming on quite severely and affecting
his head a good deal, I rode home as fast as possible to
signal for Dr. Westcott.[1] I could not get through the
cotton-field, however, without being stopped two or
three times by applications for "suthin" for this child's
boils or that one's sore eyes, all of which I referred to
the house, where I afterwards administered to the best
of my knowledge — one of my constant occupations.

Mr. Soule and C. came back, with no news from
Charleston, having found the General and his staff just
starting on a visit to the scene of action, but C. had
obtained permission to employ the men and made
them very happy the next day by telling them so.

Sept. 5. I have been endeavoring to instill habits
of cleanliness into Rose and in many ways have succeeded — she has regular days when she goes home to
wash, changes her "linen" twice a week, takes a warm
bath every Saturday, and keeps her head and feet in a
condition to which they were strangers previously. I
can see, too, that it has had a decided effect upon her
sisters. One of the important items has been pocket-
handkerchiefs, with which I provided her, and she has
to keep them in her pocket. For two or three days lately
she has forgotten this essential article, and I finally told
her that if it was forgotten the next day I should have

[1] On board the *Kingfisher*.

to send her home for it. I had forgotten all about it, till, the next morning when she came to pour the water into my tub for me, a most inordinate snuffling betrayed the absent wipe. "Rose, where's your pocket-handkerchief? have you forgotten it again?" No answer, but a hiding of the head under her arm like a duck, which often takes place when she is in fault. "Then, Rose, put the coffee on, sweep the parlor, and go home for it." This elicited, "me no gwine home," a pert rejoinder I could not understand, till on calling her to me I saw by her face how excessively green I had been. I reprimanded her with a sober face as she again repeated "me no gwine home," at the same time untwisting the handkerchief from about her waist, but when she had left the room I should have shaken the bed, if that had been my style of laughter. Robert is a great wag in his way, though we do not see so much of his fun, as, having been used to the house in "Secesh time," he is utterly undemonstrative before white people and is only gradually thawing into a little more communicativeness. But we overhear him sometimes talking with the others. A most entertaining but not quite so pleasant exhibition of it (and C. and I could not help laughing at Rose and Hester's good-natured, amusing account) was his riding after the two girls one day when he had been out for the horses, extolling himself and insisting that they should call him "Maussa" or he would ride them down, with his spurs on! Hester gave in, but Rose would n't — "him too mannish!"

There is a great deal of tyrannizing over each other. "Mind now, min', run quick or I knock you," — or "kill you dead" it is as likely to be, — is an ordinary method of getting anything done, while "cursing," as they call calling names, etc., is one of the hardest things I have to contend with in school, they are so quick to interpret any look or act into an offense and resent it on the spot with word or blow.

Sept. 9. I had a long talk with some of my big girls who had been very noisy and fighting — they do "knock" each other most unmercifully, and I can't instill any better notions into them. "Anybody hurt you, you *'bleeged* to knock 'em," is the universal response, and they have no idea of letting any difficulty be peaceably settled.

The definite reply which these people require to the ordinary salutation of Hahdy? or Huddy? into which it has degenerated here, is very amusing, and a corresponding inquiry is expected in return, to which they give the most minute answers. "Good morning, Hacklis (Hercules), how are you to-day?" "Stirring, tank you, Ma'am, how youself?" and if I had a headache I should no more think of saying "pretty well" than if I were being cross-questioned at the bar — the inquiry is so sincere and expects such a particular reply. "Dunno, Missus — tank de Lord for life," is a common rejoinder, as well as "Not so well, tank you, ma'am."

This is as good a place as any for some more examples of negro speech and negro ways. The sayings of Rose, in particular, were a constant source of interest and amusement. H. W. writes that she "tells me everything, in her simplicity, even to the fact that her father has silver money which he keeps buried, and that her mother sends her to the pen for milk before it comes up here!"

[*May* 16.] Rose commented, "You lub Miss Helen," and then in a few minutes, "Miss Helen lub you. All two (both). I love Miss Helen, too. Miss Helen one *nice* buckra. You more rough 'long er Miss Helen. Miss Helen *so* softle — when him touch me I no feel 'um — me feel you — you so strong." All this with inimitable gesture and expression and a "leetle" and "middling-sized-bear" voice that was inexpressibly droll.

[*May* 17.] As I sat down to write this morning, Rose came in to dust. "Miss Hy't, you gwine write Norf?" Yes, Rose. I told her that little Robert sent me the pictures and a letter from little Mary. It pleased her very much, and she said she wanted to see them. "Me lub Robert and Mary." Thinking I should like to get at some of her notions, I asked her, What do you mean by love, Rose? "Me dunno — brothers and sisters." Don't you love any one else, Rose? "Me dunno." Why, you said yesterday that you loved Miss Helen, and just now that you loved Robert and Mary. "Me lub dem." By this time the top of her head was in contact with the floor, when she suddenly raised herself to a kneeling posture and pointing up, said a moment after, "Me lub God," and in a few minutes, as if she were quoting, "An dem dat foller arter Christ." What do you mean by that, Rose? "Me dunno," and I found she had not the least idea. Presently she enumerated Mass' Charlie, Mass' Willyum, and Mister Philbrick in her category, and then went on with her dusting. By and by she said — "Miss Hyut, me no say your name." No, Rose. "Well, me lub you an' Miss Helen de *morer*."

Mr. Thorpe has a boy, Strappan, who is even more noted than my Rose, and who has given some remarkable answers to questions which Mr. Thorpe puts to him, and which he takes down verbatim. The only one I know is his definition of Love. "Arter you lub, you lub, you know, boss. You can't broke lub. Man can't broke lub. Lub stan', he ain't goin' broke. Man hab to be berry smart for broke lub. Lub is a ting stan' jus' like tar; arter he stick, he stick. He ain't goin' move. He can't move less dan you burn um. Hab to kill all two arter he lub, 'fo you broke lub."

[*Aug.* 15.] This morning Rose was sewing with me in my chamber, and, as she is very apt to, got talking about the time when they ran away from the "robbers" and the Yankees first came. It is always interesting, and I wish I could give you her language, though it would be little without her emphasis and expression. The first time she saw a Yankee — "Great dairdy!" she said, "So Yankee stan'?" I don't think she knew what sort of an animal to expect.

Sept. 15. When Rose came into my room this morning, she came up to my bed to ask how I was and express her contrition that she did not stay all night with me! "Me could n't sleep, me think all night Miss Hayiut sick, me should stay long him — when I go bed, me say, 'Hester, Miss Hayiut sick, I oughter stay wid her;' Hester say, 'Come, go 'long me, take you shum,' but me would n't go den!" She is very trying sometimes, but full of character, as you see, and it is hard to know just how to deal with her. I am afraid of being too lenient to her and so spoiling her, or too stern, for fear I *should* spoil her, and so losing

her affection, which ought to be the controlling influence. With all their subserviency, which I am happy
to say is disappearing, they have little idea of obedience.

Sept. 17. This morning there was no milk, as in this
benighted region if it rains they don't "pen cow" at
night, and for the same reason Abel did not catch one in
the field this morning that we might have a drop for
breakfast!

[*Oct.* 19.] The doctor wanted some wormwood, and
thinking I had heard the people speak of it, I asked
Elsie. "Me dunno, me dunno nothing; me jis' born
yestiddy!" she answered.

[*Nov.* 16.] Rose came to tell me this morning that
there was no milk. Henry had dropped the bucket
(from his head) and spilled it all. "See Henry here."
Why, Henry, where did you spill the milk? I asked in
dismay; but he looked blank till she interpreted for
him — "Which side de milk churray?" (throw away).
How, when, and *where* they do not use or know the
meaning of. *Which side,* is *where* — *What time, when* —
but they do not understand a sentence with *how* in it.

The next four extracts give a good idea of Mr. Philbrick's letters to his superintendents and of the far-
sighted, honest thought which he put on his Port Royal
undertaking. The first was written in the summer;
the others appear in their proper place in order of time.

E. S. P. TO W. C. G.

Boston, July 28. If you can induce some old man
who is a good judge, I would let him pick select cotton
all through the season for seed, going over the whole
field, or such parts of it as he finds the best cotton,

culling the best pods from the best plants. In this way you can get seed enough to plant some acres next year, which would yield enough for the whole plantation another year and of a superior quality. This is the way the most intelligent planters got up their famous varieties of seed, and we ought to be able to use as much brains as they did. Perhaps you can get some refugee to do this, without giving offense to the mass, but he must be a good judge.

I hope you will not feel it your duty to enlist in the army, for I consider your position there a very useful one and difficult to replace. I don't mean useful merely to the people with whom you come in contact, but politically, upon the solution of the great social, political problem which we have got to solve, viz., the worthiness and capacity of the negro for immediate and unconditional emancipation. I intend to publish the results of this year's operations next winter and want to be able to show that we have raised cotton at a lower price per pound than the former proprietors did, counting the interest upon their capital invested in negroes as a part of their expenses, which is no more than just.

This point, as regards the raising of cotton by free labor, Mr. Philbrick did successfully make later, as will be seen (see page 265). Another inducement to Northern capital to come South was offered by him at this time in a letter which appeared in the Boston *Daily Advertiser* on July 20. It was entitled "A New Market for Manufactures," and tabulated the results of his operations in the "shop" during the fifteen months of its existence so far. Between March, 1862, and March, 1863, for instance, a population of four hundred and twelve had spent there $3047; during the months of

May and June, 1863, a population of nine hundred and thirty-three had spent $3800; the articles bought had included a variety of dry goods, provisions, hardware, etc., almost all of which supplied needs entirely new to the blacks. The letter concluded: "It may readily be seen that a considerable demand may arise for the articles above-named and others of kindred nature, when a population of some millions shall be in a position to apply their earnings to the supply of their rapidly increasing wants. Should not the manufacturing interests of the North be awake to this?" This letter, written for the express purpose of bringing means of civilization to the blacks, was taken by many Northern friends of the negro as proof that its writer's motive was to exploit the black race for the benefit of the white. Of course, Mr. Philbrick knew perfectly well to what misconstruction he exposed himself when he told the public that there was profit to be made on the old plantations. The following letter was written in reply to a warning from C. P. W. on this very head.

E. S. P. TO C. P. W.

Boston, Sept. 24. I don't agree with you about avoiding publicity for our enterprise. I hold that the pecuniary success we are likely to meet with is the very best reason why the whole thing should be made public, for it is the only sort of success which can make our enterprise a permanent thing and take it off the hands of philanthropic benevolence, which, though well enough for a spurt, can never be relied on to civilize the four millions of darkies likely to be on our hands. If we succeed financially, it will prove that free labor is self-sustaining, and that the blacks are capable of becoming a useful laboring class immediately after leaving their masters' hands, and this fact is of vast importance. If we attempt to keep quiet, we shall incur with much more justice the accusation of being mere speculators than if we make the most of our success by bringing it before the public as a political experiment, of great influence upon our future social system, thus giving the public the full benefit of the experiment. The fact is just this. Negro labor has got to be employed, if at all, because it is *profitable*, and it has got to come into the market like everything else, subject to the supply and demand which may arise from all kinds of enterprises in which it chances to be employed. It is not likely that it can be protected on a large scale by the amount of disinterested philanthropy which happens to be present on the Sea Islands, but if it can be open to private enterprise, by an occupation of lands free from unnecessary restrictions and under a proper sense of the security of property, it can afford to *lose* some of the Methodism now bestowed upon it at Beaufort. We want first to prove that it is profitable, and then it will take care of itself.

E. S. P. TO W. C. G.

Sept. 24. Limus' seine was shipped in the schooner. I have not yet ordered any for 'Siah, for I thought it would be too late for him to use it this year, and he had better wait and see if Limus' seine was all right. Moreover, entre nous, I don't believe it will do him any good to spend his time a-fishing. It has a sort of excitement, like gold-digging, which unfits a man for steady, plodding industry, witness Limus. Now the present demand for fish will not be permanent. After the war the negroes will have to fall back upon field-labor for a living, and it will be better for them if in the meanwhile they do not acquire a distaste for steady labor and get vagrant habits. I would talk this over with 'Siah and ask him in serious mood if he really thinks best to spend so much money in fishing-gear, when he could buy land with it by and bye.

Here begins again the rambling narrative of plantation happenings.

FROM H. W.

Sept. 26. C. was very busy paying for cotton, and we found him on the piazza, sitting at a little table with the drawer full of money and the gang of women standing and sitting about at the foot of the steps, while he called them up one at a time. He paid old Nancy first, asking her how much she thought it was. "Me dunno, Massa, you knows." As much as ten dollars? "Oh yes! Massa, I tink you gib me more nor dat." Fifteen, perhaps? Five for you, Doll, and Peg, each? "Yes, Massa, I tink so." And it was pleasant to see the corners of her mouth go as he counted out $48 — which she took in perfect quietness and with a sober face, a curtsey and "Tank'ee, Massa." Sinnet was more demonstrative than anybody, lifting up hands and eyes, and ending with "Tank de Lord; I mus' go praise." Amaritta drew for her gang $78 — they have picked over three thousand pounds. C. paid out over $1000.

H. W. further reports that when C. told old Grace he had weighed altogether a bale for her, "Good God!" she cried, "me lib to raise bale o' cotton! Come along, Tim, less get some vittle."

The next letter is Mr. Tomlinson's reply to one from W. C. G., in which he had complained of negroes

who refused to pay their "corn-tax," — a rent in kind
for their private patches of corn-land, — and had suggested their expulsion from the plantation as the best
remedy.

REUBEN TOMLINSON [1] TO W. C. G.

Sept. 30. I have just read yours on the "corn question." I have told Government Superintendents, when
the people refuse or neglect to bring their corn to the
corn-house, not to interfere with them until it is all
broken in; [2] then to tell them how much is expected
from them, and give them a certain length of time to
bring it in. If it is not done, get a "guard" from the
"Jail," and go to their houses and take it. Of course
the superintendent is to use a sound discretion in
making his demand, making due allowance for failure of
"crop," etc. Your plan is in my opinion open to serious
objections as a matter of *expediency*. I have no doubt
that there are people on your places whom you would
be well rid of. If you can endure them patiently a little
while longer, I think it will be to your advantage to
do so. The Government is commencing at once the
erection of a large number of houses, and after they
are finished those turbulent and unruly people may
be disposed of without the scandal and excitement
which would otherwise accompany their removal.
After this season is terminated, you can refuse any
longer to employ such persons, and the Government
having then provided homes for them, there will be
no longer an excuse for boring you with them.

[1] A Pennsylvanian, General Superintendent for St. Helena and
Ladies Islands, since Richard Soule had resigned that position.

[2] That is, gathered.

Mr. Philbrick's advice was as follows:

E. S. P. TO W. C. G.

I am not surprised at the prospect of some meanness about the corn-tax. The negroes would be a marvelous race if it were not so. If any difficulty is encountered in collecting the tax, I should take it out of their pay at $1.50 per bushel, which is about what it costs me to send corn there.

FROM H. W.

Oct. 13. Mr. G., who had just come from the Point, told me a very nice thing about the men there. It seems that a few weeks ago Mr. Tomlinson made an address to them at church about there being five church-members in jail for shooting cattle, and after he got through, 'Siah, the foreman and elder of the Fripp Point Plantation, rose and indorsed what he had said, adding that the thing had never happened on his place. That very week an ox was shot there, and Mr. G. has been unable to find out who did it, all the men protesting that they did not know. So to-day he called them all up and talked to them, and then spoke of the ox and asked them what they thought they ought to do. One man rose and proposed to pay for it — another seconded the motion, and they passed the resolution to do so by a vote of sixteen against two! Mr. G. was very much pleased, and gave notice that if the perpetrator of the deed would come to him and confess within four days he should be let off without paying the fine.

Oct. 20. Thomas seemed much better, but very

weak, and asked me if I would not give him some liquor!
I asked if he had ever been in the habit of drinking it,
and he said yes, that he bought it by the pint at camp!
He belongs to the First South Carolina Volunteers, Colonel Higginson's Regiment. It is dreadful to think of
such means of civilization being introduced among
these poor people. It made me heartsick.

While I was dressing for dinner C. came up to ask
me if I had "any prejudice against color," as he had
asked the steward of the *Wabash* [1] to dine, "a Boston
boy who speaks English as well as you do." We found
him a very bright, intelligent young fellow and very
modest and unassuming withal — gave his name only
as "Joseph" both to Mr. Soule and C. He had come
foraging for the Admiral, and as C. found him waiting for the people to come from the field, he took him
about with him and brought up at the house. He was
on board the *Mohegan* when Port Royal was taken
and had then just come from the coast of Africa where
they had taken Gordon, the slave-pirate, on board
the barque *Ariel*, and he gave us a most interesting
account of the whole affair, as he went on board with
the Captain when he ordered the hatches to be opened
and the nine hundred blacks were discovered. C. says
he overheard Amaritta say to him, "You free man? I
t'o't so, when I see you walk wi' buckra," and old
Grace, when he asked her if she had any eggs, answered, "No, Maus — my dear," her first impression
being that as he walked "wid buckra" she must be
respectful, and then remembering that she must not
say "Maussa" to a black man. He is black as Robert,

[1] Admiral Dupont's flag-ship.

but with Saxon features. Speaking of Henry, he asked, "Is he short and stout and about my complexion?" Henry is almost white!

Oct. 22. Limus is full of amazement at the men of the Fifty-Fifth [1] and could not express his surprise at their walking up to their post-office kept by a black man, and opening their letters to read "just like white men!" They don't know what to make of educated blacks, — it upsets all their ideas on the relative position of the two races!   I expected some remarks from Rose about our sable guest — she was not here, but the next day she began: "That stranger man eat up here? Which side him eat?" In the dining-room with us. "Him free man?" Yes, he was born in Boston. "Him read and write?" Yes, as well as I can. This made her open her eyes, and when I told her that in Boston there were schools for the black children to go to just like those for the white children, where they could learn the same things, she departed with a very quiet, "Yes, Ma'am."

FROM C. P. W.

Oct. 24. Nothing happens here now, so that even this delightful country, with its charming variety of scenery and its delicious climate, its bracing air, its sparkling streams, its richness of autumnal tints, the ever-varying play of light and shade upon the steep hillsides and through the green valleys often cease to charm. For myself, I may say that even the continual excitement incident to the task of weighing cotton,

[1] The Fifty-Fifth Massachusetts Volunteers (colored), which was in camp at Port Royal.

selling sugar, or counting rails, not to mention the no
less important duty of seeing that my hat is not stolen
from my head, or the shingles off my roof, — even these
interesting and exciting occupations sometimes grow
wearisome, and fail to afford that continued gratification and satisfaction to enjoy which is the object of a
life in this Department. Although the statement seems
absurd, I must nevertheless affirm, that it is more
bother to take care of a plantation of one hundred and
twenty working hands than it is to exercise that number in the "School of the Company;" and that the
satisfaction derived from the faithfulness and honesty
of perhaps thirty is hardly sufficient to atone for the
anxiety and distrust with which one regards the remaining ninety, who lie by habit and steal on the least
provocation, who take infinite pains to be lazy and
shirk, who tell tales of others, of which themselves are
the true subjects, and from whom all the artifices of
the lawyer cannot draw a fair statement of fact, even
when it is obviously for their own interest to tell the
whole truth. "Wherefore he is called the everlasting
Niggah."

I have had my grumble, and I feel better. What I
have said "has truth in it, only distorted." I am not
actually miserable, though one might draw that inference
from these remarks. The fact is that, the novelty of this
life having worn off after fifteen months of the "useful
experience," the life, as was to be, and was expected,
loses something of its satisfaction, and one is more open
to the effect of the vexations and annoyances than when
the interest was fresh and the work new and untried.
It is not so much that one is annoyed by the work it-

self, but the imperfections of the system under which we are obliged to work grow more clear and are continually presented in various forms. The only satisfactory thing would be to reconstruct the system on the plantation, first, by turning off all the hands not wanted; second, by adopting a new system in regard to the privileges and compensation of the people. The privileges are, free houses, free land for provision crops, free use of wood, and, with certain restrictions, of the animals and implements. I should do away with these privileges, making them pay house-rent and land-rent, making them pay for their wood, if of certain qualities, and for the use of teams and implements — for their own work. Then I should increase their wages, with fixed prices for the various kinds of work. I should wish to be able to discharge any one whose work did not suit me, and remove him from the plantation. These reforms cannot possibly be instituted now, and can never be, probably, on this island. In the meantime, if the people were only honest and truthful, other matters would be of comparatively little account, but they are the most provoking set, in this respect, that you can easily conceive. They are almost incorrigible.

REUBEN TOMLINSON TO C. P. W.

Oaks, Oct. 30. I have appointed you one of a " Commission" of three, to meet in the "Study" at R.'s place on Wednesday, November 4, at 10 A. M. The first case that will probably come before you will be that of the disputed ownership of a "boat," now in the possession of one " Limus," purveyor to General Gillmore, but which is claimed by "Barkis," who lives at

Hilton Head. Both the parties have been to see me, and Barkis is not "willin'" to give up his claim.

FROM H. W.

Nov. 8. I found C. had two men locked up in separate rooms downstairs — there had been some trouble, and one, who was half drunk, had used a knife. One man he let go, the other is still shut up, and sent to see me this evening. It is dreadful to have such things happening, but it will do good for the people to find that there is some law over them.

Early in November Mr. Philbrick went down to Port Royal again to gin and export his cotton crop.

E. S. P. TO MRS. PHILBRICK.

Coffin's Point, Nov. 10. Arrived here about 6. I found people in the field picking cotton at R.'s places, and found on nearly all my fields the cotton still green and blossoming, while on most of the Government plantations the grass had stopped its growth long ago and the crop was about over. I find old Frank (the wily) in confinement in the harness-room for some row among the people last Sunday, awaiting trial. Oh, the horses, how they do look! A few months among our Northern fixings make everything look so wretched down here.

There is a circular just issued by General Saxton, pointing out the plantations which are to be sold to the negroes, and advising them to stake out their claims and build cabins on them as preëmptors, which will not attract many of my people, I think. The McTureous places, T. B. Fripp's, Hamilton Fripp's, and others are to be so sold, as soon as the necessary surveys are made. I doubt the policy of this sort of thing until the time shall have passed for the redemption of the land by the old owners, though none may ever appear to redeem. I am afraid some rows may arise from the difficulty of fixing and recording boundaries among a lot of negro squatters, should there be many such.

These plantations, about to be sold at auction to negro preëmptors, were those which had been reserved for this purpose from the sale of March 9, 1863 (see p. 171). The order of the President (dated September 16), from which General Saxton got authority for his circular just mentioned, also provided for the sale at auction of about twenty plantations in lots not to exceed three hundred and twenty acres. This latter provision, which might possibly result in preventing many negroes from owning any land at present, — since the plantations reserved for them alone were not large enough for all, — presently brought about infinite trouble, through disagreement among the authorities.

FROM H. W.

Nov. 15. The people are quite disturbed about General Saxton's new order, which Mr. French and Judge Smith have been trying to explain to them at church; — in vain, apparently, — for some of the most ignorant of our people thought they should be obliged to buy land, and came to C. in distress at leaving the plantation. Others we hear are selecting their lots, but now comes General Gillmore's order to stop all sales; I am afraid these poor people, who hate all change and "confusion," will have their brains hopelessly confused.

FROM E. S. P.

Nov. 18. General Saxton has given orders that all
work on the plantations [1] in preparation for next year's
crop shall be stopped, for he expects to give them up
either to the purchasers or the tax-commissioners very
soon. The tax men are here, as amicably disposed towards each other as cat and dog, and as they are not
remarkable for their efficiency in matters of business,
I do not think it very likely that they will accomplish
much this winter. They have two parties of surveyors
at work, but they don't seem to be doing much but
chop vines and sail about the creeks in boats.

FROM W. C. G.

Pine Grove. [*Sept.* 23.] I think you would be quite
astonished at the refinement and homelikeness of our
parlor. Bright table-cloths, a most elegant couch lately
developed, — a comfortable old sofa, pictures all around,
a fancy bookcase almost full of books, — a glass-topped
secretary with an ample supply of pigeon-holes and
writing arrangements, — papers lying around loose,
— and a wood fire burning in the big chimney-place,
— won't that do for philanthropists? One door opens
into a large dining-room, — the windows upon a portico,
looking out upon the creek winding among the green
marsh grass, with broad water and islands in the distance. For contrast now and then a pig squalls vigorously under the house, — for it is getting cold now and
the pigs eagerly seek the shelter of the "big house."

[1] Meaning, of course, plantations belonging to the Government.

It is in vain to try to keep them out, though I 've had a fence built round the house.

Nov. 14. I shall have to take to contraband pants, I 'm afraid, as I did last winter. The negroes can hardly hold me to be of gentle kind, when they see me doing their own work in their own clothes. I wish you would come down to see me, if it is only, by the sight of a white cravat and shining beaver, to convince them that I am a "boss" born. You shall have your fill of clearing up and improving, too; I need just such energy to make respectable my own premises. At present they are the pigs' playground, except on Sundays, when a lot of the plantation urchins are allowed very quietly to peep in at the windows and learn manners from white folks. At present a young fellow, who has lately waked up from a slouch into a man, is patiently leaning against the sill, waiting, I suppose, for his lesson.

FROM H. W.

Thanksgiving Day, Nov. 26. We sat down to dinner — sixteen Massachusetts people, six ministers' sons. Mr. Folsom and William Allen, Miss R. and Mr. G. went home; all the rest spent the night, and no one on a sofa. We wondered what was the last [dinner-party] as large that had dined in this old house, but Robert says he never saw such a large party here — Mr. Coffin used to give his dinners in Charleston.

FROM E. S. P.

Nov. 26. We got to R.'s house, where he told us he had been helping Mr. Wells all day before in boating

his cotton from Morgan Island to his home place.[1]
There was about $3000 worth on the island, and he
did not choose to expose the rebels to any further temptation in regard to it. It seems that Tuesday morning
the cow-minder had gone out to the pen with his milk-
pail and never returned. Search being made, the milk-
pail and his jacket were found, and some new tracks
of shoes on the beach, also traces of a bivouac breakfast and marks of a boat's keel on the Coosaw River
beach. Nothing more is known than this. The pre-
sumption is that a scouting party had come over Coosaw River and bivouacked on the beach, hauling up
their boat, and that, seeing this poor man in the morning, they gobbled him up and cleared out as they came.
He was an Edisto man, of considerable intelligence,
and it is hoped his information will not be so reliable
as the rebels might wish. Mr. Wells immediately informed Captain Dutch and got Mr. R. to help him
boat over his cotton. Captain Dutch sent a guard to
patrol the island and sent his little schooner up opposite Morgan Island in Coosaw River as an outpost.

We had an immense rush at the store yesterday, four
hundred and sixty odd dollars during the day here. R.
and Wells have taken over fifteen hundred dollars in
the three days after opening their goods. Amaritta
bought over forty dollars' worth at once, and poor
Juliana staggered off with a load on her head that she
could hardly carry. The trunks go like smoke, so do
the firkins and other domestic wares.

[1] The "Mary Jenkins" place.

Dec. 1. Uncle Nat, who has carried the plantation keys for forty years, giving out all the allowance for people and creatures, and has done no field work for that length of time, has had an acre and a half of cotton this year, and has raised the largest proportion, six hundred pounds seed-cotton per acre, of any one on the place. He lives at Pine Grove with his wife, but plants here for old association's sake, and the other day, when C. made the last cotton payment, he gave Nat's money to his sister, Nancy. The next morning Nat was up here early and took his hat off to the ground to C. "Came to thank you for what you send me yesterday, Sar — much obliged to you, Sar (with another flourish and scrape). I well sat-is-*fy*, and jest as long as the Lord give me life and dese ole arms can do *so* (imitating the motion of hoeing), I work cotton for you, Sar!"

Dec. 5. Our cotton crop is about all in, though some people are still in the field gleaning. They glean very carefully now, and don't allow a single pod to escape them. I have about one hundred gins now in running order, and expect to have fifty more, all going in another week.

Dec. 10. I rode down to see the work. It was a busy scene — a whipper on each arbor with a child atop to fill the machine, which is used to lash the dirt out of the cotton before ginning and make it easier to gin;

then the gins were all at work — the women were sort-
ing — the men packing — potato-vines were being
brought in to be weighed, carts and oxen carrying seed
—altogether such a busy piece of work as one does
not often see here.

FROM E. S. P.

Dec. 10. We were surprised by a green carryall coming down the road drawn by some army horses, hay-
fed and round. The passengers were a Mr. Paige, a
correspondent of the *Tribune*, and his friend, a Mr.
Baldwin from Cleveland. I had met them in one of
my trips between Hilton Head and Beaufort, and after
answering several questions asked them to come and
see me, but I did n't think they would take the pains.
Mr. Paige asked questions enough to pump me dry
while here, but I don't believe he will be much the
wiser, for he asked some three or four times over. I
took them down to the praise house in the evening and,
Uncle Sam being ill of "fever and pain in head," I
helped with the hymns and read a chapter from the
Bible. Old Aaron and George prayed, Doll's Will told
off a hymn from memory, and George repeated one,
as I think, from his own brain, putting in all the coup-
lets he could remember, and hunting over his brain
for each one while they were singing the last. My visit-
ors were very much interested, and were chiefly pleased
with the earnestness and simplicity of their worship,
remarking that they were fortunate in not being bothered
with doctrine. I am afraid they did n't get much of
an idea of our schools, for the only girl they asked to
spell happened to be Caroline, whom they met in the

street. She is only half-witted, you know, and did n't do her teachers much credit. I should like to see what Mr. Paige has to say about our doings in the *Tribune*. I asked him not to mention the name of this plantation, for I did n't want to call the attention of the Coffin family upon us any more than I could help. He asked me for the names of any superintendents and teachers here, but I told him they did n't care to be brought before the public.

I was curious to know how much cotton could be got from a certain amount of seed. I ginned just five pounds of cotton and had thirteen pounds of seed left, being over a peck, for it weighs forty-four pounds to the bushel. The people were very much amused to see me gin so long, and wondered that I had the strength for it. You know they consider us rather effeminate in regard to strength, but I did not find it nearly so hard work as I supposed. It is not half as hard as mowing.

Dec. 13. Mr. Wells had his cotton about half ginned when there came a posse of men from the First South Carolina Regiment, without a white officer, to hunt after deserters on his plantation. They met the men they wanted and shot them all three in broad daylight; one is badly wounded and may not recover, but the others probably will. After shooting one man they were going away to leave him, and Mr. Wells went and took care of him and sent him to the hospital.

Dec. 17. The people were all at work ginning cotton, and the new mechanic Nero, whom we found at the White place, was putting the engine in order. This engine serves as a moral stimulus to keep the people at work at their hand-gins, for they want to gin all the cot-

ton by hand, and I tell them if they don't get it done by
the middle of January I shall gin it by steam. The result
will probably be that there will be little left for the steam-
engine to do. But it will do no harm to put it in order
and then I can grind corn with it next summer. The
weight of all my cotton is now 287,790 pounds [1] in seed.
The samples which I sent to Liverpool were appraised
there as worth forty-eight to fifty pence, which, if exchange remains as high as at present, would make our
crop worth $100,000 in Liverpool. This is as much as I
had ever estimated I should realize from it.

FROM H. W.

Dec. 17. The cotton packing continues; twelve bales
are already prepared for ⌃⌃ the market, stamped with
the old Coffin trademark. \/ The initiated know what
it means, but I doubt ⌄⌄ if any one else would
recognize the significance of the headless and footless
box!

FROM E. S. P.

Dec. 27. The children came up about half-past two
o'clock on Christmas afternoon [to see the tree], but
being told not to come until sunset they hung around
outside the gate till Mr. Hall was ready for them. About
dusk they were all marshaled in by classes, and we all
helped distribute the presents. The children seemed
struck aghast with the brilliant sight, and when William
Hall wished them all a Merry Christmas, they threw up
their hands and shouted with all their might. It was n't

[1] Two hundred and sixty-five thousand pounds was "about as
much as there was raised in the whole Department" in 1862.

a cheer, but more like a yell, evidently in answer to his good wishes. The presents were taken with the usual apathy shown on such occasions, and as soon as they had time they began to compare them with each other and some to complain how they did n't get enough.

Yesterday morning we made our preparations for Hunting Island. It was a fine day, wind east, and rather warm. We had four negro oarsmen. Seven white folks made up the load, including Mr. Eustis. We landed on the Island just as G.'s boat did. After unloading our grub and firing off our guns to dry them and let the deer know that we were coming, we scattered about in various directions in search of game. I then went to see the ruins of the lighthouse in the middle of the point, a few rods from each beach. It was a brick structure and must have been over one hundred feet high in order to overlook the pine trees about it. There is nothing left now but a mass of brick and rubbish about forty feet high, covering an acre of ground. It was blown up by the rebels at the beginning of the war, and they did the work thoroughly. Great blocks of granite and plates of iron lay bedded in between the masses of brick-work, some of which are still coherent in masses, and séveral feet in thickness. It is the first real ruin I ever saw in this country. The keeper's house close by has been all torn to pieces by the negroes for rebuilding their own cabins and corn-houses.

The next extracts tell of more raids for soldiers, fresh despair, and renewed hope that they might at last be stopped.

FROM E. S. P.

Dec. 27. On getting up this morning the people were found all in a hubbub. The soldiers had been there in the night, some fifty strong, and had carried off not only Cæsar, a deserter, Abel's son, but also old Miller, Tony, and Jonas and David, neither of whom had ever belonged to any of the regiments. Of course all the people were enraged, and justly, for they have been assured by General Saxton over and over again during several months past that they need n't be afraid of any more drafting, for it was all over. As soon as we had done breakfast I walked down to the quarters to see what facts I could gather. It seemed they [the soldiers] had come by rowboats to the village creek, thinking they had got to our creek, and landed at Fripp Point. There they found no deserters, for there were none, but took all the men they could find, viz.: Pompey's boy Isaac, Fortune's boy Jimmy, and Alick's boy January. They got old Dan to show them the way to Coffin's and came along the road, arriving just after praise-meeting; they set a guard all about the houses and shot at every man that tried to run away, catching the men named above and carrying them off. Tony and Jonas got away at Fripp Point, but they carried off the others. C. and I got into our little boat with Jim to help, and rowed around to the village in hopes to find the party still there, but they had gone, carrying Dr. Hunting's cook. So we rowed back and ate our dinner in disgust. This raid will break up my ginning on this end of the island and put it back at least two weeks, for the men are so scared that they won't dare to go to work, and the women can't do much without them.

Dec. 27. Mr. Philbrick has gone up to-night to see General Saxton, and Mr. Eustis says that if he can't (or won't) stop it, he shall write to Washington. It is the unauthorized work of the officers whose commissions perhaps depend upon their keeping full ranks.

Dec. 28. I rode off for Coosaw Fort on Ladies Island, where the pickets are. I found Captain Bryant at camp. He was very pleasant and told me that the descent upon Coffin's Point Saturday night was not made by his orders, but by one of Colonel Higginson's captains. The men were brought to him, however, and he discharged all who did n't want to enlist. So I came off content.

The holidays and the hunt for deserters have so broken up the labor that nothing of any consequence can be done now till after New Year's, when I hope the work will move on smoothly again.

[*Jan.* 1, 1864.] My errand to Beaufort on Tuesday was not very successful. I could find neither Colonel Higginson nor General Saxton. So I had to content myself with writing to the latter an account of how the solddiers had been behaving here. On getting back, I found the people more quiet than I had expected. The return of the men from camp had reassured them, and most of them have gone to work again.

The year closes with W. C. G.'s reflections on the progress of the " Port Royal Experiment."

FROM W. C. G.

Dec. 27. We are busy ginning and packing. Both men and women are hard at work, and till 3 o'clock P. M. the scene is almost one of Northern industry. There is more noise, less system and steadiness. Now and then two or three break out into a quarrel, in which they excel all other people I ever saw with their tongues, — tremendous noise, terrible gestures, the fiercest looks,—and perhaps by evening they are friends again. Meanwhile the others sit still at their work, listening to it as a matter in the common course of things, — and will tell how *they* love peace and quiet; it will be their own turn next! In all their faults, — passion, lying, stealing, etc., — they are perfectly conscious of the sin; and the same ones whom it would be impossible to stop, except by force, in their tempests of rage, will when quiet talk as sensibly of their folly as any one could desire. They seem to have a very delicate conscience without the slightest principle. That this want of principle is not innate and not their own fault, I think is proved by their consciences remaining true. Their state of morals I should say is decidedly better than it was under slavery, — less of licentiousness, lying, and stealing, — and more general manliness and self-respect. But they are very far behind, in character as well as intelligence, and I suspect that most abolitionist views of their character are exaggerated in their favor. It increases the need and it does not decrease the interest of helping them, to think so. Many a talking abolitionist would be disgusted into indifference, and many a hearty hater of the talk would be surprised into interest and favor, if they lived here for six months.

It 's pretty hard sometimes to find your best men lying to you, or your most trusty people ungrateful and distrusting you, — and then again a light breaks out where you thought there was neither fuel nor fire. The most encouraging symptom is the clearly increasing influence which the best of the people are acquiring, — so that there certainly is a *general* improvement.

1864

FROM E. S. P.

Jan. 3. I don't know how low the thermometer would have stood out of doors here. R.'s was at 19°. The one in our parlor was at 28° some time after lighting the fire.

You will probably in due course of time see the tintypes of Rose and Demus. Old Judy and Minda got theirs taken some time since, but there has been no opportunity of sending them to you. As they went up all by themselves, the arrangement of their toilet was original; hence a display of jewelry rather more characteristic than tasteful.

The subject of the approaching land-sales now becomes the all-important topic.

Jan. 20. There was notice given for all the people to meet at St. Helena church on Sunday last to hear the President's new instructions about land-sales. These new orders were obtained, as nearly as I can learn, by Father French, who went to Washington at General Saxton's request to urge the matter. The plan de-

feats that of Dr. Brisbane, who meant to sell at auction.[1]
Now, as you will see by the papers, all the lands that
were bid in by the United States are offered at private
sale, to black or white, in lots of twenty or forty acres
at a uniform price of $1.25 per acre, like Western pub-
lic lands, with the privilege of preëmption, but to those
only who have resided on lands belonging to the Government for at least six months since the occupation
of the island by our forces. So this gives all the superintendents and teachers a chance to buy as well as
the negroes, but excludes all new-comers. I found
Dr. Brisbane as much disturbed as it is possible to
conceive.

Of course I stayed over with Mr. R. another night
to attend the church. It was a fine morning, and we
found a pretty large attendance, both black and white.
Parson Phillips was there and opened the services.
Mr. French followed, urging them to go ahead at once
and locate their lots. General Saxton followed, saying
but little, but urging them not to sleep till they had
staked out their claims.

Father French begged leave to differ, for he wanted
them to respect the Sabbath. Mr. Hunn followed, saying they had better do it *to-day*, for it was no worse to
drive stakes Sunday than to keep thinking about it.
He condoled them on the small pay they had been getting from Government and private speculators, saying, "What's thirty cents a day in these times for a
man who has to maintain himself and his family?"
(Great sensation among negroes, and a buzz, with
mutterings of "that's so," etc.). Then a paymaster

[1] See p. 230.

made a spread-eagle speech. Then Colonel Ellwell was called out by Mr. French. Then Judge Smith mounted the pulpit and explained to the negroes the meaning of preëmption, how it was formed of two Latin words. Colonel Ellwell contrived to mystify the people a little as follows. After expatiating on the goodness of President Lincoln, he said he was so kind he had even offered pardon to the rebels, and perhaps we should see their old masters back here some day, with a whole county of scoundrels to swear they had always been loyal Union men, etc. The whole fandango lasted till nearly three o'clock, and then we had the usual amount of shaking of hands, etc., outside. I lost no time in finding Mr. Hunn and informing him that I had paid an average of over fifty cents a day through the whole season of working cotton. If he had been a younger man, I should have said, as I thought, that it was not a true kindness to these ignorant people to say anything tending to make them discontented with the rates of pay that had been established with a good deal of care by men who had been quite disinterested and well calculated to judge of such things. In fact, I might have told him, what I certainly believe, that a much higher rate of pay than they have been receiving would tend to diminish the amount of industry rather than to stimulate it, by rendering it too easy for them to supply their simple wants. I held my peace, however, and was content to hear him apologize, disclaiming any intention of referring to me in what he had said, etc., and admitting that my case was an exception, adding that he did n't suppose I should be *allowed* by Government to pay higher rates than those established by General Saxton! We were accompanied

home from church by Mr. Eustis, and Mr. R. came as
far as G.'s. They all met here Monday, in a pouring
rain, to talk over the subject of wages for the coming
year. It was concluded to pay in money entirely instead of in molasses and bacon, believing that the days
of rationing in any form had passed, and that the negroes would be better pleased to handle all the money
and spend it as they pleased. So we raise the pay of
cotton hoeing from twenty-five cents to thirty-five
cents per old task, and add five cents more, making it
forty cents, besides the premium on the weight of crop,
which remains as before, making the average wages
about sixty or sixty-five cents for cotton work, which
we think none too high for the present prices of dry
goods, etc. Of course, the smart hands earn more than
this in a day, for they do one and one-half times or twice
as much per day as they used to, and these prices are
based upon the old master's day's work or task. I have
some men who gin fifty pounds a day and earn their
dollar, while they never ginned more than thirty pounds
for their master. I spent most of the day with G. on
his plantations, talking with him and his people about
the prospect of success with the new system. I have n't
yet found a single man on any of my places who wants
to risk buying land. They all say they had rather stay
where they are and work for me. The more intelligent foresee many difficulties in owning land, such as
having no access to marsh, or woodland, no capital
for live-stock, plows, harness, carts, etc., and they don't
like the idea of having to wait a whole year to get their
reward for planting the cotton crop. The people seemed
highly satisfied to work on and well pleased with the

prospect of higher nominal wages to talk about, and slightly higher in reality, with the privilege of spending them as they wish.

Jan. 27. Last Friday I made an expedition to Eddings Point in our little boat. Arriving about one o'clock, and leaving the boat in charge of the boys, I walked up to Mr. Wells' house on the Mary Jenkins place, about one and one-quarter miles. I went down to the nigger-house to see the people. I found the people in a state of confusion about buying land. They had got the impression at church from the earnest way in which they were urged to buy, that they *must* buy land *nolens volens*, and wanted to have my consent to stay where they were and work for me as long as they pleased! Of course I laughed and told them they were welcome to stay as long as they wished and behaved well. They seemed "well satisfy" with this, and all in good humor.

I stayed at home Monday to see Mr. Hull, who came down with another big boat-load of cotton for our people to gin. They had finished ginning what he brought last week in two days. As soon as his boat came to the landing near Nab's house, the people made a rush for the cotton, the men carting it and the women carrying the bags on their heads and hiding it, so they might have some of it to gin. It was like rats scrambling for nuts.

Mr. B. has a letter from Secretary Chase, urging that a bale of free labor cotton be sent to the Sanitary Fair at New York, and I offered to present a bale for the purpose. It will be worth about five hundred dollars; but is not a very great contribution, considering that we have two hundred of them nearly.

I see that my letter to Alpheus Hardy [1] is going the rounds, being copied in Providence *Journal* and New York *Evening Post*, with a few blunders as usual. Did you notice the expression "extend the arm of charity" was printed "area" instead of "arm," making a very absurd appearance? The Providence *Journal* put in an extra cipher, multiplying my figures by ten. In order to correct this blunder, which was a serious one, making the cotton cost ten times as much as I stated, I wrote to the editor, giving him some more information about my crop, for the benefit of the Providence cotton spinners. [2]

FROM W. C. G.

Jan. 29. Outside of our plantations, the people for once are excited with good reason. In the most awkward, incomplete, bungling way the negroes are allowed to preëmpt twenty and forty acre tracts; so everybody is astir, trying to stake out claims and then to get their claims considered by the Commissioners.

[1] A letter dated December 28, 1863, inclosing $100 for the relief of families of freedmen. The letter gives figures that prove the success of the free labor experiment on Mr. Philbrick's plantations, and concludes as follows: "I mention these things to show how easy it is to render the negroes a self-supporting and wealth-producing class with proper management; and I, at the same time, fully appreciate the duty imposed upon us as a nation to extend the arm of charity where the unsettled state of the country renders industry impossible until time is given to recognize and force to protect it. We are more fortunately situated than the people of the Mississippi valley, and have got the start of them."

[2] A letter dated January 25, 1864, and printed in the Providence *Journal* on February 6.]

These gentlemen meanwhile are at loggerheads, the land is but half surveyed, and everything is delightfully confused and uncertain. Still it is the beginning of a great thing, — negroes become land-owners and the door is thrown open to Northern immigration. Years hence it will be a satisfaction to look back on these beginnings, — now it is very foggy ahead and very uncertain under foot.

FROM E. S. P.

Feb. 4.   Sunday morning I met the whole female population on the road, coming to church. It was baptism day, and the women had all put on their best dresses, their summer muslins and turbans, making a fine show.   On arriving at the Captain John Fripp gate, by the avenue, I found a knot of young men seated there, with one of their number reading to the rest from the Testament. I asked them why they did n't go to church with the women! They said they had heard that "soldiers had come to catch we," and "we were scary." Poor fellows, what a strange life of suspense they are leading! General Gillmore has ordered a complete census of the islands, black and white men included, for enrollment on the militia lists, and no white citizen is allowed to leave the Department until after it is found whether he is wanted for military service, i. e., after a draft.

Having got the cotton all shipped, Mr. Philbrick prepared to go home, but he was not to leave without receiving from his employees more than one expression of their growing consciousness of power.

FROM H. W.

Feb. 9. The women came up in a body to complain to Mr. Philbrick about their pay, — a thing which has never happened before and shows the influence of very injudicious outside talk, which has poisoned their minds against their truest friends. The best people were among them, and even old Grace chief spokeswoman. It is very hard, but not to be wondered at in the poor, ignorant creatures, when people who ought to know better are so injudicious, — to use the mildest term the most charitable interpretation of their conduct will allow. I don't see what is to be the end of it all, but at this rate they will soon be spoiled for any habits of industry.

Feb. 14. As we went to the back steps to see Mr. Philbrick off, we found the people collecting with eggs and peanuts for him to carry. He told them that he could not carry the eggs to Miss Helen, but would tell her. Then Grace begged his pardon for her bad behavior and complaining the other day, and, collecting all the eggs which he had refused, told C. they were for him, and sent them by Rose into the house. She, with the other women, had complained of C. to him, and I suppose she meant it as a peace offering.

E. S. P. TO W. C. G.

Boston, Feb. 22. I regretted that you were not present at the pow-wow after church on the 14th. Mr. Tomlinson talked very "straight" to Pompey and others about their having no right to live on my land without working for me at fair rates. He expressed his opinion very freely about the fairness of our prices and told them they must go and hunt up another home or work for us at these rates. I promised to sign a "pass," which you can do for me, promising to Pompey or any other man who works for us that as soon as he gets a piece of land of his own, gets a deed of it, and gets it fenced in, we will sell him a cow at cost, but I would not agree to allow their cows to run at large on the plantation, and Mr. Tomlinson said I was perfectly right. During the confab I overheard mutterings among the crowd such as "we shan't get anything," "it's no use," etc., serving to convince me that the whole subject would be quietly dropped unless stirred up by some such men as J. H. and F. J. W. again. Considering the prospect of high prices of molasses and bacon, etc., I think we may find it advisable to pay fifty cents all summer for what we had promised forty. But would do nothing about it till I have made my purchases of molasses, etc., and know just how the thing will stand.

An unexpected danger in the shape of an epidemic of small-pox made its appearance in the middle of the winter and lasted for two or three months.

FROM H. W.

[*Jan.* 29.] Mr. Philbrick vaccinated all the children here last year, and the few cases we have had have been among those grown persons who were vaccinated many years ago, and have all been very mild. It may run through the place, but it is not likely to be violent, and the quarters are too far off to expose us.

Feb. 26. Rose came up as usual, but had such hot fever that I sent her home to add one more to the sick list there, where all but one have "the Pox," taken from Hester.

I expected Rose would not escape. Moreover, Uncle Sam now has it, so Robert may give out in a few weeks; but no one has been very ill, and no one yet has died here. It seems to be a milder form than that which appeared at the Oaks and at Mr. Eustis', where a number have died, or else they give them more air here, which is I believe the fact. I do not go to the quarters now at all. I can do no special good in going, and they send to me for what they want.

[*March* 21.] Monday morning just after breakfast Rose came into the parlor with a funny expression on her face and asked me if I had been into the kitchen. "Well, Aunt Betty got de Gove*ment* lump, for true; I shum yere and yere," pointing to her chin and cheek. So I went downstairs, and there was Betty on the floor, fairly in for the small-pox. I find the people call it " Govement lump," and those who have it " Union," those who don't " Secesh," while the fever which precedes the eruption goes by the very appropriate name of " Horse Cavalry!"

March 9. In the evening, a little after nine o'clock, the air was suddenly filled, as it seemed to me, with a strange wild, screaming wail. At first I thought it must be the mules; but it rose and fell again and again in such agony, as I thought, that Mr. Soule and William went out to investigate, while I opened the window to listen more distinctly. It seemed to come from Uncle Sam's house, and though now more subdued I thought it the sobbing of strong men, and that I could distinguish Titus' and Robert's voices. But the gentlemen soon came back, saying that there were evidently a good many people in Uncle Sam's house having a merry time. I

said that was strange, for he was not well, and that it
sounded so like distress to me that I should think, if I
supposed him sick enough, or that they ever manifested
grief so audibly, that he had suddenly died. Several
times before I went to bed I thought I heard the same
sound, though more subdued. As I went upstairs to bed
there began, at first quite low, then swelling louder with
many voices, the strains of one of their wild, sad songs.
Once before when Uncle Sam was sick they have had
their praise-meeting up there, for he is the Elder. But
it was not praise-night, and as the hymn ceased and I
could distinguish almost the words of a fervent prayer,
I was quite sure that, as is their custom, they were sitting up and singing with the friends of the dead, — all
of the plantation who were not watching with the sick
in their own homes. And so it proved. The night was
wild and stormy, but above the tempest I could hear, as
I woke from time to time, the strangely "solemn, wildly
sad strains " which were continued all the night through.
At sunrise they ceased and separated; the air of their
last hymn has been running in my head all day. Then
came the stir in the house — Robert making fires — I
knew his step — and then Betty at my bedside to ask
about the breakfast. "And Bu' Sam dead too," was her
quiet remark when her business was done. " I dunner if
you yeardy de whoop when he gone."

This practice of sitting up all night with the dying,
H. W. justly enough condemns as "heathenish:" "The
houses cannot hold them all, of course, and they sit
round out-of-doors in the street, the younger ones often
falling asleep on the ground, and then they ' hab fever.' "
But of course it was useless to expostulate with them;

to their minds the omission of the watch would be a mark of the greatest disrespect.

The next two extracts furnish further comments on the mismanagement preliminary to the land-sales.

FROM W. C. G.

Feb. 22. Did you know we had long ceased to be philanthropists or even Gideonites? We are nothing now but speculators, and the righteous rail against us. A great crowd of our brethren have just come down to be present at the late sales. Mr. Philbrick and the purchasers of last spring paid about $1.00 or $1.25 per acre; now prices run from $5.00 to $27.00 per acre.[1] There has been the most disgraceful squabbling among the tax-commissioners, General Saxton, Rev. Mr. French, and other authorities. The people are the victims. At first most of the lands were to be sold at auction in large lots; that brought in white settlers — and only a little was for negro sales. Then one commissioner sends up to Washington, gets orders for a Western preëmption system, and with a grand hurrah the negroes were told to go and grab the lands. The other commissioners then throw all possible obstacles in the way till they can get dispatches up to Washington too, and the answer comes back, — Preëmptions don't count, sell by auction. — And so! — This is a precious Department of ours.

March 14. The past two months have been full of unpleasant work, — the people were unsettled, discontented, and grumbling. I hope their growling is nearly

---

[1] Land on the Sea Islands is now worth $15 an acre, — $20 if it is near a road.

over, and look for quieter times soon. The disputes among the tax-commissioners have been very unintelligible and prejudicial to them. On some places I understand that the negroes refuse to have anything to do with the new proprietors. On others they have agreed to work, and the year as a whole will probably witness much more industry than either of the last two.

At about this time an appraisal was at last made of the "chattel property" which had been found on the plantations, with a view to selling it at auction. Of course Mr. Philbrick and his superintendents, who had been using these things ever since they came into possession, desired, in most cases, to buy them. At the Fripp Point auction the negroes showed their ungracious, not to say ungrateful spirit, by bidding against W. C. G. and actually buying all the mules, oxen, and cows away from him. In looking forward to the auction at Coffin's Point, where the movables alone had been appraised as worth more than Mr. Philbrick had paid for the entire place, H. W. writes:

March 6. We were doubtful how far the behavior of the Fripp Point people might affect ours, though C. was quite confident there would be no trouble — and moreover expected a good many outsiders, as R. said Beaufort people had been inquiring all through the week when the sale was to take place here, with the significant remark, "Coffin's Point's the place!" and we knew if they did come things would be run up very high. So that it was impossible not to feel a most uncomfortable anxiety all day.

March 7. Monday morning the first thing I heard was Mike in excited tones calling to C. that the Fripp people were coming over "to buy everything out de

gate " — that they would leave everything on top Massa
Charlie, but that he must not let the stranger black
people get anything.

Fortunately Mike's fears proved to be exaggerated,
and Massa Charlie got practically everything that he
wanted.

The next letter, from Mr. Philbrick to W. C. G., is
concerned with several different matters. The last paragraph will serve to introduce a number of extracts all
concerned with criticisms directed against Mr. Philbrick by Abolitionists and negroes.

E. S. P. TO W. C. G.

Boston, March 24. I hope no cases of merchandise will
be opened without carefully comparing contents with
the invoices, and if any errors are found they should
be reported immediately. I am sorry to see that a considerable deficit was found in some of the stores, which
I can only account for on the supposition of theft. I
think sufficient care has not been taken to guard against
theft from carts on road. The value of the property
lost is not a matter of so much consequence as the demoralization to the thief and to others who are encouraged to similar practices by his example. I don't think
the negroes one bit worse in this respect than the laboring classes of other countries, and not nearly so bad
as the lower classes in all large cities. But we ought
to be very careful how we expose them to temptations
which they are not strong enough to resist, till such
time as they acquire more self-respect than they are
likely to in this generation.

I shall not be able to make any dividend to the share-
holders this year. After paying my advances and set-

tling with superintendents, there will not be any surplus over the needs of the current year.

Mr. F. J. W. has been quite talkative and rides his
hobby to death,[1] concerning the rights of the negro to
have land for nothing, etc., etc., expatiating upon the
tyranny of the newly forming *landed aristocracy*, the
gigantic speculators who are grinding the negro down,
etc., etc., ad libitum. He held forth on these topics at
length at a meeting of the Educational Commission
about two weeks ago, and succeeded in making Professor Child and some others believe that the whole
labor of the Commission for two years past had been
wasted or overthrown by the recent changing policy,
which had ousted them out of their promised rights
and cast them out upon the merciless open jaws to
devour them alive, etc., etc.

E. S. P. TO W. C. G.

April 18. Just now it would seem as if the Sea Islands were to be abandoned to the negroes and wild
hogs. I had heard some things of General Birney [2]
before which led me to regard him as having injudicious sympathies, and should not be surprised at any
time to have him send you home as a "fraudulent coad-
jutor" of an unrighteous speculation, upon the repre-
sentation of Pompey and John, if they should happen
to gain an audience after dinner some day. Joking

[1] F. J. W. was in Boston at the time.

[2] William Birney, Brigadier-General and Commander of the Post
at Beaufort during one of Saxton's absences, had, on March 30, issued
an order to the effect that in all cases the negroes were to be left in
possession of the land they claimed as theirs.

aside, however, I think it would be a good plan to get Colonel S. to retract some of his nonsense, and I have no doubt he will do it at your request, for he is one of the most good-natured and well-intentioned men in the world. He is very likely to have said what the negroes say he did, indiscreetly, of course, and without dreaming what effect it might have. If the people continue to refuse to receive their money, as I don't believe they will long, I would consult Mr. Tomlinson about it. I think he will sustain us in anything reasonable. I think if Mr. Tomlinson were to tell John or Pompey that they would not be allowed to take any of their cotton and would be severely punished if they attempted it, it would have a good effect. Any way I think the matter will blow over soon. It is not strange that the negroes should act like fools when they have such examples before them as we see nowadays.

FROM H. W.

April 18. At night came Mr. Soule from Beaufort with an account of the investigations going on there concerning the tax-commissioners before Judge Smith, an agent sent by the President for the purpose. Mr. Soule found that he had also been commissioned to look into the affairs of our "concern," as the Fripp Point men had sent a petition to the President to be relieved from Mr. Philbrick's oppression! Mr. Soule and Mr. Tomlinson both saw Judge Smith, and had some talk with him at the meeting, which was a public one, and he was invited to come down here, see Mr. Soule's books and investigate all the charges thoroughly. Whoever drew up the petition (of course it had been done by a white man, but who we could not tell, for his name as witness had been omitted in the copy given Judge Smith) had so overshot the mark that it was palpably absurd to all who knew the facts, and happily Mr. Soule had found Judge Smith to be a fair-minded, able, clear-sighted person, who could not have dust thrown in his eyes.

April 21. Sat waiting the arrival of Judge Smith, when about one o'clock Robert called to me that a carriage was coming. To my amazement, instead of the Judge alone or with only a friend, a great vehicle with four white horses and "sofas inside," [1] as Rose said, dashed up to the front door with four gentlemen, Mr. Tomlinson and Mr. G. being on horseback besides. Of course I had to fly round about my dinner and get up tables large enough to seat thirteen people. By three dinner was ready and my guests at table — a very pleasant company : Judge Smith, a round, smooth-faced *gentleman* between fifty and sixty, active and wide-awake ; Judge Cooley, the new tax-commissioner, a Westerner and also very pleasant. Judge Smith took Mr. Soule's statement before dinner, and afterwards Mr. G.'s, all simply facts and with no waste of words. C. was not questioned at all. Then Mr. G. went over to the Point for the men there, for, though the Judge was satisfied that Mr. Philbrick was not a scoundrel and all of us aiders and abetters of his iniquities, we knew the men there would never be satisfied with the statement from any of us or Mr. Tomlinson, who had been talking to them for two hours that morning. Poor things, they are much more sinned against than

[1] An ambulance.

sinning. They came flocking over so closely upon Mr.
G.'s heels as to get here nearly as soon as he did, and
the session of the Court began by the examination of
John Major before tea, the others crowding about the
door and filling the piazza, quiet and orderly, but eager
listeners. Not a single one of our people came up. John
Major is a discontented, conceited fellow, who has
never worked for Mr. Philbrick, though his wife and
children have, and he headed the petition. It was
splendid to see how quickly the Judge saw through him,
when he has been only a week in the Department, and
could hardly understand what he said; but he showed
the man pretty plainly what he thought of him, telling him, when he said the Government could not find
him out [know him] that it *had* found him out, that it
had his name in Washington, and that if he thought
Secesh times were so much better, the Government
loved him so well it would let him go back to his old
master! After tea came 'Siah and Pompey, two very
different men, — intelligent, hard-working, and honest,
the former particularly truthful and reliable, men whom
we all respect, — and it was a fine sight to see these
men, only two years out of slavery, respectfully but
decidedly standing up for what they thought their
rights in a room full of white people. 'Siah only said
that he thought he ought to have fifty cents for what
he is now paid forty for [1] (about four hours work), but
that he had given his word to Mr. Philbrick for this
year and he would stand by it. He says he never signed
the paper, or saw it, but that he answered the question the two officers asked him and told his name.

[1] Cf. E. S. P.'s letter of February 22, p. 251.

Pompey afterwards stated that the two officers asked who owned the adjoining plantations and that one, — and that on being told that Mr. Philbrick had bought them all, said: "Then we need not go any further" — which looks like malice aforethought. The paper was, apparently, written at Hilton Head and there signed with the men's marks — if so, it is a forgery. Pompey's great difficulty seemed to have arisen from a misunderstanding of statements made by Mr. Philbrick, in which he considered that Mr. Philbrick took back his word, and so he had lost confidence in him and was ready to appeal to any one who promised to see him righted and relieved from his "confusion." He says, and all the men say so too, that Mr. Philbrick promised when he bought the land to sell it to them when the war was over for what he gave for it, and that when he was here last he told them he should ask them ten dollars an acre. This they all stand to, and cannot be convinced they have made a mistake, but have lost their faith because he has broken his word, — and outsiders have fanned the flame, telling them that if they did not work for Mr. Philbrick for what he chose to pay them, — and that he was paying them nothing, — he would turn them out of their homes, and more to the same effect. It was a most interesting occasion, and it was pleasant to feel that there was a man of so much sense in the Department. He tried to pacify the men, and then privately told Mr. Soule that he should advise Mr. Philbrick to pay the fifty cents.

The next day the gentlemen departed, Mr. Tomlinson going to the smaller Philbrick plantations to make the newly-ordered written contracts with the

people. By the terms of a circular issued April 1 by
General Saxton, each superintendent was ordered,
before April 15, to make to his general superintendent
and to sign a statement of the agreement existing between himself and his laborers. The general superintendent was then ordered to visit the plantation, explain the contract to the negroes, and affix to it the
names of all who agreed to the terms of it; any laborer
who objected to the terms was warned to leave his employer or stay with him at his own risk. H. W. records
the reception given to Mr. Tomlinson by the Pine
Grove people.

April 22. They were silenced, but not convinced, but
agreed for this year. Mr. Tomlinson had trouble with
the people at Mr. Folsom's and Mr. Harrison's both.
He had meant to do the job here, but could not, as C.
was away. C. did not expect any difficulty, and I suspect that he was right, for just after all had gone, two
of our men, "Useless" Monday, the stuttering cow-
minder, and Hacklis, the sulkiest-looking man on the
place, came up and, with the brightest smiles and
cheeriest manner, began to ask me so earnestly how
I was, that I felt as if I were not honest if I did not
mention that I had a slight headache. "Mebbe de confusion make you sick, sorry for dat. Not one our
people come up yere. We bery sorry for dat," — and
much more of regret, and assertion that "so long as
Mass' Charlie on de place dey satisfy." Old Monday
wished to know if the milk satisfied me, and was very
much delighted when I told him that if he had not sent
some up the night before I should have had none for
the gentlemen's breakfast, and kept exclaiming, "I
glad for dat," as if he had wished to express his sym-

pathy by deeds as well as words. Then Hacklis said,
"Come, let's go," as if they had come up simply to
assure me that our people would give no trouble. I was
touched.

The end of the story was a month later.

FROM H. W.

May 27. Mr. Tomlinson came home last night with
C. and Mr. Soule to spend the night and make the
contract with the people, so C. sent word to them to
assemble in the cotton-house yard before they went
to their work, and he and Mr. Tomlinson went down
before breakfast, so that they need not be interrupted
in their work. They were gone so long that we began
to fear some trouble — indeed C. said he expected
some "jawing," and that it would be strange if this
was the only place where there was none ; but not a
word was said — the people apparently are so ashamed
of the conduct of the women when Mr. Philbrick was
here and so indignant with the "Fripp People" that
they are on their best behavior.

FROM W. C. G.

Early May. We have been having a funny time with
our people lately. One of my plantations is decidedly
ahead of all the others in intelligence and energy. They
were so energetic about March 1 as to get a petition
sent up to President Lincoln, praying for redress against
their various oppressions. The matter was referred
to some gentlemen coming down here to make other
investigations, and two or three weeks ago they pretty
thoroughly examined our affairs. I believe the result

was pretty satisfactory. The originators of the movement were two dissatisfied men who have given me great trouble. There was much reason for some of their feeling, but very little for their complaints. As a result of the whole affair, however, I believe we all think it would be politic to increase our wages still more. At present we pay rather less than some, but our cheap stores far more than make up the difference. This, however, the people, instead of appreciating, only make the subject of more complaint.

When that was nicely settled, I made the discovery that both plantations had thought it proper to plant a great deal of corn among my cotton. I had given them corn-land for themselves, but they, in pursuance of a Secesh custom of planting a little corn between the cotton rows, had done so to an outrageous extent. And they in many cases refused to take it out. The truth is here, —that we are rather more in the power of the negroes than they in ours. I shall insist on every grain being out, but actually shall probably have to do it myself. Well — such disputes are almost the only excitement I have; better some, perhaps, though unpleasant, than none.

E. S. P. TO C. P. W.

Boston, May 3. As soon as I can get complete information from Liverpool about my claim on the insurance company,[1] I shall settle with them and be

[1] Early in April the steamer *City of New York*, carrying sixty-one bales of Mr. Philbrick's cotton, was wrecked in Queenstown harbor. The cotton was insured for $1.50 a pound, but would have brought more in the market.

ready to settle with yourself, G., and Folsom. Are you not ashamed to put in your own private pocket the proceeds of the hard labor of the poor abused negro? I think you cannot have read the *Tribune* and *Independent* lately, or you would not be so depraved.

The sarcastic allusion in this last letter to the *Tribune* and the *Independent* refers to two letters which had lately appeared in those papers respectively, the one signed "J. A. S.," the other anonymous. Both were from Beaufort, and both attacked Mr. Philbrick for a letter which he had recently written (February 24) to the New York *Evening Post*. This letter was the presentation which he had planned to make proving from his own experience that it was possible to raise cotton cheaper by free labor than had been possible by slave labor.[1] In it Mr. Philbrick had also stated his belief that the land-sales would be an injury to the negro if they enabled him to buy at $1.25 an acre land which was already worth much more and would, after the war, rise still higher in value, for such purchases would be made largely as speculations, and would destroy all incentive to labor. The points of attack selected by the writers in the *Independent* and the *Tribune* were Mr. Philbrick's rate of wages, — why did he not pay his hands $2.50 a day? — his views on the land-sales, which, they said, showed his desire to make of the negroes an "agricultural peasantry," as dependent upon great landed proprietors as ever they had been in their days of slavery, and the course he had pursued relative to his own purchases in land. "His own statements of his intentions induced the almost universal belief that he desired to buy land for the purpose of testing the industrial capabilities

[1] See p. 219. The idea was by no means new. Frederick Law Olmstead had devoted a great deal of space to proving the truth of it, and indeed had quoted many planters who admitted that, as a system of labor, slavery was expensive.

of the negroes, and when they had justified his confidence in this respect, that he would sell them the lands
in small allotments at the cost to himself." His actual
performance now, on the other hand, was to put the
price of his lands "further from their reach than
before," fixing it "according to the increased value
which their labor and proved capacity have given
them." To these three accusations Mr. Philbrick
made reply in two letters. First, as to the auction-sales,
he agreed "that the good faith of the Government
should have been kept in regard to the promised home-
steads, however we may differ in opinion as to the
expediency of making the promise at this time."
Second, as to his scale of wages, he maintained that, on
his plantations, "whenever the amount of work done
in a day approaches the standard of a day's work in the
North, the wages also approach the limit of Northern
wages, under similar conditions." [1] Third, as to his
alleged promise to sell his land to negroes at cost, he
said, "I am not aware that I have ever committed
myself to any definite plans for disposing of this land;
for I have not been able to digest or mature any plan
satisfactory to myself." [2]

There is nothing vital in these two letters of Mr.
Philbrick's which is new to the reader of these pages.
They are based on his firm belief that it was no kind-
ness to the negro to make discriminations in his favor.

Mr. Philbrick's message to his superintendents
about the increased pay demanded by 'Siah and
Pompey, and his advice to W. C. G. in the matter of
corn planted between the rows of cotton were as
follows:

E. S. P. TO W. C. G.

Boston, May 18. I have already written expressing
my assent to the rise of wages at any time when you

---

[1] (Dated April 26, in the *Independent*.) On St. Helena to-day it is
always possible to hire men for common work at fifty cents per day.

[2] Dated May 2.

shall all agree, and also write C. P. W. to-day that I should at any time assent to any change in the management, sustained by the unanimous approval of the corps upon the spot, without waiting to hear from me. You can avail yourself of the change to get rid of the corn in cotton-fields. I hope you will not pull it up yourself. I think such a step would lose more in dignity than you would gain in consistency of purpose. We must expect these people will take any undue advantage of us they think they can do with impunity, but I think such cases can be more readily reached through their pocket nerves than their moral sensibilities. Moreover, it is always better to do nothing in which we should not be sustained by the authorities, whose tender sympathies are not always judicious, as you know. I would not allow a hill of corn in the cotton-field, i. e., I would not pay the extra price till it is pulled up.

The next letter shows that the freedmen were waking up to their rights in more ways than one.

FROM W. C. G.

May 19. We had a queer scene here on Tuesday. It is probably the first time that the slaves — contra-bands — freedmen — have asserted themselves our fellow-countrymen by claiming the right of voting. A meeting was called in Beaufort to elect delegates to the Baltimore convention.[1] It was assumed that we could stand for the sovereign state of South Carolina, and so we sent her full complement of sixteen repre-

---

[1] The National Union Convention which met on June 7.

sentatives, and furnished each with an alternate. There are hardly thirty-two decent men in the Department, it is commonly believed. A large half of the meeting consisted of blacks, and *four black delegates were chosen*, Robert Small [1] among them; the others I believe were sergeants in the South Carolina regiment. At one time there was considerable excitement, and white paired off against black, — but on the whole both colors behaved very well.

The whole affair will be laughed at by the North, and it is hardly probable that the delegates will be received. I hope they will.

In this hope W. C. G. was to be disappointed. Not one of the delegates was received.

With a group of H. W.'s letters the story goes back to home life.

FROM H. W.

Sunday, May 8. I have been wanting to see a Baptism performed as it is here in the creek, and as there was to be one to-day C. arranged yesterday for us all to go up. We had a lovely drive, reaching the bridge by the church just as the Baptism began, and, sitting in the wagon where we could see and hear everything, we witnessed the whole ceremony and saw the vast crowd that had collected for the same purpose. As the last came up out of the water the people began to sing, and we moved with the crowd towards the church, which was presently filled, as many more people outside sitting about. We sat for about four hours, through all the services. The minister soon changed his clothes and

---

[1] The hero of the *Planter* episode ; see p. 46.

came in, but in the meantime the people sung. Mr.
Parker took occasion in his sermon to express very
liberal views towards other denominations of Chris-
tians, and then invited "all members of sister churches
to remain to the Communion service." There has been
so much talk and trouble about this, and all who were
not Baptists have been so vigorously excluded,[1] that
we were very glad to see the new minister take a different ground, and remained gladly. While the deacons
were arranging the Table, those who chose went out,
after which the elders went to the doors to call them
back. "Member, member, what you keep de church
waitin' for?" and again the church was filled, floor
and gallery, — I never saw such a sight, — but the
minister's earnestness and the general seriousness of
the people made it unlike a spectacle, and a serious,
most interesting occasion. Then there was a collection
taken up in the elders' hats, the people making change
while old Robert would attempt to persuade them to
leave the whole bill! Then two couples were severally
married, not both at once after Mr. Phillips' heathenish
fashion, pronouncing them all husbands and wives!

May 16. I found that the Court was to meet here at
nine o'clock. Mr. Soule asked me to be present, and I
listened all day to the examination of the various witnesses. It was very interesting; but it was very sad to see
how little dependence could be placed upon their word.
Men and boys took the oath one after the other and then
lied as if they had sworn to do so. Their ingenuity was
wonderful, and we had to come to the conclusion that
if those who we supposed spoke the truth had been on

[1] See p. 145.

the other side they would have lied as badly as the others. It has now become very important to carry the case through and discover if possible who have perjured themselves, as they must learn how important it is for them to speak the truth. But little additional light was thrown by the labor of to-day, and they adjourned at night till Thursday, at Pine Grove.

May 19. The court sat at Pine Grove, but though the moral certainty was very great, it was almost impossible to convict on the evidence, because they lied so.

A man came in great excitement to tell us that the rebels had made a raid during the night onto Morgan Island and carried off all the people. F. and R. immediately took the sailboat and went over to the gunboat to let them know.

May 22. F. went to church to find out about the poor Morgan Island people, and heard from Mrs. Wells that eleven people, men and women, had been carried off by fifteen Secesh — three of Hamilton Fripp's sons were among them. They took all the clothes, money, and eatables they could find, and told the people that they were living well and earning forty cents a day while their old mistress was starving and had no one to work for her, and they thought it was time they went to take care of her. One man escaped after his hands were tied, and one woman refused to get into the boat, and they knocked her down and left her. They have frightened poor Mrs. Wells pretty effectually by saying they should like to carry Mr. Wells off on the points of their bayonets. "That man that pays them forty cents a day." A picket has been stationed there and another on Eddings Point.

May 27. My "seamster," Maria, has a little girl who she sent me word should be my little chambermaid, and she wished me to name her. Her youngest child, Noble, I did not know, he is such a great boy, and I remarked that he was bigger than Cicero was two years ago. "Too much, Missus, him lick Cicero now," and she explained that it was because he was a Yankee child, and then she and Rose enlarged upon the general superiority of the Yankee children, who could all "lick" all the Secesh children of twice their years! It was very funny, but I daresay there is some truth in it, as the women only work when they feel able to do so, and moreover they all have a greater variety of food.

The boys returned from the gunboats with full accounts from the officers of the disgraceful abandonment of the expedition [1] and its complete failure, owing in the first place to the drunkenness of an officer and then to the failure of common sense. General Foster has arrived [2] — I hope he will prove to be somebody; this poor Department seems doomed. General Birney seems to have shown as little sense in this matter as on the negro question.

May 31. To dine at Pine Grove, stopping on the way to see if I could find any of Pierce Butler's [3] people among the St. Simonians who have settled on the deserted plantation of Hamilton Fripp. Found one woman who was nursery-maid at Mr. Hazard's, who she said was a cousin of "Butler's;" she remembered him well and his two daughters, also Mrs. Butler. "She was a

[1] One of many minor raids, very likely up the Combahee River.
[2] As General commanding the Department of the South.
[3] Husband of Fanny Kemble.

very great lady — a *very* great lady, and a most beautiful lady — slender-like : she tell Mr. Butler if he give
up the slavery, she would likes to live there, but she
could n't stan' that ; but he would n't 'grees to that,
so she goes 'way and she get a dewoce. Oh, but she could
ride hos'!" She said that Mr. Butler was a very kind
master to his servants indeed, "but sometimes he have
bad overseer."

June 15. Rode through the quarters to tell the people
myself that I was going home for a visit. "But you
comin' back dough — arter we get use' to you you must
n't lef' we — and you sarvice to we when we sick too
much." "Hi!" said old Betty, "you brudder an' sister
been eat you like one oyshter!" "Dey tink you like
one angel come down," said old Judy, "and they no
ben see you so long time."

The long letter that comes next is perhaps the most
interesting and convincing of all that Mr. Philbrick
wrote.

E. S. P. TO W. C. G.

Boston, July 8. Your long letter has received due attention, but I do not yet feel as if it would be advisable
to sell lands any sooner than I had always intended, viz.,
at the end of the war. I agree with you that the present
system is unsatisfactory and annoying, tending to develop the evil as well as the good that is in the negro
character. I had about concluded to propose next winter something like the following plan, but don't think it
good policy to promise *anything* now for two reasons :
first, such promises would be distorted and misrepre-
sented by the negroes among themselves in the interim,

so that when the time comes, nothing but dissatisfaction and growling would result; second, because something may turn up in the meantime to change my mind as to what is best. My rough plan is to sell to the people at cost all live-stock and implements we could spare, — nearly the whole, — for which they can doubtless pay cash next winter. Then divide the lands among them to be used as they see fit for the remainder of the war, they to pay either a certain share of the cotton they raise, say one half, or a certain amount of cotton, annually. (Don't like this last.) A small farm to be reserved on large plantations to be sold to or worked by some white settler, who can devote his time there and act as our agent to look after our rights, and if possible work a little cotton on his own account, experimenting and introducing improved methods of culture. It might be almost impossible for such a man to get labor, but there will be some negroes too dependent in their habits to want to wait a year for their pay and some old people and widows who would prefer wages paid monthly. This white man's farm is, however, not a necessary part of the plan, and if labor can't be got, of course it would n't succeed. Teachers and store-keepers to be kept on the ground at our expense, who will look after the houses they live in and do whatever else they can to keep things straight.

Another plan is to sell life-leases to the negroes, instead of the fee simple, disposing of the lands you propose to sell. This occurred to me as a means of avoiding the terrible and disastrous confusion which it will be next to impossible to avoid after a term of years, if the fee should be conveyed, when the purchasers die and sell or change land as they will to a certain extent in time. It

is bad enough to trace a title and find out whether it is
good for anything here in systematic New England,
and difficult enough, too, to fix boundaries and maintain them against encroachments ; but it makes my
orderly bones ache to think of a time when, after some
men now purchasing land shall die, leaving two or
three sets of children, some born under wedlock and
some not, some not their own but their wives' children,
some even of questionable parentage, and some who
were never heard of before, all claiming a slice of the
deceased man's land, and of course all claiming the
best. Suppose it was bounded by a "stake and stones"
as of old here, minus the stones which are absent; suppose some of the claimants think best to set up a new
stake where one has gone to decay, and suppose they
are not over exact in placing it; or suppose, as is more
than likely, their neighbor thinks the new stake en-
croaches on him and pulls it up entirely, stamping on
the hole and putting it in according to his own ideas,
etc., etc., ad infinitum. Now, as you must admit that
all this is likely to occur, and worse too, would such a
state of things tend to bring about a healthy and rapid
development? Any one who has watched the minute
subdivision of lands among the French peasantry
knows that after a few generations a man has not land
enough to live on or work economically, and hence a
vast amount of time and energy is wasted in France
for lack of organization; — that, too, where they have
an administration of justice the most minute and exact
to be found in the whole world, an organization of the
judiciary which reaches to every man's case, however
minute or inconspicuous. The life-lease system would

avoid these troubles, but would be open to this objection, a serious one, too, viz., the negro ought to feel that in building up a home for himself, it shall be a home for his children, for he has too little of the feeling of responsibility for his offspring, which is one of the best stimulants to good order and civilization.

The future value of the lands is a question I don't think of much consequence, neither is the question of profit to the present holders to be considered, when conflicting with the future welfare of the community. If we only had clearness of vision, the wisdom to see what would really be best for the masses, I sincerely believe that it could readily be adopted without in any way prejudicing the present profits of the holders. You speak of the probability of having less cotton planted for us in case your plan is followed. I should n't consider that of *any consequence whatever*, except that, as a general thing, the amount of cotton planted will always be a pretty sure index of the state of industry of the people, and their industry will always be the best measure of their improvement. It might take them some time to find out that cotton was the best thing for them to work on, but present prices are fast teaching them this fact.

The objection noted above against a life-lease is a serious one, and perhaps sufficient to balance those future annoyances likely to grow out of selling the fee.

I do not agree with you in what you say of the *unnatural* dependence of these people. I don't see any people on the face of the earth of their rank in civilization who are so independent as they are.

I don't see the justice of the claim to the soil now made in their behalf by Mr. J. A. Saxton [1] and others, and with which you seem to sympathize somewhat. The fact is that no race of men on God's earth ever acquired the right to the soil on which they stand without more vigorous exertions than these people have made. This is apparently the wise order of Providence as a means of discipline, or the misfortune of man, as a consequence of his failings, perhaps both; but I cannot see why these people should be excepted from the general rule. If they *have* acquired the necessary qualifications to be benefited by becoming landholders, then there is no reason for delay; but here is the very point of difference between us, whether they would be in the long run so benefited.

As to price, I never considered the question of profit to myself or those I represent as of consequence in fixing the price. It is no doubt an expression of this kind which gave rise to the general belief, claimed by some whites as well as blacks, that I would sell at cost, "was bound" to do so, etc. It did not occur to those who so believed that I could have any good or disinterested reasons for selling for more than cost. It may be difficult to fathom one's own motives in such cases, but I can say honestly that I do not believe in the success of a system of selling to any people any property whatever for less than its market value, with a view to confer a lasting benefit upon them. That is, I think the immediate ease which such a course would confer would beget idleness and unthrifty habits when compared with a system by which every man should be

[1] Compare J. A. S. on p. 265.

required to pay full price. No man or race of men ever truly appreciate freedom who do not fight for it, and no man appreciates property who does not work for it, on the same terms with those around him. I think they would be better off for paying ten dollars an acre for land, if the land is worth it, rather than one dollar, because they would use the land for which they had paid full price more economically, would be likely to get more out of it, and would be taught a feeling of independence more readily than by being made the recipients of charity.

In this case, however, we have a complication of circumstances entirely unique. We have a number of people who have bought land at a rate fixed by Governent, and a certain amount of "discouragement" would ensue if our people were charged more per acre than their neighbors for similar land. They could n't be expected to see the justice of such an arrangement, and it is difficult for us to explain why it should be so. This is a very strong argument for selling cheap, for we should avoid any course which we should not be able to easily prove just, when dealing with such a defenceless people. Of course there would be a grand howl among the so-called philanthropists at the mention of any plan on my part of selling at any rate above cost, witness the sensation produced by my letter to the *Evening Post*; but I don't care much for that, and ought not to care at all. We could n't sell the land as you propose [1] without calling forth a similar howl

---

[1] Evidently G.'s suggestion was practically for the plan Mr. Philbrick did in fact adopt finally, that of selling some of his land to negroes and some to white men. The price at which he sold to the negroes was determined by the ideas here expressed.

from this sickly sympathy, which would have me sell all the land and would accuse me of a tendency to aristocracy if I retained any lands to be disposed of otherwise. Of course the negroes would n't be satisfied either. I don't expect to satisfy them by any course which would be consistent with common sense. I think it possible that I may fall into such a plan as you suggest after I get down there next winter. In the meantime I don't want to make any promises.

The next three letters are full of the irritation engendered by unintelligent orders from official superiors.

FROM C. P. W.

July 17. Do people look with any interest toward this Department, either for military achievement or civil improvement? The former require better men — generals — than we are blessed with; the latter may come, — after the war.

Do people expect much of the negro of Port Royal? Let them expect. It is amusing to hear M. W.[1] She understands all the peculiarities of affairs down here with wonderful quickness and penetration; I have learned to respect her judgment and opinion. To hear her rail at these people, and slip out sly hints about the conduct of the "friends of the freedman" is a treat.

Rose was sitting disconsolately on the wood-box the other evening; I began chaffing her about her melancholy looks. She did not say much, but presently she asked if I had heard from Miss Harriet again; I told her no, and she heaved a big sigh, and asked when she

[1] A mulatto, educated in the North, who had gone to help at Port Royal.

would come back. "Mass' Charlie, no one *know* how
I miss Miss Hayyut. If my own *mudder* go Nort', I no
miss her mo'." I asked her if she missed Miss Harriet
more than I missed my "farmly," whom I had n't seen
for so many months. She could n't tell. "Ebry man
hab e own feelin'."

Aug. 17. The unexpected opportunity to send off
my letter was the visit of one Lewis Keller, from
the provost marshal's office at Hilton Head; he came
down to make inquiries concerning deserters, able-
bodied men, etc., etc. He also obtained a map of the
island, with plantations marked thereon. The provost
marshal, I am sorry to say, is conceited, opinionated,
and wanting in common sense and discretion. He has
ideas which, if founded on anything, rest on reports
only, and very vague reports too. He thinks, or rather
(as the notion, once in his head, must stick there) he
is certain, that there is communication between the
negroes who buy at our stores and the rebels; that there
is a camp of deserters (black and white) on Hunting
Island, and that these deserters are employed in carrying supplies to the main; that the proximity of our
stores to the rebel country is a dangerous state of things,
not only inciting the rebels to come over, but likely to
supply them with all they want if they do come. Also
he thinks that the negroes have no business to have
guns. Also he does not see what they can want with
all the stuff sent on the *Kelley*. Now the *Kelley* arrived
just before the regulations which allowed plantation
supplies to enter insurrectionary districts. The treasury agent at once offered to permit the *Kelley's* cargo
to come on shore. The provost marshal, who by this

time appeared to be very willing to "help us all he
could," took the invoice to General Foster, and came
back with permission to land all of some things, one
half the dry goods, one third only of the grocery supplies, flour, bacon, etc. We shall probably have to sell
the rest at Hilton Head. Very provoking. Some of the
supplies were small enough as they were; what is left
will be about a mouthful apiece all around; e. g., one
hundred and eighty barrels of flour came; my share
would be about thirty-five. I could have sold twenty-
five whole barrels, and peddled out the rest in six weeks.
My share of sixty barrels will be about twelve! The
provost marshal could not see what the people wanted
of so much provision. Yet he has at his office the census of all these plantations, besides a written statement
prepared by Mr. Soule of the amount bought at these
stores within the last six months and the lists of purchases over five dollars at a time (we have to keep these
lists, as one condition of keeping store).

Besides restricting the quantity of goods, all the
stores are to be closed except those at R.'s and Folsom's. I may sell what I have on hand, but not take
in anything more. Ignorance, stupidity, and conceit.

E. S. P. TO C. P. W.

Boston, Aug. 24. The recent assumption of authority
by the military officials seems to have extinguished the
Treasury Department in Port Royal. It is a difficult
case to reach, for this officious intermeddling bears the
semblance of earnest and zealous watchfulness of the
public interests. Any representations at Washington
will avail nothing, so long as Colonel H. cherishes the

idea, or pretends to, that it is not for the public welfare to have us sell bacon and 'lasses at Coffin's Point. Any permission from the Treasury Department which would appear to him as too lenient would only give him another chance to exercise his authority, which tickles his vanity and makes him appear a big man. A difference of opinion between him and myself would hardly be listened to at Washington, so long as it is upon a subject on which his superiors think him qualified to judge better than myself. Suppose the Secretary of the Treasury were to allow goods to be taken from Hilton Head without restriction, General Foster and Colonel H. would still think the rebels would get them, and, having the power in their own hands, would not be likely to allow us to avail ourselves of any such privileges. I should like to have the question asked him, "How the Coffin's Point people are to get supplies?" If we are forbidden to keep a store there, it certainly cannot be forbidden us to send a wagon-load of goods there for the supply of that plantation whenever needed, which will answer our purposes well enough. In order to avoid any trap-springing by parties who might think it a smart thing to tell Colonel H. we had not discontinued the store, it would be best to have a plain talk with him on the subject. We don't want to *keep store*, but supply the plantations, and need not keep any considerable stock on hand at these "exposed" points.

The next group of letters returns to the subject of negro recruitment. By this time various Northern States, in despair of finding enough men at home to make out the number of recruits required of them by the general Government, were getting hold of Southern negroes for the purpose, and their agents had appeared in the Department of the South, competing for freedmen with offers of large bounties. At the same time General Foster made up his mind that all able-bodied negroes who refused to volunteer, even under these conditions, should be forced into the service. If the conscription methods of the Government up to this time had not been brutal, certainly no one can deny that adjective to the present operations. Yet it will be seen that experience has tempered the indignation of the superintendents, though not their distress.

FROM C. P. W.

Aug. 9. Lieutenant-Colonel Rice, agent for Massachusetts, has come. After looking about a little, he does not think the prospect of getting recruits *very* brilliant, but his agents are at work in Beaufort streets, and may pick up a few men. He intends to send native scouts on to the main to beat up recruits; $35 a man is offered for all they will bring in. Colonel Rice intended to come down here to-day, but had to go and see General Foster and Colonel Littlefield,[1] Superintendent of Recruiting. (He — Colonel L. — calls it recruiting to conscript all he can lay hands on.) There is to be, not a draft, but a wholesale conscription,[2] enforced here. Lieutenant-Colonel Strong of the First South (Thirty-Third United States Colored Troops)[3] enrolled all colored men last month. It is possible, if the men

[1] Colonel Milton S. Littlefield, Twenty-First United States Colored Troops.

[2] Foster's order was dated August 16.

[3] "The First South," as the First South Carolina Volunteers was always called by the negroes, had in the spring been enrolled among the United States Colored Troops as the Thirty-Third Regiment.

can be made to understand this, that a few can be induced to volunteer, but I hardly think that many will be secured, either by enlistment or draft. Colonel Rice comes down here this week. Mr. Soule (just returned from Beaufort) describes him as a pleasant man, simple in manner, with great good sense, shrewd enough, and of an inquiring turn. He has gone right to work, not bidding for men, but offering the whole bounty, etc., at once, and at the same time he is trying to find out all he can about things and people here. I long to "shum" and keep him over night.

FROM W. C. G.

Sept. 23. I'm glad to say that my plantations have at last contributed their share to the regiment. With two or three exceptions all my young men have gone, — twenty, more or less, — which has deprived me of at least half my stock of labor. They are carrying out the draft with excessive severity, not to say horrible cruelty. Last night three men were shot, — one killed, one wounded fatally, it is thought, and the other disappeared over the boat's side and has not been seen since, — shot as they were trying to escape the guard sent to capture all men who have not been exempted by the military surgeons. The draft here is a mere conscription, — *every* able-bodied man is compelled to serve, — and many not fit for military service are forced to work in the quartermaster's department.

Oct. 12. You ask more about the draft. The severity of the means employed to enforce it is certainly not to be justified, nor do the authorities attempt to do so, — *after* the act is done. The draft here is carried on by

military, not civil, powers. We have no civil laws,
courts, officers, etc. Consequently the only way in
which public operations can be accomplished is by
issuing a general order and instructing the provost
marshals to see it carried into execution. The only
agents to be employed are necessarily soldiers, and the
only coercion is necessarily that of guns and arbitrary
arrests. The state of society — as far as regards the
draft and also many other things — is one in which
most men conspire to escape the voice of the law; so
that, when such unfortunate occurrences happen as
the late shooting affair, there seems to be nothing for
it but indignation and sorrow, and perhaps an examination into the circumstances to discover if they justified
recourse to such extreme action: e. g., the shooting
seems to have stopped further proceeding in the draft.
If there were any civil power here, such things would
be as unjust and horrible as they seem. As it is, each
case has to be weighed by itself and may prove better
than it seems. The Massachusetts recruiting agents,
of course, have nothing to do with enforcing the draft.
But their presence seems to have increased its activity
and their bounty contributes to its success. Nearly all
my men have gone voluntarily (i. e., felt they must go,
and, for the bounty offered, concluded to go without
violence), and all are constantly writing home letters
expressive of great satisfaction.

The letter following from T. E. R. (one of Mr.
Philbrick's superintendents, frequently referred to in
these letters as "R."), gives a capital idea of the plea-
sures of living under military rule.

T. E. R. TO C. P. W. (AT HOME ON A VISIT)

St. Helena Island, Oct. 17. An order was issued just before or about the time you left to take away all the boats, to prevent intercourse with the rebels; so they attempted to enforce it, but, after the first day, boats all went out into the *mash* or up on dry land in the bush, and then alas for *General Order* or any other man. Several applications were sent to General Saxton in reference to the matter, and these he forwarded to Foster, and he let his dignity down easily by permitting all the boats taken to be returned and all not taken to be retained, on the presentation to the provost marshal of *triplicate* certificates describing the owner (age, height, color of eyes, hair, complexion, and occupation), describing boat (a pine dugout), certifying to the strict loyalty and *good citizenship* of the owner, signed by general superintendent, and approved by general commanding. Is n't that red tape to perfection? They never went to Coffin's to take the boats, nor did they ever go there to get soldiers — strange, when it is thought by many that there is nearly a regiment on that plantation. Perhaps they feared *Coffin's Battery*.[1]

The next letter is from H. W., at the time of her return with C. P. W. to Port Royal.

FROM H. W.

Coffin's Point, Nov. 12. There had been so much delay and uncertainty over our arrival that Rose had

[1] See p. 187.

gone home, but Rodwell stopped to tell her we had come as he went down with the cart, and she exclaimed, "Pray day come for me go see Miss Hayiut." In the morning she came early into my chamber, bright and eager. I knew Robert was black as the ace of spades, but they both of them did look blacker than anything I ever saw before, but it was good to see them.

The next group of extracts is again occupied with the everyday events of plantation life.

FROM W. C. G.

Nov. 12. As usual I managed to miss the last mail. Now that the W.'s and their party have returned, perhaps we may be assisted into greater punctuality. Fortunately for us they live farther from the human race by two and a half miles than ourselves, and can't reach it without passing within half a mile of our house. Politeness usually obliges them to come up and take our budget. We live on our friends in a great many ways here. Without attempting any system or intending to set a wrong world right, we realize all the best fruits of socialistic communities. If any one has anything good, he is expected to enjoy only a small piece himself; and most things that are done have a reference to our united, not to any individual interest. Our own geographical location is such that we are peculiarly fitted to receive the benefit of this interchange of good offices, — while we can hardly reciprocate as we ought to.

FROM C. P. W.

Nov. 19. Alden and I were put on Plantation Commission work as soon as we got here, had a session

Wednesday and tried several cases. The untrustworthiness of these people is more apparent and troublesome than ever. I feel as if it would not be safe to allow them to gin the cotton — it seems certain that a great deal of it would be stolen. Their skill in lying, their great reticence, their habit of shielding one another (generally by silence), their invariable habit of taking a rod when you, after much persuasion, have been induced to grant an inch, their assumed innocence and ignorance of the simplest rules of *meum* and *tuum*, joined with amazing impudence in making claims, — these are the traits which try us continually in our dealings with them, and sometimes almost make us despair of their improvement — at least, in the present generation. It is certain that their freedom has been too easy for them, — they have not had a hard enough time of it. In many cases they have been "fair spoiled."

FROM H. W.

Nov. 27. Rose is a trump. She does all my cooking neater and better than I have ever had it done — makes bread and biscuit and puddings as well as I could myself, and until this morning, with our help, of course, has done the chamber-work too. With those three children I have got along as well as I could ask. I begin to appreciate what and how much they have learned the last two years.

[*Dec.* 11.] Over seventy children at Sunday School. I had a very nice time with them indeed, and was much struck with their progress in general intelligence. Their eager, intelligent faces and earnest attention and interest

in all I said to them were a great contrast to anything
they would have manifested two years ago. Indeed, I
could not have talked to them, and they would not have
understood me if I had, in anything like the same way
that I did to-day.

Nov. 23. We saw Mrs. Vaughn, who seems to find
life here very hard, and repeats the inevitable experience of all those who have ever had anything to do
with the blacks previously, that these are the most
degraded and barbarous of their race in the country.

We met C. Soule and Captain Crane,[1] with their two
servants, coming down to spend Thanksgiving. We had
a right pleasant evening. Captain Crane played and
sung, and we were very glad to hear the piano, and he
to touch one.

FROM W. C. G.

Nov. 27. On Thanksgiving Day we gathered together
all our friends, — all our "set," at least, — and sat
down, twenty-six of us, together, to eat turkeys and pies.
It was a rather formidable thing to attempt, with negro
servants and St. Helena supplies, but we had quite a
good time, and have done our duty in giving the party.
It is probably the last time that we'll all meet together.
Those who are to stay next year are all bemoaning their
fate; together we have had a very courteous and friendly
circle, — rather peculiarly so for such a rough kind of
life and surroundings, — and the loss of so many as
will go will probably rob the work here of much of its
pleasantness.

----

[1] Both in the Fifty-Fifth Massachusetts Volunteers (colored).

War, in the person of the triumphant Sherman, was again drawing near, and the two young officers of the Fifty-Fifth had barely celebrated Thanksgiving with the people from home when they were summoned to take their part.

Nov. 28. C. brought word that all the troops had been sent to Savannah to meet Sherman, and that citizens were on guard at Beaufort.

Dec. 1. To-night comes C. from Beaufort with news of the Grahamville fight.[1] It is said we have been twice repulsed, and the fight is not over.

Dec. 2. A cart came down from R.'s and brought a note from him to the effect that Captain Crane, who was with us such a short time ago, has been killed in the fight at Grahamville, but that C. Soule was unhurt.

Dec. 3. The rumors with regard to the expedition are various and contradictory, but the impression seems to be that we have been whipped, but hold on and have intrenched at Grahamville.   Mr. and Mrs. Soule are cheerful and brave, but very anxious, and it makes our hearts sink to hear the guns as we do. Pray God we may succeed this time and Sherman may come through. It will be such a day as has not been seen in this Department since Dupont took the place.

Dec. 4. We have repulsed the enemy since we intrenched, and deserters say Sherman is coming.

Dec. 6. Captain Crane found that his company was left behind at Morris Island, but begged so to go,

[1] The battle of Honey Hill (near Grahamville), fought November 30.

that Colonel Hartwell [1] took him on his staff, sending a Captain Gordon, who had just come from the North, to take charge of his company. Colonel Hartwell was wounded and Captain Crane killed in one of the first charges, in which our troops were repulsed, so that Captain Crane's body was left in the hands of the enemy. To-night we hear that ten thousand troops have come from Fortress Monroe to reinforce us, and deserters tell of Sherman's advance and successes. You may imagine we are all on the *qui vive*, and anxious, for we hear all the firing.

Dec. 11. Savannah is in Sherman's hands and Pocotaligo in Foster's. We hope and trust this is no South Carolina rumor.

Dec. 15. To-night Mr. Soule brings word that Sherman breakfasted with Foster yesterday morning, on a boat that came to Beaufort to-day.

Just after Christmas Mr. Philbrick went back to Port Royal to see to shipping his cotton.

FROM E. S. P.

Dec. 28. Arrived this evening. No fellow passengers that I knew. Most of them were Sherman's officers who had left him at Atlanta for various reasons and now come to join him. Very pleasant men, with a degree of hearty good sense and whole-souled patriotism that was truly refreshing.

[1] Of the Fifty-Fifth Massachusetts.

1865

The Georgia refugees — Sherman's army at Beaufort — Discontent of the negroes about wages — W. C. G.'s work at Savannah for the refugees — Return home of most of the letter-writers — The death of Lincoln, its effect on the negroes — End of the war and return of the planters — Stealing of cotton by the negroes — Superintendents "demoralized on the negro question."

FROM E. S. P.

Jan. 1. Yesterday morning I had a talk with Mr. H.[1] in the yard, where he is at work framing the school-house. I like him very much. He is a somewhat rare combination of a refined gentleman, without much education, but very well informed and wide awake, and a modest and quiet industry with the most practical common sense. He is truly interested in the negroes, without the least bit of sentimental or ill-advised sympathy. He is very glad to come here and take charge, and I think he is the best superintendent I have had here at all.

I saw some of the people who came about the house by chance during the day, and who seemed truly glad

[1] F. H. was to take charge of Coffin's Point on C. P. W.'s leaving permanently for home a few weeks later. In connection with Mr. Philbrick's words about him and in preparation for his own letters, it is worth while to record something he had written in the autumn:

Oct. 7. St. Helena. I am slowly recovering from my three weeks' sickness, — more buoyant and hopeful than ever before. I seem to have a new birth, with new aspirations, and new views — particularly in regard to life and its duties and prospects among the freed people of South Carolina.

If *God* is not in it, then I am laboring under hallucination.

to see me. They have got quite over the land-fever, and say they prefer to work along as they have, wherein they begin to show sense. Rose is still the only cook and does very well, except that she sometimes bakes potatoes longer than she boils hams, etc., etc. I suspect H. helps her put things together somewhat. The Christmas tree was to have been last evening, but the rain prevented. C. P. W. has gone up to bring down Mr. Eustis and his two ladies to dine. The house being an elastic one, I suppose it can be made to hold several more people than at present, if they will only bring their own blankets. The old diet of sweet potatoes and hominy, ham, fresh pork, and waffles, holds its sway yet, with grunnuts in the evening, of course.

FROM H. W.

Jan. 2. At sunset we all adjourned to the cotton-house, where the tree was all ready to be lighted. It was a very pretty sight, and after we had let the children in I sent word that the grown people might come and see, if they liked. Then, before anything was cut down, the children sang a number of the songs I have taught them, standing in classes, the smallest in front, their little eager faces irresistibly comic. The older people soon filled up the building, making rather a crowd, and a less manageable one than the children alone; but they were pleased at the sight, and when the noise became overpowering, I could stop it for the time being by starting a song, which the children would instantly catch up. Then I let the children sing some of their own songs in genuine, shouting style, a sight too funny in the little things, but sad and disagreeable

to me in the grown people, who make it a religious act.
It is impossible to describe it — the children move
round in a circle, backwards, or sideways, with their
feet and arms keeping energetic time, and their whole
bodies undergoing most extraordinary contortions,
while they sing at the top of their voices the refrain to
some song sung by an outsider. We laughed till we
almost cried over the little bits of ones, but when the
grown people wanted to "shout," I would not let them,
and the occasion closed by their "drawing" candy
from C. as they passed out. I daresay this sounds
pleasant, and I know they all had a good time; but if
you could have looked in, you would have thought it
Bedlam let loose!

The "Georgia refugees" referred to in several of the
subsequent letters were hundreds of negroes who had
followed Sherman's army northward. "They are said,"
says C. P, W., "to be an excellent set of people, more
intelligent than most here, and eager for work. They
will get distributed onto the plantations before a great
while."

Jan. 6. Miss Towne gave us quite an interesting
account of the Georgia refugees that have been sent
to the Village. The hardships they underwent to march
with the army are fearful, and the children often gave
out and were left by their mothers exhausted and dying
by the roadside and in the fields. Some even put their
children to death, they were such a drag upon them,
till our soldiers, becoming furious at their barbarous
cruelty, hung two women on the spot. In contrast to
such selfishness, she told us of one woman who had
twelve small children — she carried one and her hus-

band another, and for fear she should lose the others she tied them all together by the hands and brought them all off safely, a march of hundreds of miles. The men have all been put to work in the quartermaster's department or have gone into the army, and the families are being distributed where they can find places for them.

FROM E. S. P.

Jan. 8. Miss Towne told some amusing stories of the Georgia refugees. Some of them, being very destitute, were bemoaning their condition, and wishing they had never left their old plantations, feeling rather abashed at the responsibility of taking care of themselves. The old Edisto people, who have been there a year or two, encourage them, saying, "Look 'o we," "We come here wi' noffin at all," "Now we have money for cotton and all the tater and hominy we can eat," etc. One woman said, "Bress the Lord, I have striven and got enough to give *seven* gowns to these poor folk." So it seems they do what they can for the new-comers. I guess these Edisto people, who have their own recent destitution fresh in mind, are more kind than the natives of St. Helena, who are rather inclined to be jealous of the new-comers, who make the labor market rather easier than before.

Jan. 6. *Monday.* I had a talk with the people, who came up to see me in a crowd in the forenoon. They seemed jolly, and had no complaints to make about the past, but wanted higher wages for the future. I talked with them very quietly for an hour, told them I would give higher wages if I felt sure the price of cotton a year hence would pay me as well as the past crop,[1] and told them if they wanted to share this risk with me, I would give them a share of the cotton for their wages. They all objected to this except one or two of the men, who said they would like such an arrangement, but their *families* could n't wait so long for their money. On the whole they preferred wages, and therein showed their sense, I think. I find that when my last cargo arrived in the *Redwing*, the people who had worked for me had their pockets full of money and bought what they wanted, but the men who had been cultivating cotton on their own hook looked on with envious eyes and empty pockets, creating a very general impression in favor of the *wages system*. Under this impression, I think they will fall to work gradually at similar wages to what I have been paying, but will probably lie idle a few weeks to think about it, in hopes I will offer more.

Tuesday morning. I heard that the schooner was at Fuller Place to take our cotton. We have been at it ever since till yesterday noon, when we put in the last we had, nearly filling her up. There was about half of it negro cotton, brought from one hundred and seventy-six different proprietors, for whom I act as agent in forwarding and selling it. I drove over to spend the night at Mr. Wells' house on Wednesday. He had gone to Morgan Island to receive and stow away some one hundred and fifty Georgia refugees, which were

---

[1] The crop of 1864 had cost Mr. Philbrick about $1.00 a pound, and he thought it quite possible that the crop of 1865 might not fetch more than that in the market. It will be seen that his fears were more than justified.

expected by a steamer from Beaufort. After he had waited for them all day, they arrived about sunset, and he spent half the night there in the rain, stowing them in houses and getting their baggage up from the steamer, which lay at anchor in the river discharging into small boats. They came from the shore counties near to Savannah, and brought a good deal of truck, beds, and blankets, and some rice and peas. Mr. Wells gave them rations for a week, and I suppose will continue to do so, for they can't get anything to eat till next harvest in any other way. The able-bodied have all been taken either by the rebels or our Government for fatigue duty and quartermaster service, so those who come here are all women, children, or cripples, such as we had before. They will doubtless be so glad of a home, however, that they will do a good deal of work. Of course it is not an economical class of labor, for it takes too much land to feed the non-workers to allow a great deal to be planted in cotton. In the morning I walked out with Mr. Wells and sold him both the plantations of which he has had charge for me, viz., the Jenkins place, where he lives, for $1600 or $10 per acre, and Morgan Island for $1200, or about $5 per acre, which is more than any one would have given a few weeks ago, when we could n't get a negro to stay there for fear of the rebels. I daresay he may do very well with it now, but it is a vexatious thing to get rations to them in such an out-of-the-way place, and, after all, young Mr. Fripp may make them another visit some night and carry off some more negroes.

FROM C. P. W.

Jan. 8. Howard's [1] corps came to Beaufort early last week, and carpenters and engineers have been busy putting the Shell Road [2] to the Ferry in order and building a bridge across the Ferry. It looks as if a move were to be made towards Charleston or the interior soon. Beaufort presents a lively spectacle; the Western soldiers are rough, unkempt customers, whose hair, falling over their shoulders, suggests vows of abstinence from the shears till they shall have accomplished a great work. The first few days of their stay in Beaufort were marked by acts more amusing to the soldiers than to the owners of property "lying round loose." The first night was chilly, and three thousand feet of lumber furnished bonfires at which the soldiers of the "movable army" warmed themselves. Shopkeepers do a tremendous business, and their shops look "fair dry;" but they do not always get pay for their goods, but are requested to look on the battlefield for their money. The troops were paid off just before leaving Atlanta, and are "flush." Bread is very scarce. The troops fared very well on the march, — one continued Thanksgiving through the richest part of Georgia.

The schooner *Horace* for New York, with the rest of our cotton and the first of the negroes', is loaded. The negroes' crops did not turn out very well, as a general rule; want of manure and careless working being the principal causes; the caterpillar did a great

---

[1] General Oliver O. Howard.

[2] The only thoroughfare by land from Beaufort to Charleston. At Port Royal Ferry it crosses the Coosaw.

deal of damage.   They seem somewhat discouraged at the prospect of having to wait so long for their money; but the advance paid them on shipping the cotton (a dollar a pound of ginned cotton) will be a great help to those who have done well.

It is an excellent thing for the property here that Mr. H.[1] is here to keep it in repair.   He is a regular trump, the best man down here.   I feel more contented at leaving the place with him than with any one here.

If I could have a place down here all to myself, and have what help I wanted, I think I should stay another year and try the experiment on a little different plan. But, as Mr. Folsom said one day, when we agreed that it would be pleasant to stay and hard to leave, "But, after all, one must remember that one has an immortal soul."

FROM H. W.

Jan. 11.   Mr. Soule, coming from R.'s, tells us that a salute fired the day before was for Stanton's arrival, come to confer with Sherman.

The next paragraph suggests that the Secretary of War had come for something besides a conference with Sherman; at any rate, he took speedy action in one important direction.

FROM H. W.

Jan. 18.   We stopped at Miss Towne's new school-house to see them all in it, and found to our pleasure that General Howard was addressing the children. General Saxton, too, was there, in his new major-general's straps.   I was very glad to see General

[1] F. H.

Howard, who has superseded General Foster here. He has a very nice face indeed, and his one arm seemed to make quite an impression on the children. Stanton has been investigating the conscription business, and Foster's removal is the result, apparently, while Saxton has been promoted.

The next letters, Mr. Philbrick's last from Port Royal, contain various pieces of Sea Island news, chiefly in connection with his plans for the next year and his difficulties with his laborers.

FROM E. S. P.

Jan. 9. I started for Coffin's Point, meeting a long procession of the people on the way to church. More than half the number were in sulkies or some sort of go-carts, with all sorts of animals pulling them, mostly quadrupeds that had once been horses, — and some might still bear that name. I had to stop and shake hands every few rods, of course. I have spent most of the day at Fripp Point, with Mr. York. Mr. G. had not been able to collect the rent of corn-land there, to be paid in corn, most of the men refusing to pay. He had withheld enough from their pay to cover the amount of corn due. I took over the money due, with the pay-roll and corn-list. After a long talk on the part of Pompey and John Major and others, which I listened to patiently, most of them still refused to bring their corn. But I felt pretty sure that when some began they would all do it, and so opened the door of the corn-house and told the willing ones to bring in their corn. Jack came first, then Katy, Louisa, and Moll. Pretty soon John Major came along with a cart-load,

and all the rest followed but Pompey. Then I began
to pay off the women for ginning and preparing their
cotton. All went smoothly except that Celia wanted
her "yellow-cotton-money" [1] "by himself," and as I
could n't tell exactly how much the "yellow-cotton-
money" was, I had to take her money all back and tell
her to go over and see Mr. G. After paying the others,
however, Celia came up and concluded to take her
dues. They all took their money excepting Pompey,
who stoutly refused, and I came off without paying
him. Then came the talk about next year. I introduced
Mr. York as having leased the plantation for the year,
which fact was received with less dissatisfaction than I
expected; but when it came to talk about prices, which
I left for Mr. York to settle, they all demanded *a dollar
a task*, evidently having been preparing their minds for
this for some time back. Then followed the usual
amount of reasoning on my part, enlarging upon the
future uncertainty of prices of cotton, etc., but we made
little or no impression on them. They had evidently
been listening to an amount of talk about the wealth
I had acquired at their expense, and felt aggrieved
that they were not making money as fast as those who
planted their own cotton, on Frogmore and other
places. I told them that the proceeds of last year's
crop had all been expended by me in carrying on this
year's work, but they would n't believe it. John Major
said he knew very well they had been jamming the
bills into that big iron cage (meaning my safe at R.'s)
for six months, and there must be enough in it now to

[1] "Yellow cotton" was cotton which for any reason had been
stained in the pod.

bust it! It had been raining for the last half-hour pretty steadily, and we finally withdrew, the choir of hands hanging about me, singing out "A dollar a task!" "A dollar a task!" as we went off.

Jan. 15. I went out and introduced Mr. Jackson on Tuesday morning to the Pine Grove people, who expressed very little surprise or feeling of any kind, but met him with the same cry which had greeted me and Mr. York at the Point about *a dollar a task.* I left him with them and rode over to Cherry Hill with old Mr. Waters. The Cherry Hill people received us very well. Tony had a long list of grievances to relate, for Mr. Folsom had had him in jail for a fortnight for refusing to bring out his cotton, raised for me, which he kept in his own house. I listened quietly, and then told Tony I could n't go behind the decision of the court, but if he had any other matters in dispute with Mr. Folsom he had better come up to the house in the evening and we would talk them over together; but he never came, probably from a sense of guilty conscience.

Primus and Mike and several other negroes were there [in Beaufort], buying horses from officers and men in Sherman's army, titles very uncertain, for they mostly belong to the quartermaster. I advised them not to buy a horse till the ownership was certified by an officer, but they were too much in a hurry for that and hooked on to the first quadruped they could find offered for sale. The fact is that thousands of horses are attached to this army which are picked up by the privates in their march through Georgia, and which these privates pretend to own, and sell without authority, pocketing their money as fast as they please.

Some of them are very good horses, and some are not.
The town was crowded with the army, on a general
leave to ramble about, and new troops continually
arrive. One entire corps marched over Port Royal
Ferry yesterday, and two more army corps are said
to be following. Some twenty steamers arrive daily at
Beaufort direct from Savannah, bringing the troops and
wagons, artillery and animals. So you can imagine what
a confusion appears in the streets as they disembark
and march out to camp. The greater part of the whole
army seems to be coming around this way and marching
over the Ferry towards Pocotaligo. Secretary Stanton
is said to have arrived from Savannah at Beaufort last
evening. It seems that Primus and the other negroes
were about to get their new horses over the Ferry, when
the provost marshal sent down a guard to seize men and
animals, and marched them all off to the guard-house
for the night. The horses will probably be taken away
from them and the men allowed to pursue their way
this morning, with more sense and less money than they
came with. I don't pity them much, for they were fairly
warned, and their eagerness to own horses, for which
they pay from $200 to $300 each, is perfectly absurd.[1]

[1] Concerning this horse-buying fever Mr. Philbrick has elsewhere
an amusing anecdote:

[Jan. 8.] The latest case of destitution I have heard of was the case
of old Robert at the Oaks, cow-minder, — you remember him. He
and old Scylla applied to Mr. Tomlinson for rations, pleading utter
poverty. It turned out next day that Robert and Scylla's husband
were in treaty for Mr. Fairfield's horse, at the rate of $350! They
did n't allege *inability* to pay the price, but thought they would look
around and see if they could n't get one cheaper. I daresay it will
end by their buying it.

Later. An interesting scene has just taken place. May's Comba knocked at the door and asked me to come out in the entry a minute. Thinking there might be some domestic trouble, though she looked smiling, I went out and found about twenty women (representative women) about the door. Comba disappeared in the mass with a giggle, and old Grace spoke up, about as follows: "I 'se come to you, sir " — pause — " I 'se been working fer owner three years, and made with my chillun two bales cotton last year, two more this year. I 'se a flat-footed pusson and don't know much, but I knows those two bales cotton fetch 'nough money, and I don't see what I 'se got for 'em. When I take my leetle bit money and go to store, buy cloth, find it so dear, dear Jesus! — the money all gone and leave chillun naked. Some people go out yonder and plant cotton for theyself. Now they get big pile of money for they cotton, and leave we people 'way back. That 's what I 'se lookin' on, Marsa. Then when I come here for buy 'lasses, when Massa Charlie sell he sell good 'lasses, then when Mister W. sell he stick *water* in 'em, *water enough.* Molasses turn thin, but he charge big price for 'cm. Now I 'se done working for such 'greement. I 'se done, sir." Whereupon chorus of women join in like a flock of blackbirds all talking at once. After a while I got a chance to say about as follows: "If any one wants to work on this plantation I will give them so and so (naming terms), but if any one don't like my wages, they may go and find better, but they can't use my land to plant their corn and 'tater on. That 's my rule." Chorus interrupts with discordant shouts: "I stay right here, sir — I will work this land

for myself, sir — I will sell the cotton," etc., etc.
Amaritta and Petra stood silent all this time, and finally
Amaritta quietly asked me to repeat my terms, which I
did. She repeated them after me word for word, but
said nothing more, only nodded and grunted a sort of
assent. The chorus became wilder and more noisy, and
I walked off into the house. Presently Demus came
to the door and said Amaritta wanted to see me by
heself. So I went to the door, and Amaritta called Tilly,
Petra, and one or two others. Thus said Amaritta:
"I 'se work for you dis lass year, sir, what I was able.
I been sick, you know, wi' small-pox and did n't get
much strength all summer, but I don't mind much
what them people say, sir, they 'se got no manners.
Now you say you 'll give so and so (carefully repeating
my terms). Well, sir, I 'se come to say I 'se 'gree for
work. I 'speck to work, sir. I want to lay my bones in
dat air bush (pointing to cemetery), and don't want
to go nowhar else ; that 's what I wanted to say, sir."
Then the other two or three women chimed in with
smiling faces and said the same in fewer words, and
so I bid them good-morning. I told them, too, that if
some of those people who made so much noise did n't
look out, they would get turned off the place, just as
Venus and her gang got turned off last year. The fact
is, they are trying to play brag, as such people often
will ; but they will all go to work in a few days, I feel
sure.

Jan. 17. Mr. Folsom went over to Port Royal Island
with Mr. G. on Sunday, taking their own horses, and
rode over Sherman's pontoons at Port Royal Ferry,
without a challenge, and then up the mainland as far

as Pocotaligo Bridge, around which the 17th Army Corps is encamped, in full possession of the railroad. Mr. G. called here an hour ago on his way back, and told some of his experiences. He says they were taken for "Secesh" by our own troops, all the way, just as we all are in Beaufort, for the officers themselves seem to be hardly aware that we are all Yankees, taking us for the old residents of the island, made loyal by our experiences.

Every one wonders what brought Secretary Stanton here. He seems to have done something, at any rate, viz., hauled General Foster over the coals severely for his negro conscription last summer, promoted General Saxton to a brevet major-general, with enlarged powers; and, report says, put General Howard in place of General Foster. The newspapers will tell you all I know, and more, too, without doubt. Mr. Tomlinson, who was about disgusted with things here as he found them when he came back from the North, and had concluded to go to Philadelphia to take some position offered him there by the Philadelphia committee, now thinks he will remain here, — for which I am very glad. Very few men could be so useful as he in this place; for though he has a weak spot on the question of negro character, he has a vast deal of good sense in detail, and is perfectly unimpeachable in his stern regard for justice, never allowing himself to be *used* in any way for the furthering of the designs of interested parties. No one who has not spent some time under martial law knows how hard it is and how *rare* for men in office to follow such a course, unswerved by either flattery or ambition.

Jan. 22. General Saxton came over to the St. Helena church last Sunday, and set all the Edisto people into a stew by telling how he was going to send the black troops there to defend the islands, and how they might all go back to their "old homes," etc., forgetting that they were not natives of Edisto, but only refugees when there, and that they were now more comfortably settled here than they were there in 1862. The Georgia refugees are coming along by hundreds and thousands, and he "wanted to make room for them," etc. Of course the Edisto people all say the General has ordered them to pack up and he will carry them back, etc. So, many refuse to work, but pack up and sit still, waiting for the General to come along and tote them across the sound! The Georgia negroes are a superior-looking set to those of these islands. Many are taken in outbuildings, etc., and have given a good start to labor by giving the impression that if the old residents don't work, *somebody else will.* They have gone to work for Mr. York at Fripp Point, and here for Mr. H., and all along the road generally. George Wells has got over a hundred Georgians on Morgan Island doing well, and I guess the rebs won't trouble him, they are too busy.

Mr. Tomlinson is to take the place on General Saxton's staff formerly held by Captain Hooper, but without military rank. C. F. Williams is to take Mr. Tomlinson's place here.

We hear by your letter the list of the passengers lost on the *Melville.* All our worst fears are confirmed, and you were right in supposing that it was our acquaintances who were lost. This miserable steamer I once talked of coming on, by her previous trip, but gave it up when I found her character.

FROM W. C. G.

Jan. 23. I think I suggested in a previous letter the possibility of my staying here. Sherman's operations have opened a wider sphere for negro work and thrown a great number of refugees into our hands. And his approaching campaign will have a similar effect. General Saxton has been appointed "Inspector General," with control of all negro affairs from Key West to Charleston and thirty miles inland. The first thing proposed is to recolonize Edisto and the other deserted Sea Islands with the refugees, and men are wanted to assist in their settlement. I have been offered a situation of this kind, or rather the General has simply asked a few of us to stay, and Mr. Tomlinson, Folsom, and myself will all remain for the present at least. I know nothing more than this, but I look forward to a rough life, something like our first year here. I shall probably go to Edisto in a day or two. There will be no danger from attack, etc., as a regiment is to be stationed there. The island is described by all as the finest and healthiest of all the Sea Islands.

If there is any movement afoot in Boston for the assistance of the negro refugees that Sherman's operations throw into our hands, it can be of the greatest benefit. The efforts three years ago were made chiefly for persons left in their own homes, and with their own clothing and property, besides their share of the plunder from their masters' houses. And in many cases too much was given. But now hundreds and thousands

are coming in, shivering, hungry, so lean and bony
and sickly that one wonders to what race they belong.
Old men of seventy and children of seven years have
kept pace with Sherman's advance, some of them for
two months and over, from the interior of Georgia;
of course little or nothing could be brought but the
clothing on their backs and the young children in arms.
Since their arrival in comparatively comfortable quarters, great sickness has prevailed, and numbers and
numbers have died. The Government gives them
rations, and has tried to give out clothing. But if
clothes, cooking utensils, etc., can be sent by Northern
friends, nowhere can generosity be better extended.

Savannah, Feb. 16. As you see, my destination has
been changed. General Saxton needed a kind of colonization office here, and I am sent as an assistant. How
long this will continue my headquarters I don't know.
I am writing in a very large and fine house formerly
occupied by Habersham, rebel. It is full of fine furniture. Our office, too, is one of the City Bank buildings.
The prices are regal, too — $15 per week for board, *e. g.*

Mar. 7. The work at the office continues the same
in kind, and the stream of waiters increases. We hope
to send quite a company off to some of the more distant
islands before long, but are terribly embarrassed for
want of transportation. First, no steamer! then no
coal! And when one can be had, the other can't. General Saxton is still, as ever previously, left to get round
on one leg. His work is of course always inferior in
importance to the needs of the military service, so there
is never an absence of reason for refusing him what he
wants. "Bricks! — without straw," has so far been

the usual fortune.   Soon a gentleman is going out towards the Ogeechee to report numbers and condition there.   It seems to be a Central Asia, from the population that swarms in for rations.   Compared with those who apply, few are allowed them.   No one who can show a finger to pick with and reports an oyster to pick, is allowed to come on the Government for support.

Here follows the last letter from G., written three months later, not long before he came away.

FROM W. C. G.

Savannah, June 9.   Our business has slacked greatly, and is now mainly kept up by recent refugees from the up-country.   We have stopped more than half the rations, and almost every family within a dozen miles has been represented at the office and been furnished with the proper papers.   But slavery still exists in the interior and is spending its last moments in the old abominations of whipping and punishing.   Of course it is nearly dead, — the people know they are free and the masters have to own it, — but the ruling passion is strong in death.

W. C. G. left the South in June; H. W. and C. P. W. had gone several months before him.   The letters written at intervals during the next two years are mostly addressed to the latter by F. H. and T. E. R.   They report the gradually changing conditions and increasing difficulties of plantation superintendence.

R. SOULE, JR., TO C. P. W.

Coffin's Point, April 29.   Mr. H. is getting on pretty smoothly, though he has occasionally to take a dose of what Mr. York calls "Plantation Bitters," in the shape of complaints, faithlessness, and general rascality on the part of the "poor negroes."

E. S. P. TO W. C. G. (IN SAVANNAH)

Boston, May 1. You will see by the papers all about the fall in prices. The Liverpool cotton men had lost twelve millions sterling upon the depreciation of their cotton in store before they heard of the fall of Richmond and Lee's surrender. There is a terrible panic there, and some of the best firms are failing. After things have come to an equilibrium, and the manufacturers begin to buy cotton for spinning, there will be a demand for ours, but it may take several months, for they have n't got to the bottom of the trouble yet.

The affairs at St. Helena seem to be progressing quietly. The chances are that all the cotton we raise this year will cost nearly if not quite as much as we shall get for it. I advanced a dollar a pound on the negroes' cotton, you know, and it has cost me about twenty-five cents a pound more to gin it, etc., etc., while I am offered less than a dollar. Query: how much commission shall I get for doing the business?

T. E. R. TO C. P. W.

St. Helena, May 6. The Coffin's Pointites had a gay old blow-out over at church, owing to Mr. Williams' telling them that they must pay Mr. Philbrick for pasturing their horses. They called Mr. P. a thief, robber, liar, and everything else that was bad.

The death of Lincoln was an awful blow to the negroes here. One would say, "Uncle Sam is dead,

is n't he?" Another, "The Government is dead, is n't
it? You have got to go North and Secesh come back,
have n't you? We going to be slaves again?" They
could not comprehend the matter at all — how Lincoln
could die and the Government still live. It made them
very quiet for a few days.

Secesh are coming back quite freely nowadays and
looking about as much as they please: Old Ben and
young Ben Chaplin, several of the Pritchards, and Captain Williams, that owned a plantation on Ladies Island.

The negroes begin to clamor about the final payment
for their cotton, and we have to tell them that the
probabilities are that there will not be any more. Then
they think we have cheated them, and so the world goes
in South Carolina. Rather a thankless task.

F. H. TO C. P. W.

Coffin's, May 21. The honesty of this people and
their disinterested benevolence are as apparent as ever.
Please don't exaggerate these valuable qualities, either
in the papers, to the Educational Commission, or in
your private conversation; because it is better that
those who are interested in the welfare of these people
should not be deceived into the notion that they are so
nearly perfect as to need no further expenditure of
benevolent effort. Of course, we know the great danger
of your wreathing your account of them in roses and
laurel. One's enthusiasm is so excited in their behalf
by a few years' residence here, that his veracity is in
great danger of being swamped in his ideality, and
his judgment lost in his admiration. So pardon my
warning to you.

The McTureous lands have recently been sold, and about every family upon this place has got its five or ten acres. I tell them they had better move or build houses upon their lots and be independent of "we, us, and co." But the idea seems to meet with little favor. A good many of them are expecting these lands to be offered to them the coming year, now that the war is about over, Dr. Brisbane, General Saxton, and others assuring them that such was Mr. Philbrick's promise when he bought them. I think there would be some important advantages to white proprietors as well as black laborers, if they had some ten acres of land of their own, — at least enough to raise their own provisions upon, and to keep their own hogs and horses upon. Such an arrangement would rid us of many annoyances, and help define the rights of each party.

" G 's article," referred to in the next letter, was entitled " The Freedmen at Port Royal," and appeared in the *North American Review* for July, 1865.

R. SOULE, JR., TO C. P. W.

Coffin's Point, Sept. 10. G.'s article is well written and interesting. He was evidently disposed to report as favorably as possible for the negroes, while at the same time he seems to have suspected that the reader would be a good deal impressed by the darker shades of his sketch, and the conclusion of the whole is: There is ground for hope, but the case is a pretty desperate one. A conclusion to which, I confess, my own observation and studies lead me, whichever way I turn.

The furor among the negroes here just now is to have

a Union Store, and they are contributing their funds for this purpose. They propose to put up a building for the store near Smallwood's Bakery (at the corner where village road branches from main road), and to make Mr. Smallwood President of their Corporation! This project will probably have one good effect in the end, namely, to open their eyes to see some things which nobody can make them see now.

F. H. TO C. P. W.

Coffin's Point, Sept. 18. Cotton is opening well now, but we have rather unfavorable weather for picking and drying. The caterpillars have finally run over a good deal of ground, doing some damage, hard to tell how much.

R. thinks he don't care to try the experiment of cotton-raising again — the risks and vexations are so great. I find that feeling quite general here this year among planters. William Alden says it is his last year. I doubt whether he pays expenses this season. His cotton is late, and now the caterpillars are destroying it.

F. H. TO C. P. W.

Sept. 24. Much of my time has been occupied of late in service on Plantation Commission. The most important case is still on trial, — that of the stealing of twelve hundred pounds of seed cotton from Mr. De Golyer. There is a "cloud of witnesses" — a very dark one — and it is hard, as yet, to discern in it any glimmering of truth.

T. E. R. TO C. P. W.

St. Helena Island, Sept. 25. With the dry weather
of July and the wet weather now, with the worm, we
shall lose a third sure of our crop, if not more.

The negroes on the island are very quiet — all
absorbed in a scheme of establishing a "St. Helena
Protective Union Store," J. Smallwood, President.
They have got the frame out and on the ground. I
have a great deal of curiosity to see the working of the
thing, for they never did succeed in the North among
intelligent white people. If they can read and write, or
*keep a Union Store, I think they ought to have the right
of suffrage.*

Nearly all the Secesh are back in Beaufort, confidently
expecting that they will get their land back in season
to plant next year.

All the Georgians will go back this fall, but all the
people Fuller [1] *took* with him (excuse me, I should say
went with him) will return here in a few weeks. Fuller
has n't any cotton this year, only corn and potatoes.
When he returned from here he told them the people
down here were very poor and in miserable condition;
nevertheless, they seem willing to come down and
share the misery of freedom to staying up there with
Fuller in comfort. At the time he was here, 17th of June,
he never had said a word to the people with him that
they were free, and did not until they made a plan
among themselves to go up to him in a body and make

---

[1] Fuller, of Fuller Place, who had succeeded in keeping with him
on a plantation elsewhere the negroes he had induced to accompany
him when the war broke out.

him tell them. Then Fuller took the old driver one side and told him he wanted him and all the people to stay with him and plant another year, and wanted him to use his influence to persuade the people to stay. So next morning he called them all up and had them stand on his right hand, and as he called their names he wanted those who were willing to stay with him another year to step over to his left hand. So he commenced with Old Gib, the driver (January's father). He turned right round and walked towards the negro quarters. Fuller says, "Why, Gib, you will stay, won't you?" "No, Sir." Then he went through the whole list, and every one marched straight home and none to his left hand, much to his disgust.

The next extract reports E. S. P.'s final decision as to the price for which he should offer land to the negroes.

E. S. P. TO W. C. G.[1]

Boston, Oct. 5. C. F. Williams has gone down to finish surveying my land, and will cut up and sell for me to the negroes about as much land as they have been in the habit of using, — good, arable land, at $5 per acre, where they are not already provided.

R. S., JR., TO C. P. W.

Coffin's Point, Oct. 9. I have no reason to complain of my people for any extraordinary delinquencies, for they have worked as well as we shall probably ever be able to get these negroes to work; but I have frequently had occasion to be vexed at their slow, shiftless habits and at their general stupidity. It is a very great trial

[1] In Europe.

to any Northern man to have to deal with such a set of people, and I am satisfied that if Northerners emigrate to the South and undertake agriculture or anything else here, they will be compelled to import white laborers. In the first place, they will not have the patience to get along with the negroes, even if there were enough of these freedmen to do all the work. But, in the second place, there will not be one quarter enough of them to supply the demand there will be for laborers when the uncleared land at the South is brought under cultivation. The old slaveholders could never get hands enough, and yet they cultivated only about one tenth of the land that is fit for cotton.

It need hardly be said that this prophecy has not yet been fulfilled.

E. S. P. TO W. C. G.

Boston, Oct. 15. I have had a letter from Charleston written by a lawyer on behalf of Captain John Fripp and his three daughters! The writer says but little about his legal rights, but appeals to my "sense of justice and generosity," to see if some compromise can't be made. He does n't say exactly what he wants, but intimates that both parties could profit by such an arrangement and save the vexations of a law suit. I don't see exactly what he has got to give, except his old title, which he probably values a good deal higher than I do. I wrote him telling him I was hampered in acts of "generosity" by the fact that the present title was not in me alone, but that about a dozen other gentlemen were interested, and asked him to make us a definite proposition. You may see by the papers that General

Howard is sent by the President to see if he can recon-
cile the claims of the negroes on Edisto and other islands
with those of the former owners who clamor to be rein-
stated in their position. I guess General Howard will
have a tough job. I don't envy him.

Nov. 21. There is a large number of old planters
who are offering their lands at very low rates, and so
many tempting chances are offered to Northern men.
The tide of emigration southward does n't yet set very
strong, however. I think the great drawback is the
feeling that the South is still intolerant of Yankees.
The rabble and the young men are still clinging to the
hope that they are going to have their own way about
managing the nigger, somehow or other, as soon as
they get rid of the United States forces, and they know
very well that Yankees who come among them will not
agree with them about the best way of "making him
work," for they won't believe that he will ever work
till he is *made* to. Now, to tell the truth, I don't believe
myself that the present generation of negroes will work
as they were formerly obliged to, and therefore the race
will not produce so much cotton in this generation as
they did five years ago. The change is too great a one
to be made in a day. It will take many years to make
an economical and thrifty man out of a freedman, and
about as long to make a sensible and just employer out
of a former slaveholder. It is not at all likely that the
Southern community will tax itself to educate the negro
yet for a good while, and I have my doubts whether the
system of education thus far carried on through the
benevolence of Northern and English communities can
be kept up much longer. It is a laudable and a noble

work, but I fear it can't be sustained after the novelty is over. There seems to be a lethargy creeping over our community on this subject, which is very hard to shake off. The feeling is somewhat general that the negro must make the most of his chances and pick up his a, b, c's as he can. Moreover, there is a mass of ignorance in the South under *white* skins, which is likely to give us more immediate trouble, politically, than the ignorance of the negro, for that latter is not as yet armed with the suffrage. Of course there is not much enthusiasm about sending teachers South to teach the poor whites, so the negro suffers from the magnitude of the undertaking, from his remoteness from view, and the general disposition among mankind to let everybody hoe their own weeds so long as they don't shade one's own garden.

I hear that General Howard went to Edisto with the view of reconciling the squatter negroes with the claims of the former owners, as requested by the President, but that the task was rather difficult, as you may imagine; and though the former owners had promised to "absorb" the labor, and provide for the negroes' wants, etc., they found the negroes had ideas which they were not quite prepared for, and, in short, got so disgusted with the prospect of getting the said negroes to work for them under the new order of things that they did not seem so anxious to "absorb" them as before, and as General Howard did not feel like driving off the negroes to put the old owners in possession, he left things pretty much as he found them,[1] except that the old owners, who went there confidently expecting to have

[1] By President Johnson's instructions.

all their own way, went off with a flea in the ear. I have nothing more from the Charleston lawyer, but Mr. Tomlinson reports that Charleston lawyers told him they did n't see how to get around our tax-titles, though they would doubtless carry them into court as soon as they have courts, and give the lawyers plenty of work.[1]

Dr. Clarence Fripp began to practice medicine on St. Helena, living with John Major, but afterwards got a contract surgeon's berth from General Saxton, and is now in the Village, next door to his old house, now occupied by Miss Towne! He made a professional visit at Coffin's Point and dined with them!

A picture of Clarence Fripp on his return to St. Helena, and a glimpse of his situation from his own point of view, are given in a letter to the New York *Nation* from Dennett, a special correspondent (see page 320). Dennett writes that, among the Northern soldiers and traders in the hotel at Hilton Head, there was also "a person who had the easily distinguishable appearance and manners of a South Carolinian. This gentleman, a person of some fifty odd years old, dressed tolerably well in a suit of grey clothes, with a large display of crumpled linen at the collar and cuffs of his coat, sat before the stove smoking, and talking very freely about his present poverty and his plans for the future." After explaining that he had left St. Helena when Dupont forced an entrance, leaving his plate and furniture behind, and that his plantation had been sold, Dr. Fripp set forth the situation in which he now found himself. "Some Massachusetts man had bought it,

---

[1] The original owners of the Sea Island plantations were subsequently reimbursed by Congress for their loss (minors receiving again their actual land); but inasmuch as the sums paid them did not include the value of their slaves, they considered the payment inadequate.

and he did n't know when he 'd get it back. . . . Up in
Greenville he soon spent all his money to support his
family, but if he 'd had money he could n't have saved
his property. How was he to come back inside the
Yankee lines and pay the tax? The Commissioners
knew very well it could n't be done; the sale was a perfectly unfair thing." In coming back now to Beaufort,
he said "he hoped to be able to pick up a little medical
practice; but if his profession failed him, he supposed
his son and himself could put up a cabin somewhere in
the vicinity, and get fish and oysters enough to live on."
He even talked of circulating a handbill at Greenville
asking for money for his needs, and Dennett adds:
"This gentleman, it is currently reported, has made
several visits to the plantation which he formerly
owned, and the negroes living there have collected for
his use nearly a hundred dollars." [1]

T. E. R. TO C. P. W.

St. Helena, Dec. 10. Your letter has been a reminder
of my duty, but cotton ginning is my only excuse. It
has proved much more of a bore this year than usual,
for it is nothing but *tief, tief,* all the time. We do not
get more than one fifth [2] of the weight of seed cotton
after it is ginned, and the probabilities are that they
steal the balance; but we are perfectly helpless, for we
cannot prove it against any of them. I have had about
a bale of cotton stolen at the "Oaks" since I put it in
the cotton-house. I can assure you there is nothing to
be made this year.

We had a call from Dennett (correspondent of

---

[1] New York *Nation*, November 30, 1865.

[2] The cotton when ginned should have weighed between one
third and one quarter as much as it weighed before ginning. See
p. 236.

Nation) on his Southern tour, a few weeks ago. He said he was disappointed in not getting better reports of the negroes here on these islands, for he had been looking forward to this place, feeling sure he should find something good to offset the many evil reports he had heard of them all the way down through the country.   He thinks Mr. Soule and Mr. H. very much demoralized on the negro question.[1]

General Gillmore was removed for being unfriendly to Freedmen's Bureau, and General Sickles is now in command. He told Saxton [2] to let him know what was wanted and he should have it, so things are moving on very smoothly now.   Tomlinson [3] has been on a trip through South Carolina to see what the condition of the people was and at what points he could establish schools. They have them started in nearly all the principal points.   He says the whites do not know that they have been whipped yet, and many of the negroes don't know they are free.

Mrs. Bryant has opened a pay school [at T. B. Fripp's], older scholars paying one dollar per month and young ones fifty cents. She has about sixty scholars.   Alden has opened a store on the place.

[1] In one of his letters to the *Nation* (December 14), Dennett quotes Richard Soule as saying that he thought the past four years had encouraged and confirmed the faults of the negro. "Demoralized on the negro question," therefore, seems to mean, not that Richard Soule and F. H. were finding the negro worse than they had thought him, but that they considered that present conditions were rapidly making him worse.

[2] General Saxton was Assistant Commissioner for South Carolina under the Freedmen's Bureau.

[3] Reuben Tomlinson had been made State Superintendent of Education.

The negroes' Union Store is raised and covered, but I guess will never be stocked.[1]

R. S., JR., TO C. P. W.

Coffin's Point, Dec. 17. I suppose you have heard that our plantation operations here this year have been a failure. Nobody has raised more than half a crop. The drought in the early part of the summer and the caterpillar in August and September contrived to diminish the yield. Most of the planters, however, thinking that two bad seasons will not come in succession, are making vigorous preparations for next year in the way of gathering marsh-grass and mud. I have about concluded to sell or to lease Mulberry Hill, and if I succeed in doing either I shall probably go home about the first of February.

There is a universal feeling of dissatisfaction, not to say disgust, with our colored brethren here at the present time, on account of the extraordinary development of some of their well-known characteristics. They are stealing cotton at a fearful rate. Captain Kellum of Dathaw lost a whole bale a few nights since, and to-day Mr. Williams, who has just come down from R.'s, tells us that the cotton-house has been broken into and one packed bale cut open and about one hundred pounds taken out of it and carried off! This bale belonged to Mr. York. We none of us feel secure against these depredations.

---

[1] The Union Store was finished, stocked, and operated, but its life was brief. From the first, its vitality was sapped by the claim of the stockholders to unlimited credit; then a dishonest treasurer struck the death-blow.

Two of the thieves at Coffin's Point were caught with ginned cotton in their houses, Peter Brown and William White. Before Mr. Towne could apprehend them they escaped to the main. Another, Jonas Green, had cotton-seed hid away in his corn-house. He was caught, and a Plantation Commission sentenced him to two months' imprisonment. This is the first fruit of making land-owners of the negroes. While they raise cotton of their own and no restraint is put upon them in making sale of what they bring to market, it is impossible to ferret out their robberies in most cases. Such rascality on the part of the negroes is more discouraging than caterpillars and drought.

F. H. TO C. P. W.

Coffin's, Dec. 26. I expect my sojourn at Coffin's Point is nearly closed. The attractions of the place or the people are not sufficient to keep me here another year. The climate is bad enough, the general "shiftlessness" of the people is disgusting enough; but when I see that the disposition to steal the crop is very general, that the people have done and can do it with impunity, I am discouraged about cotton-raising here. I believe they have not taken any of ours since it has been packed, but large quantities of it before. And as they all raised cotton on McTureous [1] for themselves, they could mix and secrete it very successfully.

Mr. Soule has this moment learned that his cotton-house has been entered and cotton stolen, but to what extent has not been determined.

I think Mr. Soule will be glad to get away from this

[1] See p. 312.

"Sodom." He is too good a man to be worn out by the barbarians of this latitude.

R. S., JR., TO C. P. W.

Coffin's Point, Dec. 31. How well Grant appears in everything he writes as well as in everything he does! In the *Weekly Advertiser* just received by me, I find his report of his recent Southern tour,[1] and, if I mistake not, he intimates pretty clearly that General Saxton has not managed his Department judiciously.

Mr. Philbrick has made an effort to sell the most of the plantations. As yet, however, no purchaser has appeared, and he has now about concluded to dispose of them as follows: to lease Fuller Place to N., R., and W. (the new firm who have purchased the stock on hand in store), and Cherry Hill[2] to Mr. Waters, to intrust the management of Homestead to the latter gentleman, and that of Coffin's Point to Mr. H. for account of E. S. P., and to let Mr. Williams sell the whole of Corner[3] and Fripp Point to negroes. I have leased Mulberry Hill to Mr. Waters.

Negroes continue to steal cotton, and we continue to be helpless against their depredations.

[1] This was Grant's famous "car-window" report, in which he stated his belief that "the mass of thinking men at the South accept the situation in good faith."

[2] Mr. Waters bought Cherry Hill and lived there for a short time.

[3] "Corner" was the Captain John Fripp place.

Mr. Philbrick's sales to the negroes — Persistent discouragement with the negroes — H.W.'s visit to Coffin's Point in 1868 — Tribute of the negroes to Mr. Philbrick.

E. S. P. TO W. C. G. [IN EUROPE]

Boston, Jan. 12, 1866. The Freedmen's Aid Societies have all consolidated, and lately have united with the big Orthodox society for helping refugees, the latter class being no longer so needy except that the poor whites need education as much as the blacks, and I have made up my mind that we can't help the blacks much except by helping poor whites at the same time. The combination enlarges the begging field immensely, and by putting white and black schools under the same control will give negro schools a sort of footing which they would n't otherwise have, after our troops get scarce. The old feeling has already blossomed out and borne fruit in Louisiana, where all the freedmen's schools have just been extinguished or snuffed out at a single pinch, except in New Orleans city, one lady teacher being shot through the head.

A sweeping order has mustered out over a hundred generals of the Volunteer Army, General Saxton among the rest. I don't know who takes his place in the Freedmen's Bureau. This institution will probably be continued by Congress with enlarged powers, but it is but a drop in the bucket, after all.

C. F. Williams is busy sharing out land. He sells the

whole of Fripp Point in small lots to the negroes of both
places, and some others from outside. The whole place
measures only four hundred and sixty acres, bought
for seven hundred and fifty, and the Captain John
Fripp place is only four hundred and sixty instead of
one thousand for which I bought it! By the way, the
old man is dead, leaving his three daughters in poverty,
to earn their living as they best may. Julian Coffin has
visited Mr. Soule, etc., asking leave to go into his old
room, to take some of his father's old books, and left
after a few hours, since which none of us have heard
anything further of them.

There seems to be less law than ever there. I am
about making representations at Washington to see if
I can't get some improvement.

I lost about $2800 on the negro cotton ginned in
New York, and paid over about $2500 on account of
the cotton which they ginned there! I also lost some
$2000 on cotton taken from Mr. —— in Beaufort, he
turning out a knave. Our crop of 1864 paid our Company a profit of about $19,000. I shall just about pay
expenses on the crop of 1865, not much more, I think.
The caterpillar and the drought did n't leave much
cotton.

T. E. R. TO C. P. W.

Feb. 3, 1866. I am a *gentleman of leisure* and, like
most every one else here, am living on the interest of
what I have lost. I am no longer a member of the noted
firm of N., R., and W. We dissolved January 1, and
N. and W. continue the business at the old stand. I
decided that there was not salt enough for three cer-

tainly. There is no money here to speak of, and what there is will go to Beaufort where there is liquor sold or given away. I have also given up cotton-planting; it is not a very lucrative business when it brings only sixty-six cents.

I made arrangements with Mr. Pope to still occupy this half of the house free of rent until August, if I wished, and was calculating on having a rich time seeing a native plant cotton with these island negroes, but alas, my hopes are all blighted, for every blessed soul but one man and his wife has moved away and will not work for him; so he has decided not to move here until after we are gone. He has sent one man here who was an old servant and has been with him all the time, and he is very industrious, works from morn until night; it is quite refreshing to see him. Pope was the only one of the natives who bid off places at auction [1] that came to time in paying up; so the places were put up again and bought by Northern men.

The present planters are in a dubious frame of mind these days over the prospect for another year, for it is very hard to bring wages down, and one cannot get his money back at the present price of cotton, so most of them will work on shares;[2] but that is a sure way of running a place all out, for the people will not manure it sufficiently to keep it up. Mr. Eustis is always good-natured, and is about the only man here who is not utterly demoralized on the negro question.

[1] At the auction referred to, the Government offered for sale the plantations which had been reserved for the support of schools.

[2] A negro who worked a plantation "on shares" was independent of the owner, merely paying a rent in cotton.

F. H. TO C. P. W.

Coffin's Point, Feb. 16, 1866. Really the people have
met with a great change of late, since I have sent away
Anthony Bail. They love and respect me *hugely*, which
I hope will last another whole week.

Dr. Oliver and Captain Ward, who have bought
"Pine Grove," have taken the usual disgust for the
people. They have got it bad; say they would not have
bought here had they imagined half of the reality.
They have some friends who would have bought
Coffin's Point if they could have made a favorable
report of the people. But they tell them not to think
of buying to use the labor that is now here. I say the
same when I say anything about it, though I have no
friends who think of buying here.

T. E. R. TO C. P. W.

May 21, 1867. I don't suppose we shall be able to
make any new additions to your collection of negro
songs.[1] They sing but very little nowadays to what
they used to. Do you remember those good old days
when the Methodists used to sing up in that cotton-
house at Fuller's? Was n't it good? They never sing
any of them at the church, and very few in their praise-
meeting.

Crops on the island are looking worse than I ever
saw them at this season before.

We are all American citizens now, and there has been
an effort to form a Republican party, but it has not

[1] Afterwards used as the nucleus of *Slave Songs of the United
States.*

succeeded very well yet. They are too suspicious to be led by the whites, and there is not sense enough in themselves to go ahead.

The last extract in the series is from a letter written by H. W. exactly one year later, when she made a trip to Port Royal, staying with Miss Towne and Miss Murray at St. Helena Village. The tardy tribute of the negroes to Mr. Philbrick makes the story complete.

FROM H. W.

Thursday, May 21, 1868. When I inquired at breakfast if I could have Jacob's horse for the day, I found that, as he was in use for the crop, Miss Towne had already had her horse put singly into their rockaway for school, and Miss Murray's into the chaise for my use. So when they started for school, I followed along in company as far as the end of the Village road, where Mr. N. now has a store, and, turning on to the more familiar road, soon found myself crossing the creek over Mr. Philbrick's bridge, — one of the very few in decent repair, — and on my way to Captain John Fripp Homestead. The entire absence of gates, and as a consequence of pigs, or *vice versa*, made my drive an easy one, and I did not have to get out once. It had seemed hot early, but light clouds and a fresh breeze kept it cool all day. I turned up the familiar avenue to Folsom's, after passing through one field in which the houses are still, though more scattered. The avenue was clean and trim, and the house corresponded, — a new piazza and steps all freshly painted, fresh paint inside, and paper on the walls made every-

thing look uncommonly spruce. The schoolroom
is now the parlor, and my sofa and cushion grace it
still!

Mr. Alden met me very cordially at the foot of the
steps, and I went in to see the other occupants, Mr. and
Mrs. Waters and their son. I had a pleasant call and
talk, and then, refusing their earnest invitation to spend
the day, as Coffin's Point was my one object, I pursued my lonely way. Trees cut down, and houses
moved and built in the middle of the field, with the
absence of fences, gates, and pigs, were the most noticeable changes, and I drove along, meeting no one,
until I came to the pine woods on the right opposite
old Frank's ground, just before you turn into the Pine
Grove field. The woods were all thinned out, logs
lying in every direction. Hoeing the corn planted there
were two women I thought I recognized, and, walking
the horse, I leaned forward to see who was the man
further on. Then I stopped and asked him whose the
land was he was working, when he began an account
of how "it used to be McTureous and Mr. Thomas
Coffin buy 'em," [1] which I cut short with — "Yes, I
know that, but is it your own now ? What is your name ?"
" My name Able, ma'am; dis lan' mine, yes, ma'am " —
and then — "Oh! my Lord! Der Miss Hayiut, an'
me no know um!" and he dropped his hoe and came
scrambling and running to the road. Sarah and Elsie,
whom I had just passed, and Martha further on, came
out at his call, grinning and pleased, and then he and
Martha began directly upon what I had done for

[1] Before the war.

Rose,[1] their gratitude, and willingness that I should
keep her forever. Then they talked of how hard
the last year or two had been, and there were many
reiterations of "Ebery word Mass' Charlie and Mr.
Philbrick tell we come true." "Tell 'em tousan howdy
over for we — long too much for shum. We fin' 'em
out now."

A few steps more brought me into the Pine Grove
field, and I turned towards the house, followed by half
a dozen small children, only one of whom I knew or
knew me, — little Abigail. Towards the house whom
should I come upon but Flora and her Sarah, a great
girl. She was pleased as could be, but told me I should
find no one at the Grove. Old Monah was dead, and
all the old people had bought land and lived at the
Point. They were working for Mr. Ward, glad enough
to earn a little ready money for food. I went on to see
Mrs. Vaughn, and as she had not come up from school,
walked down to the praise-house, seeing no one I
knew but old Binah.

School had dispersed, so I walked back to the house,
and dined there, and then for Coffin's Point. Once
inside the line — for the gate is not — I met the familiar breeze of the Big Pasture, but its altered face.
The houses are back as far as the creek on one side
and the woods on the other, — two or three quite large
and with piazzas, — the praise-house near the corner of
the wood. I was a long time passing through it, for they
all dropped their hoes and came down to shake hands.
I got Uncle George to follow along with hammer and

---

[1] Rose had been living with H. W. in the North, and was now at
Port Royal with her, also on a visit.

nails to mend the chaise, as the floor was so broken I could not put my feet on it, and the bag of oats had dropped through on the way. I had tied the halter to the dasher and wound it round the bag, so there was no loss. The dilapidation was a pleasing reminiscence of old times, and George was pleased enough to earn a quarter by patching it up. Then I drove on to the house, where are only a Mr. and Mrs. Sinclair left in charge. Mrs. S. was very polite, and asked me up into our old parlor, which did not look as pleasant as in the old time. Garibaldi was out at pasture, so I could not have the ride I coveted while my horse was eating his dinner. As I had never been into the schoolhouse since it was finished, I borrowed the key and walked down to it. As I pulled the rope to hear the sound of the unused bell, Robert came in, quiet as ever, but greatly pleased, and asking many questions about Mass' Charlie and Mr. and Mrs. Soule. I found the people were coming up to be paid, so I went back to the yard and stood there as they came up to the schoolroom door, across which was the old school table, with Primus behind it, and Mr. Sinclair, looking over his list. Then I walked on the beach, and Robert put my horse in and I drove off.

Mike had followed me up the road, loud in his regrets for the "good ole times when Mass' Charlie and de fust gang white people been here." "Mr. Philbrick de fustest man in de worl'. General Bennett [1] could n't — could n't — fetch de fust feathers round his heart!" whatever that may be.

[1] General Bennett was managing Coffin's for the owner, who had bought it of Mr. Philbrick.

CONCLUSION

WHEN the end of this record is reached, undoubtedly the feeling uppermost in the mind of the reader is one of disappointment. At first blush one is ready to believe that the members of the little colony, in proving the free negro capable of raising cotton to good advantage, had still more completely proved him unfit for freedom. Yet the more one reflects on the story, the more plainly one sees that the discouraging state of things described in the later letters was merely the inevitable result of Emancipation, and would have been the same had any other race been concerned, whatever its characteristics. The ferment of Freedom worked slowly in the negroes, but it worked mightily, and the very sign of its working was, as a matter of course, unreasonableness, insubordination, untrustworthiness. This result might have been foreseen, and probably was foreseen. It was not a pleasant thing to contemplate, nor is it pleasant to read of, but it proved nothing as to the powers and possibilities of the negro people. It is not probable that any of the "missionaries," however discouraged, came to think that the black man was too stupid or too dishonest to become a self-respecting member of society. Nor does it appear that W. C. G. was justified in fearing that their efforts were worse than wasted, inasmuch as the negro might have acquired manhood more rapidly if left to himself from the start. They had established two facts, the very foundation-stones of the new order in the South; that the freedman would work, and that, as an employee, he was less expensive than the slave. Their reward was not in any one's gratitude, but in their own knowledge that they had served their unfortunate fellow-beings as far as, at the moment, was possible. And it must not be forgotten that some stayed on, putting their energies where there was no question, even, of waste or of ingratitude. There is no telling the service done for the Sea Islands by the education that has been given to it these forty years, or indeed by the mere presence of the women who have devoted their lives to this service.

Looking at the letters as a whole, perhaps the reader finds that the chief impression they have made upon him is that of profound respect for the negro wisdom shown by the writers. Keenly as they felt the past suffering and the present helplessness of the freedmen, they had the supreme common-sense to see that these wrongs could not be righted by any method so simple as that of giving. They saw that what was needed was, not special favor, but even-handed justice. Education, indeed, they would give outright; otherwise they would make the negro as rapidly as possible a part of the economic world, a laborer among other laborers. All that has happened since has only gone to prove how right they were.

INDEX

INDEX

Aaron, 235.
Abel, 65, 66, 141 n., 145, 212, 218, 239, 330.
Abigail, 331.
Abolitionists, hostility to. See Army Officers; Hunter; Saxton.
Advertiser, Boston, 62, 219, 324.
Africa, 203, 225.
Alden, William, 286, 313, 321, 330.
Alex, 86, 87, 95.
Alick, 31, 239.
Allen, William, 232.
Amaritta, 88, 144, 187, 212, 222, 225, 233, 304.
Andrew, 103.
Anti-slavery people, hostility to. See Army Officers; Hunter; Saxton.
Antony, 95.
Ariel, The 225.
Army Corps, 17th, 305; 18th, 150 n.
Army officers, hostility of, to anti-slavery people, 108, 115, 122, 308. See also Negroes, hostility of army officers to; Hunter; Saxton.
Army Life in a Black Regiment, 104 n., 131 n., 133 n.
" Arnie," Miss, 127.
Atkinson, Edward, 53, 62, 101.
Atlanta, Georgia, 290, 297.
Atlantic, The, 2, 9.

B——, Mr., 247.
Bacchus, 64, 65, 121, 123, 126.
Bacchus, foreman of Morgan Island, 203, 204.
Bail, Anthony, 328.
Baldwin, Mr., 235.
Baltimore Convention, 1864, 267.
Baptisms, 145, 146, 249, 268.
Barkis, 228, 229.
Barnard, James M., 162, 163.
Barney, Hiram, 2.
Barstow, Major, 163, 164.
Bay Point, v, 13, 29, 35, 37 n., 41, 73, 79
Beaufort, N. C., 82.
Beaufort, S. C., vi n., 6, 9, 16, 31, 39, 45, 46, 47, 53, 54, 61, 71, 72, 82, 83, 92, 93, 98, 100, 104, 106, 108, 117, 122, 127, 128, 129 n., 134, 141, 150, 155 n., 167, 170, 175, 186, 187, 196, 197, 202, 207, 211, 221, 235, 240, 255, 257 n., 258, 265, 267, 282, 283, 289, 290, 295, 297, 301, 302, 305, 314, 320, 326, 327.
Beaufort River, vi n., 6, 71, 116, 117.
Beaufort Sound, 203.
Beauregard, Fort, v, 5, 37, 61.
Becca, 126.
Ben, 95.
Bennett, General, 332.
Betsey, 185.
Betty, 61, 252, 253, 272.
Betty, 144.
" Biffert," 49, 82.
Binah, 27, 44, 45, 157.
Bingham, Quartermaster-General, 132.
Birney, William, Brig.-Gen., 257, 271.
Black Draft. See Draft, Black.
Boston, vi, 117, 118, 141, 168, 190, 205, 220, 225, 226, 250, 256, 257 n., 264, 266, 272, 307, 310, 315, 316, 325.
Boston syndicate, 140, 172, 208, 258, 275, 316.
Boutelle, Captain, 205, 206.
Brannan, John M., Brig.-Gen., 86, 94, 108, 122.
Brisbane, Dr., 129, 164, 244, 312.
Brown, Peter, 323.
Bryant, Captain J. E., 185, 187, 240.
Bryant, Lieutenant O. E., 188.
Bryant, Mr., plantation superintendent, 108, 116, 122.
Bryant, Mrs., 115, 321.
Bundy, Dr. Francis, 142, 143, 188, 196, 197.
Bundy, Mrs. Francis, 141, 142.
Burying-place, 65 n., 66.
Butler, Pierce, 271, 272.
Butler, Mrs. Pierce. See Kemble, Fanny.

Cæsar, 184, 239.
Caroline (1), 16, 17.
Caroline (2), 87.